Walter Andrew

PHILIP CAPUTO is a former journalist and Pulitzer Prize winner who has written numerous works of nonfiction, including *A Rumor of War*, one of the most highly praised books of the twentieth century, which is read widely in colleges throughout the country. His novels include *Acts of Faith, The Voyage, Indian Country, Horn of Africa*, and his most recent, *Crossers*. He divides his time between Norfolk, Connecticut, and Patagonia, Arizona.

Also by Philip Caputo

Additional Praise for *The Longest Road*

"[Caputo] keeps the narrative moving with his observant eye and mordant sense of humor."　　　　—*The New York Times Book Review*

"[Caputo] gives us a view not only of the 17,000 miles he traveled but of the many people with whom he spoke. The novelist and multi-award-winning journalist, whose *A Rumor of War* was one of the defining books of the Vietnam era, should get it just right."　　—*Library Journal*

"A continental tale that is always engaging and frequently reassuring."　　　　—*Publishers Weekly*

"This reporter has more stamina in him than your average twenty-one-year-old. . . . Caputo creates captivating portraits of a wide variety of communities."　　　　—*Kirkus Reviews*

"Get ready to buy your copy, because you will enjoy Caputo's road adventure across America."　　　　—*The Bismarck Tribune*

"A new travelogue for a new millennium."　　　　—*The Kansas City Star*

"A perfect vacation book that's funny and erudite at the same time."　　　　—*New Haven Register*

"Not just an entertaining travelogue, but a thoughtful look at where we are today."　　　　—*Between the Covers*

"A book of this nature—full of road knight-errantry, striking personal reflection, and the color of plentiful places—may never have been done so vividly before."　　　　—*The Goldendale Sentinel*

"It's a good ride, and a good read."　　　　—*Minneapolis Star Tribune*

THE
LONGEST
ROAD

Overland in
Search of America,
from Key West
to the Arctic Ocean

PHILIP CAPUTO

Picador   Henry Holt and Company   New York

www.picadorusa.com
www.twitter.com/picadorusa • www.facebook.com/picadorusa
picadorbookroom.tumblr.com

Picador® is a U.S. registered trademark and is used by Henry Holt and Company under license from Pan Books Limited.

For book club information, please visit www.facebook.com/picadorbookclub or e-mail marketing@picadorusa.com.

Map by Laura Hartman Maestro

Designed by Meryl Sussman Levavi

The Library of Congress has cataloged the Henry Holt edition as follows:

Caputo, Philip.
    The longest road : overland in search of America, from Key West to the Arctic Ocean / Philip Caputo.—First edition.
        pages cm
    ISBN 978-0-8050-9446-6 (hardcover)
    ISBN 978-0-8050-9696-5 (e-book)
    1. Caputo, Philip—Travel—United States.   2. United States—Description and travel.   3. National characteristics, American.   4. United States—Biography.   5. United States—Social life and customs—21st century.
6. United States—Social conditions—21st century.   I. Title.
    E169.Z83C37 2013
    973.93—dc23

                                                                    2012050451

Picador ISBN 978-1-250-04874-5

Picador books may be purchased for educational, business, or promotional use. For information on bulk purchases, please contact Macmillan Corporate and Premium Sales Department at 1-800-221-7945, extension 5442, or write specialmarkets@macmillan.com.

First published in the United States by Henry Holt and Company

First Picador Edition: May 2014

10 9 8 7 6 5 4 3 2 1

For Livia, Anastasia, Sofia, and Lindsay

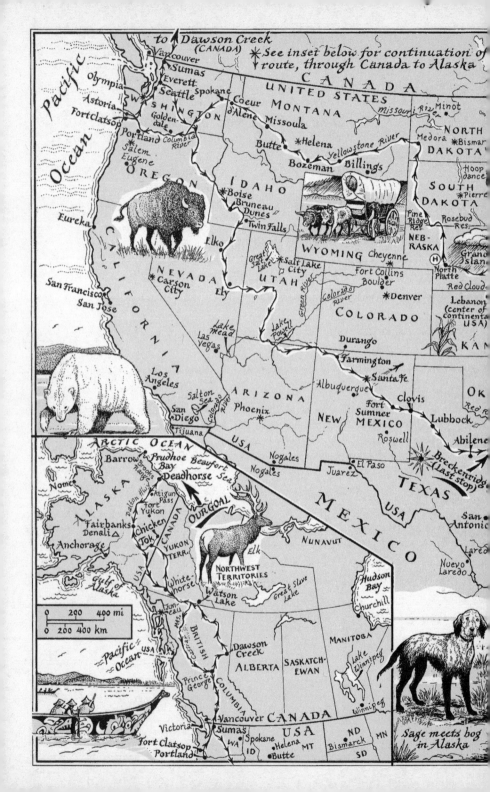

PREFACE

THE IDEA HATCHED ON BARTER ISLAND, A WIND-SCOURED ROCK in the Beaufort Sea that was almost not an island; the channel separating it from the Alaskan mainland looked so narrow a center fielder on one side could have thrown to a second baseman on the other. It was as remote and barren a place as I'd ever seen, its surface unblemished by a tree, shrub, or bush. But it wasn't lifeless. It was in fact peopled by two hundred Inupiat Eskimos and a handful of whites who lived in Kaktovic, the only settlement within 150 miles. Kaktovic had the architectural charm of a New Jersey warehouse district: a dirt airstrip, a hangar, houses like container boxes with doors and windows.

All in all, the perfect spot to hide from a court summons, although that wasn't why I was there that afternoon in September 1996. Along with three friends, I was on a layover after a hunting and fishing trip in the Arctic National Wildlife Refuge; we were waiting for a bush plane to fly us back to Deadhorse, where we'd left our pickup two weeks earlier.

In the lounge of the Waldo Arms, the island's one hotel—*hotel* is an exceedingly generous term for what appeared to be a few double-wides bolted together—we lunched on turkey soup and watched the Dolphins play the Cardinals on satellite TV.

The thick soup was welcome after two weeks of MREs supplemented by lean, gamy caribou. A change of clothes, a shave, and a hot bath would have been still more welcome, but those luxuries would have to wait. After we landed in Deadhorse (its name is of uncertain origin), we faced an eighteen-hour drive to Fairbanks down the Dalton Highway, almost five hundred miles of potholed dirt and gravel.

"Keep an eye out for polar bears," cautioned Walt Audi when, bored with hanging around, I decided to go for a walk. Walt owned the Waldo Arms and Audi Air, the flying service that had brought us to Kaktovic and, we trusted, would soon take us out. Somewhere in his sixties, with a white goatee and white hair foaming out from under a beret, he looked more like a tourist's picture of a French painter than a bush pilot. He explained that Barter islanders practiced whaling Melville style, putting to sea in small boats armed with harpoons. The dead whales were towed ashore to be butchered, which attracted polar bears. If no blubbery scraps were available, they might settle for a fresh human.

I thanked him for the warning and went outside, passing a DEW-line radar station, now a Cold War relic. Earlier, Walt had mentioned that he'd come to Kaktovic thirty-four years ago on a contract to refiberglass the dome.

"And I stayed," he'd added.

Naturally, I asked why. He thought for a moment, as if he'd never considered the question, and replied without a hint of irony, "I don't know."

For a while, I strolled along the shore, a strip of dirty sand littered with huge trees washed up from God knew where. A bitter wind blew in from the Arctic Ocean, ice floes sailed by on lead-colored waters cold enough to kill you in just slightly more time than it would take a bullet. Across the channel, the Romanzoff Mountains rose a mile high, snow blanketing the slopes almost all the way down. It was a little past Labor Day and already full winter.

In my mind I fled to another island, Key West, where I'd lived in the seventies and eighties, indulged in gin and controlled substances, caught a lot of fish, and burned through two marriages before I left to avoid incinerating my third. But instead of thinking of that, I imagined the palm trees, bougainvillea spilling over gingerbread porch rails, dazzling seas under a subtropical sun.

Not wishing to tempt any beach-combing polar bears, I ambled back into Kaktovic and down an avenue covered in tundra grass. It led to a red, rectangular building raised on piers to keep it from melting the permafrost. An American flag fluttered from a pole slanting from the front wall; beside it, metal letters spelled HAROLD KAVEOLOOK SCHOOL.

That's when the idea began to form. My thinking ran something like this: The Inupiat schoolkids here pledge allegiance to the same flag as the children and grandchildren of Cuban immigrants on Key West, six thousand miles away. Native Americans and Cuban Americans on two islands as far apart as New York is from Moscow, yet in the same country. How remarkable.

I felt then a heightened awareness of America's vastness and diversity. And a renewed appreciation for its cohesiveness. In an itinerant life, I'd traveled through more than fifty foreign countries. A lot of them, riven by centuries-old hatreds, all too often delaminated into ghastly ethnic and sectarian wars. Lebanon in the seventies. The Balkans in the nineties. Sudan since the dawn of time. What a marvel that the huge United States, peopled by every race on Earth, remained united. What held it together?

In a little while, I would be in Deadhorse, on Prudhoe Bay. Lying at the end of the Dalton Highway, Deadhorse is as far north as you can go by road in the United States—some 250 miles beyond the Arctic Circle.

My thoughts flipped back to Key West and a buoy-shaped, concrete monument at the corner of South and Whitehead Streets. It marks the southernmost point in the continental United States: a mere seventy miles north of the Tropic of Cancer.

With enough time, gas money, and nerve, I could drive from the southernmost point to the northernmost reachable by road. At one end, I would look upon the Gulf Stream and the Southern Cross, and at the other the Arctic Ocean and the Northern Lights. I would leave my country for part of the journey, but not my language or my culture. And possibly I would discover along the way what Inupiat Americans and Cuban Americans and every other kind of American had in common besides a flag.

I'd driven cross-country more times than I could remember, but it was always east to west, west to east, as most transcontinental travelers have done since the first wagon pulled onto the Oregon Trail. Certainly this drive would be the longest road trip I'd ever attempted.

The longest road. The idea brought on a rush of restless blood, stirred my imagination . . . and, cicada-like, went dormant, not to be reawakened for fourteen years.

Southern Cross

The author and his wife, Leslie, at the southernmost
point in Key West, Florida.

1.

I DON'T KNOW WHY MY DREAM FELL INTO SUCH A LONG SLUMBER. However, after careful investigation, I can identify what woke it up.

At the root was a condition I've suffered from for most of my life. I trace its origins to my childhood in the forties and fifties, when my father, a traveling machinist for the Continental Can Company, maintained and repaired the machines leased to canning factories in central and northern Wisconsin. He would leave our home in suburban Chicago in the late spring, and when school let out for the summer he returned to fetch my mother, my sister, and me to spend the next three months with him.

After the suitcases were stowed in the trunk of the company car, always a no-frills Chevrolet, we would head north on U.S. 45 or U.S. 41, then two-lane blacktops. Some kids would have been sad to leave their friends for the summer, but that moment when we swung onto the highway never failed to fill me with a tingling anticipation. We lived in different places over the years—backwoods cabins without indoor plumbing, lakeside cottages, houses in towns with Indian names like Shawano, or French names like Fond du Lac, or plain-vanilla American names like Green Lake—but the destination never excited me as much as the getting there. I loved to feel the wind slapping me through the open windows, and to inhale the strong smells of manure and silage as the Chevy rolled past corn and pea and beet fields speckled with the straw hats of the migrant workers who brought a touch of the exotic to the midwestern countryside—Mexican braceros, tall Jamaicans. I loved watching farmhouses whiz by, barns decorated with faded advertisements for feed companies and chewing tobacco, and the landscape change from field and pasture to somber pine forests jeweled with lakes.

Long ago, when I was a correspondent in the Middle East, I spent a couple of weeks wandering the Sinai Desert with bedouin tribesmen and an Israeli anthropologist familiar with their culture. He told me that their migrations were not always dictated by the need to find water or better grazing for their herds; sometimes they struck their tents and began to move for no discernible reason. He was forced to conclude that they were animated by an impulse, perhaps lodged in their nomadic genes, to get going, it didn't matter where.

I knew the feeling.

My father died on March 2, 2010, at age ninety-four. My wife, Leslie Ware, and I were at our house in Patagonia, a small southern Arizona town where we spend part of each winter, when my sister, Pat, phoned with the news from Scottsdale. My father had gone to live there with her and my brother-in-law after my mother's death in 2001. His passing, my sister said, had been quick, painless, even serene, so I felt more grateful than mournful as Leslie and I drove to Scottsdale for the memorial service. It was held at a spanking-new, faux-adobe mortuary that could have been mistaken, from the outside, for an upscale desert spa. Before the service began, I spent a few minutes alone with my father in a back room. He hadn't been dressed yet, and he lay on a steel gurney, a sheet covering him to the neck to hide his nakedness and the embalmer's incisions. His hair had been combed, a pleasant expression put on his face, makeup applied to restore his complexion to its former ruddiness. The cosmetics were so artful and he'd been around so long that I had a hard time believing he was really, truly gone. It became easier when I laid a hand on his forehead, cold as a rock in winter.

I spoke to him nonetheless, on the off chance that he could hear me, telling him that I would always remember him, that I would miss him, that although we'd had some sharp differences I'd never stopped loving him. Then I reminisced about the trip we'd made to Wisconsin a year after my mother's death. We'd gone to Shawano Lake to look for the beach where I'd taken my first steps in 1942. He wanted to see it again.

Our only guide was an old photograph showing my mother holding my hand as I toddled uncertainly in the sand. There in the mortuary I reminded him of how amazed we'd been to find that beach, hardly changed in sixty years. As we stood on it, he'd grown nostalgic and talked about his early days on the road, traveling from cannery to cannery with his oak toolbox, its felt-lined drawers crammed with the precision instruments of his trade. "There was nothing like it," he'd said, wistfully. "To be in a car with everything you need, nothing more, and an open road in front of you."

No two people could have been less alike than my father and Jack Kerouac, yet there had been the same spirit in the words he'd spoken as in those Kerouac had written: "Nothing behind me, everything ahead of me, as is ever so on the road."

My father's death plunged me into melancholy reflections on old age and the brevity of life, even one as long as his. In a less-than-celebratory mood, I marked my sixty-ninth birthday later that spring, after Leslie and I were back at our home in Connecticut, where we live most of the year. The milestone of seventy was coming up fast. In this era of longer life spans, you can kid yourself at sixty that you have plenty of time left, but *seventy* has the unmistakable ring of mortality. You quit cigarettes and hard partying years ago, you eat healthy servings of fruits and vegetables, you take your Lipitor faithfully, you exercise, and still you wake up at the hour of the night when it's impossible to entertain illusions, and you can almost see him at the foot of your bed, black wings spread as if about to enfold you.

Nothing behind me, everything ahead of me . . . Well, a lot of my life was behind me . . . and ahead?

As if struck by an electrical charge, the sleeping cicada born on Barter Island cracked its shell, rose in flight, and began to buzz insistently in my ear. By road from the subtropics to the Arctic.

I went to my laptop, looked up directions from Key West, Florida, to Deadhorse, Alaska. A map of North America flashed on the screen. A blue, diagonal line zigzagged across it, marking the most direct route from the southernmost to the northernmost point—5,475 miles, according to the driving directions. And that was one way, not to mention that I would have to drive from Connecticut to Key West—1,486 miles—just to get to the starting point. Then, of course, I would have to return to Connecticut from Deadhorse—4,780 miles. The total distance—11,741 miles—gave me sticker shock. Round it up to twelve thousand. Almost halfway around the world! It seemed slightly mad, but then it might do me good. To make such an epic road trip, discovering places I'd never been, rediscovering others, never knowing what I'd find beyond the next curve or hill, would be to recapture the enchantment of youth, a sense of promise and possibility.

The cicada chirped incessantly in my head. I clicked back to the first map. Looking at it brought on a mixture of eagerness and reluctance. The buzzing grew more shrill. *If you don't go now, geezer, you never will.* I listened to my inner cicada, and the uneasiness subsided. If I'd learned anything, it was that the things you do never cause as much regret as the things you don't.

But I didn't decide to go purely for the adventure. Fourteen years earlier, standing in front of the Harold Kaveolook School, I'd asked, What held the nation together? What made the *pluribus unum*?

Now I revised that question—would it continue to hold together?—because the America of 2010 wasn't the America of 1996. I'd been living in it the whole time but in some ways did not recognize it.

The worst economic calamity since the Great Depression. Foreclosures, bankruptcies, millions of homes under water, and millions of people out of work. The wages of the employed stagnant, except for CEOs, investment bankers, and the practitioners of casino capitalism on Wall Street, all of whom were making more money than ever. People were angry. In Texas, crowds at a political event had called on their governor to secede from the union. In Nevada, a candidate for a U.S. Senate seat had suggested that if conservatives like herself didn't get their way they might resort to armed insurrection. Strangely enough, much of this fury wasn't directed at the financial mandarins who had brought the nation to the edge of the abyss; no, it fell on citizens like the aging engineer who, afflicted with Parkinson's disease, was mocked and abused at a Tea Party rally in Ohio because he supported health-care reform. That was the America I didn't recognize—spiteful and cruel.

In geology, a rift is a long, narrow zone where stresses in the earth's crust are causing it to rupture. In North America, one such formation is the Rio Grande Rift, which is pulling apart at the rate of two millimeters a year. You might say, with considerable license, that it's very slowly tearing the continent in half. I couldn't help but see it as a metaphor for the stresses that seemed to be ripping our political and social fabric. But was the country really as fractured as it appeared in the media? As bitter and venomous? It wasn't my intention to take the pulse of the nation; the United States is too big, too complicated a mosaic of races and nationalities and walks of life to have a single pulse or even two or three. But I thought I'd ask people, when possible, the question I'd put to myself: what holds us together?

2.

PLANNED TO GO IT ALONE BECAUSE I'D FALLEN IN LOVE WITH THE image of myself as a solitary knight-errant of the road. My sole companions would be my two English setters, twelve-year-old Sage and her much younger cousin Sky.

Leslie was supportive. Her only objection was that I would make the trip without her. Seeking a little more support, I consulted other family members. Reached by phone in Tampa, elder son Geoff said, "Cool," but had some qualms about my traveling alone.

From his home in Tallahassee, younger son Marc expressed no reservations. "I think you're fucking nuts," he said.

From the start, my heart was set on an Airstream, as American as the prairie schooner, its bright aluminum body and rounded lines reminiscent of early racing airplanes, which is no accident; the first Airstream to roll off the assembly line, in 1936, was called the Clipper and was modeled on a design created by Hawley Bowlus, designer of Lindbergh's *Spirit of St. Louis.*

An Airstream is wanderlust made visible and tangible. It sings with Walt Whitman, "Allons! . . . come travel with me" . . . sings of lonesome highways stretching on and on.

I cannot count the hours spent surfing print and online classifieds for an Airstream I could afford. No luck. Eventually I e-mailed Airstream's CEO, Bob Wheeler, at the company's factory in Jackson Center, Ohio, pitching my travel plans—and myself. I told him I would write about the journey, and touted the publicity value if the company leased me a trailer or sold me one at a discount. Ignorance and egotism led me to presume that this was an offer he would not refuse. I didn't know then that the first vehicle occupied by the Apollo 11 astronauts upon their return from the moon had been a modified Airstream; nor that carpeted, wood-paneled Airstreams furnished with leather chairs, TVs, and DVD players are installed in air force cargo planes that fly the president and other American officials the world over.

Thus Wheeler and his marketing people considered my offer one they could refuse, and they did.

By holiday season, I was still trailerless and growing anxious; I hoped to depart from Key West sometime between late May and early June, leaving time to reach the Arctic before the snow fell and road travel there became a matter for the experts on the TV show *Ice Road Truckers*. I'd begun to consider alternatives to an Airstream when a friend introduced me to Rich Luhr, who lives in Tucson.

In his late forties, dark-haired and slender, Luhr is the founder and publisher of *Airstream Life,* a magazine dedicated to respectable vagrancy, a lifestyle summed up in the gerund *Airstreaming.* He's lost count of how many times he and his family have crisscrossed the country in their thirty-foot trailer.

I should point out that Airstreamers form a subculture almost cultic in its attachment to the trailers; in its exclusivity (there are Airstream parks that will not permit non-Airstreams past their gates); in its rituals and in its specialized lingo, which can be as opaque to an outsider as nautical jargon to a landlubber. Airstreamers disdain recreational vehicles of all other makes and models. Disdain chills into contempt when it comes to bus-size, boxy RVs with garish exteriors and interiors so loaded with luxuries they are for all practical purposes condominiums on wheels. As a leader in the cult, Luhr refused to listen to any talk about substitutes. He was going to help me find an Airstream.

We fell into a routine: I would scan the classifieds, then e-mail him with candidates. Very few were acceptable. This one was too big; that one overloaded with aftermarket gewgaws; this other one had the following defects. Luhr was a discriminating judge of trailer flesh. Whenever he gave one a rare thumbs-up, its price moved me to give it a thumbs-down. I began to despair of finding a Goldilocks Airstream—and found myself encouraging my own discouragement.

A long journey is more attractive when imagined than in reality; the closer I came to the start date I'd set, the more I felt a coldness in my feet, while an argument went on in my head, in stereo.

It's too far, said a voice in the right speaker, *it will take too long* [three to four months, I'd figured] *and cost too much. Besides, you're too old.*

It announced a headline: AGING WRITER'S REMAINS FOUND IN MIDDLE OF NOWHERE.

Buck up! replied the left speaker. *Every year you drive from Connecticut to Arizona and back without a problem. And you're not circling the drain yet.*

In early March, Luhr e-mailed with good news. He'd met a woman, Erica Sherwood, who restored and sold antique Airstreams from her home in Breckenridge, Texas. A burnished 1967 Caravel on her Web site caught my eye. At nineteen feet, it was ideal for a guy and two dogs. But then there was the asking price: $24,500. Private owners almost never lease their Airstreams, but I phoned Sherwood asking if she would and was surprised when she agreed. We settled on another vehicle in her inventory: a renovated 1962 Globetrotter, also nineteen feet, but with higher clearance that would be better on rough roads.

Leslie flew home to Connecticut while I remained in Arizona, where I bought a 2007 Toyota Tundra, a pickup capable of hauling a boxcar, and then a hardtop shell for the truck's bed to provide a home for the dogs. After Sherwood's lawyer drew up a lease agreement, she drove eight hundred miles to Tucson and delivered the Globetrotter to Luhr's house. I met her and the trailer there at the end of March.

Sherwood is a *presence*, a six-foot, blue-eyed blonde of thirty-seven who'd played guard for the women's basketball teams at Baylor and Abilene Christian universities. As for the trailer, a roof-mounted air conditioner slightly spoiled its aerodynamic lines, but it was otherwise a compact beauty, so polished that I could have shaved in it without missing a spot. Inside, it was equipped with a minifridge that ran on propane or electric power; a galley with a sink, counter, and three-burner propane stove; a dinette in front that broke down into a bed; a sofa in back that pulled out into another bed; a stainless steel shower stall-cum-toilet, and a small, chip-burning stove for heat, all compressed into about 150 square feet. Luhr and Sherwood took me to a Tucson Walmart and a camping supply store for essential equipment: tools, a 30-amp power cord, a water hose, a flexible sewer hose, stabilizer jacks, a hydraulic jack, work gloves, butane lighters, and sundry other articles. Sherwood had told me that her Web site's domain name, Nomadica, was intended to encapsulate a footloose, minimalist mode of travel. But after the buying spree I began to wonder just how minimalist it was going to be.

I was introduced to the routines, procedures, and terminology of trailer life: hitching up, hooking up, leveling and stabilizing, dry-camping (done in wilderness areas lacking sewer, water, and electricity hookups).

Luhr presented a manual he'd written—*The Newbies Guide to Airstreaming*—and opened it to the chapter on checklists. There were two daily departure checklists, one for the outside, one for the inside; ditto for arrival. Total items to be checked: thirty-five. I was starting to feel as if I were in my first day of flight school.

More terminology followed. *GVWR*, for Gross Vehicle Weight Rating, meaning how much the trailer weighs (the Globetrotter was 3,100 pounds); *Net Carrying Capacity*, meaning how much weight could be put into the trailer; *GAWR*, for Gross Axle Weight Rating, meaning how much weight the tow vehicle's front and rear axles could take. The trailer's *tongue weight*—the weight it exerted on the tow vehicle's axles—could not exceed either axle's maximum rating. Happily, Luhr reported after a look at the specs, the Globetrotter's tongue weight was a scant 340 pounds, while the Tundra's GAWR was 4,000 pounds (front) and 4,150 (rear).

Nevertheless, I nearly wept as the Whitmanesque romance of the open road was crushed under, well, the weight of all this technical information.

But Luhr and Sherwood burbled on, and such was their enthusiasm, such their joy in overcoming my ignorance, that I morphed from flight trainee to heathen in the hands of two chipper missionaries bringing my benighted soul into the fold.

The convert, having been catechized, was now to be baptized. I put theory into practice by hitching up the Globetrotter to the Tundra. Herewith the procedure. The truck had to be backed up till its *hitch ball* was directly under the trailer's *hitch coupler* (lining them up was a tricky maneuver). Then the *hitch jack*, electrically powered in newer trailers, manually operated in antiques like the Globetrotter, was cranked, lowering the coupler over the hitch ball. The assembly was secured with a padlock inserted through a hole in a lever, this to avoid becoming unhitched at, say, fifty or sixty miles an hour. Two *safety chains* were shackled to a sturdy bracket on the Tundra as an added precaution; should coupler and ball part company, the chains would keep the trailer and the tow vehicle together long enough for the panic-stricken driver to pull off the road.

The next step was to attach the *breakaway switch*, a black box with a braided cable fixed to the Airstream's A-frame. The cable was clipped to the same bracket as the safety chains. In the event that everything failed, causing trailer and tow vehicle to undergo a sudden divorce, the cable would pop out of the box, activating the trailer's brakes so it didn't careen down the highway by itself.

Finally, the *brake controller* was plugged in. This device consisted of: (1) an electrical box installed under the truck's rear bumper and wired to its brakes, lights, and turn signals; (2) a power cord and plug wired to the trailer's electrical system. Connect (1) to (2) and the trailer brakes would be activated when I applied the tow vehicle's brakes. Also, the brake lights and turn signals of tower and towee would operate as one.

I drove out for a test run, under Sherwood's supervision, past the city limits into the desert, back again for some experience at urban towing. The Tundra pulled the trailer so easily that I sometimes forgot it was there.

"I wouldn't drive this fast," Sherwood cautioned, diplomatically, as I zipped through a construction zone. She spoke with a lilting Texas drawl that often caused me to not pay attention to *what* she was saying because I was listening to the *way* she said it. "And remember when you're changing lanes that you're about twenty feet longer than you're used to."

After overnighting in the Globetrotter, it was time to go. Sherwood came out of the house with Luhr and ceremonially draped a set of keys on a cloth lanyard around my neck. I was now an Airstreamer. Then she passed her palm across the trailer's shining skin and said, "Now, Phil"—adding a syllable to my first name—"I want you to treat her like a beautiful lady who bruises easily."

I thought of the great distance the beautiful lady was going to cover, of the bruising time she was bound to have going up and back down the Dalton Highway, and said that I'd do my best.

3.

STARTED ON A SHAKEDOWN CRUISE, HEADING EAST ON I-10 FOR the Florida panhandle. The plan was to leave the Globetrotter at a friend's farm near Tallahassee while I tied up loose ends at home in Connecticut.

It was Sage, the twelve-year-old English setter, who convinced me that I shouldn't try the journey solo. Sage was a spry elder but no longer able to jump into or out of the truck bed. Removal and reinsertion had to be done four times a day—the morning walk, the evening walk, and two rest stops in between. Each time, she writhed and kicked as if she thought I was going to toss her into a wood chipper. Eight daily wrestling matches with sixty-four pounds of squirming dog was wearing, but it did simplify my life by reducing my wants to a stiff nightcap and a motel room with a king-size bed.

So it went on the drive to Tallahassee, but without the martinis and the motel rooms. (On the first night, in Las Cruces, New Mexico, I settled for a beer from the Globetrotter's minifridge and for its bunk—sized for a king provided he was as thin as a fence post.) On the morning of day three, camped beside the Llano River in the Texas hill country, I was struggling to lift Sage into the truck when a flock of fat, white domestic ducks waddled past. Instantly, she twisted out of my arms and took off after them. Wild ducks would have flown; those barnyard degenerates ran, fleeing into the dense rushes bordering the Llano, Sage in pursuit.

"No! Sage, no!" I hollered, pointlessly—she was deaf as a brick.

I thrashed through the rushes to the riverbank and saw the ducks swimming with the slow current, Sage paddling right behind, her pretty head held high above the slate-green water. I ran downstream, keeping up with the procession, and noticed that the ducks were more clever than they looked. They would swim at a leisurely pace for a few seconds, allowing Sage to almost catch up; when she got to within a yard, they would take flight and land ten or fifteen feet farther on. She would paddle faster to close the gap, then they would fly again. Their plan became clear to me, though not to Sage: they were going to lure her on until she quit or drowned from exhaustion.

Stumbling along the bank, I shouted to her, waved my arms, tossed rocks to get her attention. Several people from the campground had gathered to watch this amusing spectacle. By now, she was about a hundred yards from where she'd leaped in, and although she was tiring, she showed no signs of giving up, nor that she'd caught on to the ducks' tricks. English setters have three things in common with English aristocracy: they are generally good-looking, love to hunt, and are not terribly bright. It looked as though I was going to have to strip down to my underwear and plunge in after her. Instead, I flung another stone, aiming for a point a foot from her nose. It wasn't a major-league pitch; the missile landed on her skull. It did no harm; in fact it did a lot of good. Distracted from her quarry, she turned and saw me, frantically giving the hand signal to come. She swam across the river, clambered up the bank, and vigorously shook herself off at my feet. I wanted to hug her but figured she'd regard that as a reward for bad behavior, so I snapped a leash to her collar, jerked her toward the truck, and scolded, "You goddamn, thick-headed, pea-brained moron, don't *ever* do that again!" She looked up at me with umber eyes that seemed to ask, "What are you so worked up about?"

I related this misadventure to my friend Guy de la Valdene when I arrived at his Dogwood Farm two days later. He advised me to take Sky for companionship and leave Sage home with Leslie or put her in a kennel.

That was the sensible thing, but if I were sensible I wouldn't even be taking this trip. Sage was not a coddled pet; she'd been my hunting dog for a dozen years. We'd chased grouse, pheasant, and quail everywhere from Canada to the Mexican border, from Montana to New Hampshire. We'd shared hardships and occasional dangers; one time, lost in the Arizona mountains on a night when the temperature plummeted to sixteen degrees, we'd huddled together beside a fire and heard the menacing cough of a nearby mountain lion.

We were comrades, and I couldn't imagine leaving her at home, much less incarcerating her in a kennel for four months. Likewise, I couldn't imagine taking care of her and Sky while towing an antique trailer for thousands of miles. The solution was obvious. Still, I was reluctant to let go of that knight-errant image. With my wife beside me, I would not be an adventurer but merely one more senior citizen "seeing the country." A tourist. On the other hand, it had occurred to me that Leslie's absence would make the lonesome road a bit too lonesome, and such a long separation might put a strain on our marriage. I phoned her and asked her to join me, if she could swing it with her employer. She could; intuiting that I would come to my senses, she'd already explored taking a leave of absence with her boss, who, to her surprise, was all for it. She'd been with *Consumer Reports* magazine for twenty years; she'd earned some time off. Soon, things were settled. She arranged for a working leave: she would put in twenty-five hours a week, editing stories on her laptop, staying in touch with the office by cell phone and e-mail. As for her arrangement with me, she volunteered to look after Sage and Sky, conferring upon herself the title "dog wrangler."

I left Guy's place on April 11. Late that afternoon, while bypassing Charleston, South Carolina, I heard a lively radio debate about the city's plans to commemorate the 150th anniversary of the beginning of the Civil War. Someone argued that the ceremonies were going to be too festive for such a somber occasion. Another person was incensed about the "Secession Ball" that had been held four months earlier to mark South Carolina's departure from the Union: white men and women garbed in period tuxedos and gowns, celebrating their forefathers' defense of black slavery, he said. No, another voice chimed in, not in defense of slavery but of states' rights.

That this discussion was taking place at all perplexed me. Issues that I thought had been resolved ages ago still had the power to touch hot buttons.

And not only in the Bethlehem of the Confederacy. The following day, as I picked my way through traffic on the Washington Beltway, I was listening to another talk show and heard "secession" once again. This time, it came from both sides of the political divide. Out in the Arizona I'd left a week earlier, the Republican-led state senate was considering legislation that would empower Arizona to invalidate any federal law it deemed unconstitutional. If it passed (it didn't), Arizona would for all practical purposes have declared itself independent of the United States. The proposal had upset people in Democratic Pima County, which includes Tucson and is as big as Vermont. Led by a lawyer (who else?), the county's citizens had started a movement to break away from Arizona and form a new state, Baja Arizona.

Baja Arizona? Oh, that was wondrously weird. And unsettling. I'd lived through the sixties, but the divisiveness now, in these times of recession at home and war abroad, seemed graver still. Secessionist balls and squabbles about states' rights in South Carolina, a separatist movement in Arizona. Did I hear, or merely imagine I heard, ever so faintly, the great American rift creaking as it widened?

4.

WITHOUT A DESIGN, A JOURNEY BECOMES AIMLESS WANDERING. I spent days planning the trip in my Connecticut office and damn near went blind, squinting at road atlases and Google maps. Plotting routes through western Canada and Alaska was easy—there were only two or three—but the Lower 48, with some three million miles of road and highway, presented bewildering webs of red, green, yellow, and blue lines meandering all over the place. I felt like a shopper staring at a hundred different brands of breakfast cereal, not sure which one to pick.

Sitting on my desk was a copy of *The Journals of Lewis and Clark*, edited by Bernard DeVoto. Once we were west of the Mississippi, we would retrace, as much as was possible by road, Meriwether Lewis and William Clark's voyage up the Missouri River, across the Rockies, and down the Columbia to where it ended, on the Oregon coast. From there, we would proceed to the Canadian border, then take the storied Alaska Highway to Fairbanks, and, finally, the Dalton to Prudhoe Bay.

That left east of the Mississippi. Once again, Lewis and Clark guided me. While staring at the Rand McNally atlas, I noticed the Natchez Trace Parkway, bordered by green dots to indicate that it was a scenic highway. It led through Mississippi and Alabama into Tennessee, where, near the town of Hohenwald, the words *Meriwether Lewis Monument* appeared in tiny red letters. I remembered reading that the explorer had died on the Natchez Trace while on his way to Washington in 1809. The monument marked his gravesite. Not far from it, U.S. 412 ran westward across Tennessee and over the Mississippi into Missouri. That settled it— Lewis's grave would be a waypoint.

To get there, we would traverse the Everglades via U.S. 41, head up Florida's Gulf Coast, cross the Panhandle into Alabama, hop into Mississippi, and join the Natchez Trace at Tupelo, birthplace of Elvis Presley. This north-by-northwest route was intended to give the trip coherence. That said, unforeseen circumstances, or a whim, were bound to take us off course.

I had only one hard-and-fast rule: avoid interstates. They are predictable and boring, and their uniformity somehow erases changes in landscape; you can drive six hundred miles, from forests into desert, and feel that you haven't gone anywhere. In a sense, you haven't. You have no idea about the lives of the people in the towns and cities you've bypassed at seventy miles an hour.

On the afternoon of May 19, Leslie, the dogs, and I pulled into a campground on Stock Island, split from Key West by a mangrove channel scarcely wider than an alley. From Dogwood Farm, we'd made a two-day haul down the Florida peninsula through squalls of flying ants called lovebugs. Hitched back to back, they mate in midair, boiling out of the woods and marshes by the trillions. They went at it on our side windows, entertaining Leslie no end, and splattered against the windshield till we could barely see the road and had to stop at gas stations to refill the windshield washer. I liked slaughtering them; after all, they're so repulsive they can't even look at each other when they're having sex.

The drive down the Overseas Highway through the Florida Keys had been frustrating—bumper-to-bumper traffic turned what should have been a two-hour trip into four—and more frustrations attended our arrival in Key West. I couldn't back the trailer into our assigned parking space; with a single axle and a short hitch, the Globetrotter jackknifed at a twitch of the steering wheel. That was one of the reasons I couldn't back it in. The other was that I didn't know what I was doing, a deficiency overcome by finding another, more accessible space. There, I discovered that the cap to the campground's sewer line was frozen shut by encrusted salt and sand. No amount of whacking with a rubber mallet would loosen its grip. A strapping young guy from the staff answered my summons for help; he took a steel hammer to the cap as if he were trying to kill something and it came free.

Time to connect the sewer hose. In my eagerness to escape swarming mosquitoes in the Everglades that morning, I had forgotten to close the valves to the holding tanks; so when I knelt to open the outlet under the trailer's back end, guess what splashed into my lap? Another mishap cleaned me up. The onboard water tank needed to be topped off. With one end of the water hose screwed to the camp's faucet and the other end shoved into the tank's fill hole, I opened the spigot all the way. The water pressure must have been set to fire hydrant standards, because the hose leaped from the tank, swayed in midair for a moment, then writhed across the ground like a psychotic cobra, spitting all over me. This wasn't all bad; aside from its hygienic effects, it cooled me off—the heat and humidity were Amazonian.

I'd no sooner recaptured the deranged serpent and reduced the flow to a trickle than I heard a shrill squawking, accompanied by a shriek. The latter came from Leslie, the former from the propane leak alarm, a device designed to protect the Airstream's inhabitants from asphyxiation or from blowing themselves up. I rushed into the trailer. How could there be a leak with the propane tanks shut off and no appliances running? An answer came to me. Leslie had brought Sage and Sky inside and switched the air conditioner to high to cool them off. Suspecting a power surge, I switched off the AC, reset the alarm, then turned the AC back on, setting it to low. The hideous squawk was silenced. Having shown so much ineptitude earlier, I was perhaps inordinately proud of myself for managing this crisis. Nevertheless, I fumed.

"Maybe this trailer idea wasn't so excellent. I'm spending all my time on this damned thing. I feel like calling this whole trip off!"

Familiar with my tantrums, Leslie gave me a knowing look mixed with a little skepticism. "I told you that we should stay in motels."

From the moment she'd set eyes on it, she hadn't been one to rhapsodize over the Airstream: "Looks like a Jiffy Pop bag." I'd christened it "Nomadica," after Erica Sherwood's Web site. I really liked the exotic sound, but Leslie thought the prosaic "Ethel"—after Lucy and Ricky Ricardo's neighbor Ethel Mertz—was more appropriate. Her rigged survey sample of friends preferred that name, and that was how the Tundra, which I wanted to call "Gray Hawk," was christened for Ethel's husband, Fred.

"And I told *you*, we're not staying in any goddamned motels," I snapped.

"Chill," Leslie said.

That's no easy thing when the air temperature equals body temperature, but I gave it a try, strolling around the campground, which was really a resort. Palm trees, rustling in a languid breeze, lined tidy avenues of crushed gravel. I confirmed an observation of Leslie's: giant RVs with model names and logos all wrong for the setting. The "Montana" bore a drawing of a snowy mountain range; the "Teton" displayed another mountain range. In vain, I looked for a "Florida" with a picture of a swamp. Couples of a certain age lounged in camp chairs amid their toys—jeeps and powerboats on trailers hitched to their outsize motor homes. Our tiny, tinny, spartan Ethel distinguished Leslie and me from these indolent, luxury-loving vacationers in their glossy land yachts, or so I believed. We were road warriors, bound for the Arctic Ocean. And so, through self-inflation, I restored my self-respect.

Dripping sweat but figuratively chilled out, I returned and had a reasonable conversation with Leslie about what to do next. Although we planned to stay in Key West for a few days, we decided to launch the journey formally with a swing past Mile Marker Zero and the Southernmost Point. That left us with a problem we were to confront over and over in the next four months: take the dogs or leave them in the air-conditioned trailer? We remembered the warning Bill Poppell gave us before we left Dogwood Farm.

Bill is the caretaker and all-around majordomo of the place. He's an older man with a keen practical intelligence and a Florida panhandle accent thicker than motor oil. Glancing at Sage and Sky, he'd asked skeptically, "Y'all gone to bring them dawgs?"

Leslie and I nodded.

"Uh-huh. Fine-lookin' bird dawgs. Ya love yur dawgs?"

Of course we did.

"We all love our dawgs," said Bill. "And they love us. Never leave ya. Know of a dawg follered us once when we was takin' a truckload of swine to an auction, way off down a whole bunch of bad road. After we got there, there he come, a bigole pot-licker dawg like yours there."

The moral of the story was soon in coming. "He dahd one day of heat stroke. Y'all want my advice, ya leave them behind. Y'all be makin' a mistake to take 'em. The mistake would be, ya leave 'em in the trailer, and the ahr conditioner cuts out, and ya got two daid dawgs."

Resolution: Sage and Sky went into the backseat atop a covered pile of gear, and we drove into town, the AC blasting. And Leslie had learned a new adjective: *bigole.*

When I first saw Key West, thirty-five years earlier, it had the look of a funky, isolated Caribbean outpost, especially in the summers, when there wasn't much for tourists to do except sweat. Its vibe was somewhere between raffish and decadent. A rowdy working seaport and navy town, home to Cuban exiles and the descendants of Bahamian settlers (nicknamed "Conchs," after the mollusk), it was also a bohemian enclave for writers and artists, a refuge for homosexuals and runaways—guys fleeing child support payments, good girls escaping bad husbands, bad girls good husbands—and a haven for drug smugglers (as it had been for rumrunners, wreckers, and pirates in earlier times), all crammed together on eight square miles. "Dodge City on the Gulf Stream," the novelist Thomas Sanchez called it for its outlaw ways, though he might have added Greenwich Village to the mix.

Almost all of that is gone now. The shrimpers and the navy sailed away years ago, the gay population was ravaged by AIDS, the *contrabandistas* are dead, in prison, or gone straight. Many Conchs left, too, unable to afford living in a destination resort. To paraphrase a line from a David Allen Coe tune, Jimmy Buffett doesn't live there anymore, although there is a bar called Margaritaville, and other drinking establishments play that song till you're ready to sledgehammer the jukebox.

Key West has become an imitation of its former self, its eccentricities commoditized for sale to tourists. That "character" you see with a parrot on his shoulder is about as authentic as vinyl siding, employed to provide local color. Gargantuan cruise ships dock two or three times a week, disgorging passengers by the thousands to troll the cheesy T-shirt shops on the main drag, Duval Street. And with all sorts of diversions to keep visitors occupied, like parasailing and jet skiing, tourist season is year-round, clogging the streets with autos, bikes, motor scooters, and pedestrians.

I was losing my cool in the downtown traffic, cussing and mumbling that tourist town was the terminal stage in a town's life cycle. Yet—I couldn't deny it—the island retained a seductive beauty. Hibiscus and frangipani daubed their colors along the narrow streets; bougainvillea draped like purple bunting over walls and gingerbread verandas, and royal poinciana—the "flame of the islands"—displayed scarlet blossoms against a sky of pure light, the empyrean.

We turned off Duval onto Whitehead Street and, at its intersection with Fleming, passed a green-and-white sign bolted to a telephone pole: M.M. 0, it read, for Mile Marker Zero. Because Key West can be reached only by driving south, it is thought of as the end of the road. In fact, it's the beginning, for M.M. 0 marks the start of U.S. 1. Maybe the island is the beginning *and* the end, the alpha and the omega.

We proceeded up Whitehead to a concrete monument shaped like a bell buoy and painted in bands of coral, black, and yellow separated by white stripes.

90 MILES TO CUBA, read the legend.

Below it, in capital letters: SOUTHERNMOST POINT. CONTINENTAL U.S.

That made it official. I set Fred's trip odometer to zero. The four of us, a pair of humans, a pair of English setters, were under way.

5.

THE NEXT MORNING, BEFORE THE SUN GREW HOMICIDAL, WE walked the dogs down a paved path along Smathers Beach, on the Atlantic side. Sage and Sky were difficult to walk on lead; being hunting dogs, they instinctively chased things, and all attempts to train them to trot along, like the sedate suburban dogs owned by my Connecticut neighbors, had failed. Advancing age had made Sage more manageable. Sky, on the other hand, was fifty-odd pounds of explosive energy. If she spotted a bird or squirrel, or if her keen nose scented something interesting, she lunged like a sled dog and could jerk you off your feet, sending you flying. Leslie had nicknamed her "Wackadoodle."

Aside from their companionship, I'd brought Sage and Sky as ambassadors, hoping they would attract attention and open the door to conversations with strangers. In a moment, they fulfilled their diplomatic function.

"Oh, they're beautiful!" a female voice said from behind us as we were about to load the dogs into the truck. "What are they?"

We turned and saw a middle-aged woman, her honey-blonde hair pulled straight back. She had extraordinarily blue eyes and freckled cheeks, and she spoke in a voice that brought to mind high fiddle laments echoing through shrouded hills.

"English setters," I answered.

"May I?" Gesturing to pet them.

"Go right ahead. They're sponges when it comes to affection."

Looking at the dogs, she asked, "May I?" Then at us: "Got to get the permission of the babies, too."

Apparently, Sage and Sky granted it. She tickled their ears and rubbed their bellies and accepted their slobbery kisses. "Oh, how I miss my baby. A golden retriever. We had to leave him behind with my stepson."

"Where would that be?"

"Huntington, West Virginia." The woman introduced herself—Jenita Meyers—and asked where we were heading. I expected her to be impressed when I replied, "The Arctic Ocean," but she merely smiled and said, "That's exciting," as if I'd told her we were going to Disneyland.

"My husband and I are travelin' cross-country, too," she went on. "We walked here."

"*Walked*? From West Virginia?"

"Not all the way down to here. We walked as far as Jacksonville, and we were worn out by then—I'm forty-four and Scott's fifty-three—and I told Scott, 'That's it.' We hopped a bus to Key West. Scott's dad is retired here. We're camped out in his backyard. We bought a couple of bikes, and when we're through here we're going to bike to California."

It was about six hundred miles from West Virginia to Jacksonville, and a good three thousand from Key West to California. No wonder she was underwhelmed by our plans.

"Through with what? . . . If you don't mind my asking."

"We did ministry in the Universal Life Church back in Huntington, and one day this spring, God just slapped Scott upside of the head and told him to get rid of everything and to start walkin' the country and helpin' out people in need of it, and that's what we did. Left a five-bedroom house with a big kitchen and a Jacuzzi."

Here comes a religious sales pitch, I thought, and composed the same polite but discouraging smile I put on whenever Jehovah's Witnesses appear at the front door. I was relieved when Jenita said that she and her husband were not out to reap converts but to comfort the homeless and persuade drunks and drug addicts to amend their lives.

Their main field of endeavor was Higgs Beach, about half a mile down the shoreline from Smathers. Higgs is a kind of derelict's Riviera, providing a target-rich environment for anyone seeking alcoholics and junkies.

"People drinking from daylight till dark," Jenita told us, dismay in her voice. "You go there at eight a.m. and they're already drunker'n monkeys."

I wanted to point out that they were probably drunk from the night before, but it seemed too fine a distinction.

"One young woman panhandled us for food, and three days later we saw her again, drunk!" Jenita said, shocked that she and her husband had been hustled. "And women selling themselves for drugs or alcohol. We saw a man drive up to Higgs, give a girl some money, and they walked out into the water and she looked like she was sittin' in his lap, but that's not all she was doin'. I said to myself, *I can't look at this, and I can't listen to this, F-this and F-that, GD this and GD that.*"

Curious about Scott's Pauline moment, I asked if I could talk to him. Sure, Jenita replied. He was off with a young homeless man they were trying to wean off weed, but he would be back in about an hour.

If Scott Meyers was a missionary, he was one who'd adopted the native mode of dress: a baseball cap, mirrored sunglasses, T-shirt, baggy shorts, and flip-flops. Lean and wiry, he wore a reddish-blond goatee dusted with gray.

The young man with him, Eric Walsh, was the homeless pothead, although, tanned and well fed, with shrewd, alert eyes, he did not fit the image.

We moved off the scorching street to a thatch-roof ramada on the beach, where we sat at a picnic table. Jenita took rolling papers, a plastic rolling device about the size of a can opener, and a pouch of "natural" tobacco from a backpack.

"Smoking is our one vice," she said, and produced two filter cigarettes, each one looking factory made. "Roll your own, you smoke less."

Eric bummed one from her. As she turned it out, I asked Scott about the divine summons. His answer suggested that earthly troubles had opened his ears to the call.

"It's this economy," he said, puffing on the cigarette. "Everything is down. I felt like I was gettin' nowhere."

He'd grown up in a prosperous household. His great-grandfather started a moving company that stayed in the family for three generations. Scott was learning the business from the bottom up as a long-haul trucker in the eighties when deregulation of the trucking industry enabled rivals to undercut the firm.

"Things went south, and we went out of business," he said.

His first marriage broke up. He went to work in construction and later landed a job with a Huntington contractor. He and Jenita, also divorced, had married six years ago. They were doing fairly well, renting the five-bedroom house with the Jacuzzi from Scott's employer, until the housing bubble popped and the Great Recession came crashing down. Work was wherever Scott could find it, and he couldn't find much.

"This past March, I was sittin' at a bus stop, feelin' like I was gettin' nowhere, like I said, and that's when God smacked me upside of the head. He said, 'What're you doin' here, miserable? You've got to sell everything you have and start walkin' the country, go out and lend a helpin' hand to those who need it.' That night, I came home and told Jenita."

"I was in the kitchen, fixin' supper," she said. "And I said, 'God smacked you upside of the head? Did you *fall* on your head?'"

I tried to imagine your conventional middle-aged, middle-class housewife listening to such an outrageous proposition, much less agreeing to it. But Jenita, sweet and innocent in some ways, was as tough as a hickory nut in others, and anything but conventional.

"I was raised up poor in a real big family," she said, and then ticked off a roster of brothers, sisters, half brothers, and half sisters. "I was born at the head of a holler in a house with no indoor plumbing. You wanted water, you went to the well. You had to go to the bathroom, well, honey, go out the back door, bathroom is the second tree on your right. I worked as a nurse for a while. I pumped gas and worked in maintenance—honey, I can hang you Sheetrock smooth as a baby's bottom. I can use a chain saw, I can kill your supper, gut it, clean it, and cook it."

Scott removed his sunglasses, revealing eyes that matched Jenita's bright blue, and picked up the thread of their story.

"We sold the car, the silverware, our clothes, the furniture. We downsized again and again, and it felt so good to get rid of material things, it was liberating."

"How do you get by? It must be tough."

"It was for me at first," Jenita said. "I'm a sweepaholic. After living in a big house, with no house to clean, I started sweeping sidewalks."

Scott said, "We've got the money from the sale of our possessions, and I've got skills. I drove a truck for a living, I know contracting work, I pick up odd jobs."

They were not trained counselors, but they had experience ministering to the addicted. From the way they described Huntington, I gathered that it's not the West Virginia John Denver sang about. Methamphetamine is the drug of choice in most of small-town and rural America, but crack is the plague in Huntington.

"The crack comes from Detroit," Scott said. "Dealers from there sell it in Huntington for five times what they'd get in Detroit. I've seen them with MONEYNGTON tattooed on their knuckles. That's what they call it, 'Moneyngton.'"

Jenita preached to the neighborhood kids that it was a sin to use crack. They called her "Aunt Cheetah" for the time she ran down a gang of punks who'd tried to break into her van. Another time, Aunt Cheetah caught a runaway girl prostituting herself for crack.

"Gave her a job cleaning our house. End of the day, she told me she was goin' out, and I knew what for, and I told her, 'No, you ain't.' Then she said she had to call her parents in Kentucky. She did, and then she took a shower, and while she was in there, I hit REDIAL and talked to her parents, and told them, 'I'm Reverend Meyers, and I've got your daughter right here, if you want to come collect her.' They did, and I still get postcards and letters from them. She's clean now, she's got a job."

If you think the Meyerses have a pretty high street IQ, you're right. But, Scott said, Key West had introduced them to a whole new dimension.

"I've known social alcoholics, but these people are professionals. You think you know the world, you get down here and know you don't."

"We saw one young woman somebody said looked like a man," Jenita said. "Right there in the open, she dropped her drawers and said, 'Do I look like a man?'"

She told tales of people down on their luck, way down, victims of the current economic wreck: a couple from Ohio, both fifty-eight years old, who'd been laid off from an auto plant, went through foreclosure, and were now on the street. A man who'd lost his wife and his job and had come down to the Keys to drink himself to death.

"Some of these stories just rip your heart out," said Scott. Then a skeptical expression played over his narrow, angular face. "But you don't know what's a real story, what's a hustle."

Eric begged another cigarette, and Jenita manufactured it in her little machine. She and Scott then excused themselves for a moment, leaving me with Eric, who so far hadn't spoken a word beyond his cadging smokes.

He was twenty-eight, the adopted son of a well-to-do family in Rockford, Illinois, and, he declared, "homeless by choice."

"I can go where I want, I'm a free man. I'm not like most homeless people. I don't panhandle. I do work. I've worked barges in New Orleans, I did house painting in Las Vegas. Look at this"—motioning at the panorama of green sea and white sand and palm trees—"People pay thousands, millions, to look at this. I do it for free."

"In other words, you're kind of an old-fashioned hobo."

"Whatever," he said, shrugging. "I've been doing it for eight years, and it's hard. Not just finding something to eat and a place to sleep, but making sure your stuff doesn't get stolen. You lose your driver's license or your state ID or your Social Security card, and you're done. And you've got to watch your health, physical and mental. Being homeless isn't for the mentally defective."

Here's a sharp survivor, I thought, and asked if he'd benefited from Scott and Jenita's counsel.

He gave me a canny look. "I'm teaching them a lot."

The Meyerses went off to spend the night in a homeless shelter on Stock Island to, in Scott's words, "learn firsthand what these people are going through." I did not see them again. I admired them for turning their backs on a culture that enshrined consumption and self-indulgence, knowing I wasn't capable of so radical a renunciation. Thinking of Scott at the bus stop, and the epiphany he experienced in the moment of despair, I recalled a line from Tolstoy's short novel *The Cossacks*: "Happiness lies in living for others." They seemed happy, this couple who'd tramped out of West Virginia with nothing but what they carried on their backs and a zeal to aid the marginalized. They probably would not rehabilitate many people with their ad hoc methods, but the attempt was what mattered. Their mission, whether or not it had come down from heaven, restored to their lives the purpose and meaning lost with the loss of Scott's employment. In trying to save others, they saved themselves.

Before leaving Key West, Leslie and I wanted to get a photo of ourselves at the Southernmost Point and to see the Southern Cross.

At the point, we joined a queue of tourists waiting to take photos. When our turn came, a balding, fortyish man behind us agreed to snap our picture. We posed beside the monument, he clicked Leslie's Nikon, and we returned the favor. Noticing his accent, I asked where he was from. He pointed seaward. "From there, Cuba."

Mario Rodriguez wasn't a tourist—a Cuban citizen has a better chance of getting a ticket to the moon than permission to visit the United States—but another escapee from Fidel Castro's tropical Alcatraz and, as of last year, a citizen of the United States.

I expected Rodriguez to tell of a perilous flight by sea, but his tale showed that the hope of freedom did not dwell only in the breasts of the desperate. He'd belonged to the Cuban elite, the beneficiary of perks denied ordinary citizens, like foreign travel and permission to study abroad. At eighteen, he was sent to East Germany to earn degrees in mathematics and business administration. There, he met and married an Ecuadorian woman and worked in what he termed *economic research* until East Germany, with the fall of the Berlin Wall, vanished from the map. He and his wife then moved to her native country, where Rodriguez taught math at a university and later established his own market research firm. His work, and vacations, took him all over the world, thirty-five or forty countries, he told me.

He'd heard about a U.S. law that allowed any Cuban who managed to get here to obtain a green card if he stayed one year and a day; after five years, he could apply for citizenship. In 2004, he got a visa from the U.S. consulate in Quito and flew to Miami. That's all there was to it.

His undramatic departure made him an unusual Cuban immigrant. What draw did the United States have on someone so privileged?

"The situation in Ecuador was not good," he said in a boyish voice. "It was not secure. I was, you know, how can you say when somebody takes you and asks for money?"

"You were robbed?"

"Yes, I was taken for two days . . ."

"You were kidnapped and held for ransom."

"Okay, yes."

"Do you know who kidnapped you and why?"

"No, and I don't want to know. After that, I decided to come to the United States. I love Ecuador, it's a nice country, but the situation there isn't right, so I came to this country because it's the opportunity country."

"And your wife came with you?"

"No. She died in Ecuador. Of cancer," he replied flatly. There was a whole other story, but I sensed it was not one he cared to tell.

Now Rodriguez was living near Fort Lauderdale, a substitute math teacher in a high school, hoping to qualify for a university teaching position. He did not, unlike Cuban émigrés of an older generation, feel the slightest moral obligation to liberate Cuba. He was just happy to be here.

"I traveled all around the world, but I always say this is the country where I want to live, because the freedom we have here, you know, we never have that freedom in other countries. To develop your self-realization. There is crisis, I know, economic crisis, but the United States is the best country in the world. I think so."

Someone had told me, years ago, that Key West's latitude was the northernmost from which the Southern Cross was visible. I had glimpsed it just once, in 1980, while on a night swordfishing trip in the Gulf Stream. It hung a hand's width above the horizon in the southwest—four stars like the points of a crystal kite.

On our last night, looking for the asterism, Leslie and I walked on Higgs Beach, where Scott and Jenita Meyers did God's work. Somewhere underfoot the bones of nameless slaves lay in a mass grave unmarked except for the brass plaque that told the story of how three U.S. Navy frigates had rescued them from Confederate slavers and brought them to Key West. The slave ships were captured out in the Caribbean, with more than a thousand Africans on board, in conditions so wretched that 264 of them died of disease within days of breathing the air of liberation. You can only wonder who they were, cast into a ditch and covered with sand beside the sea looking eastward toward the continent they'd left in chains.

White Street pier juts a couple of hundred feet into the ocean, and we strolled to its end in the breathless, humid dark. A few people were fishing, seated on camp chairs or stools beside plastic bait buckets, poles braced against the railings and the lines shimmering like spider's silk in the pier lights till they vanished into water that looked like a sheet of wet tar. Far out at sea, the lights of buoys and channel markers blinked white, red, green. We looked beyond, to where black water dissolved into black sky, and scanned right to left, left to right. The Summer Triangle—Deneb, Vega, and Altair—glimmered high up. A haze veiled the horizon, or maybe it was the faint light dome of Havana ninety miles off. But we never saw the Southern Cross.

6.

ECADES BEFORE STARBUCKS WAS A GLEAM IN ITS FOUNDERS'
eyes, *café con leche* was a staple in the Florida Keys. It's the equivalent of a latte, but with a higher octane rating. I bought two *grandes*
at Sandy's Café on White Street, where Cuban patrons were knocking
back *buchis*—shots of heavily sugared espresso—which made the Spanish
they were speaking sound like a language lesson recorded for 33 rpms
but played at 78.

I returned to the campground with the *grandes* to caffeinate Leslie
and me through the to-do items on our departure list.

"Y'all gonna go all the way to Alaska in that little thing?" asked Harry
Wade, a trailer-park neighbor who was giving us a hand. Harry, a retired
homicide detective from Alabama, was traveling with his wife in a sleek,
new RV as tall as a boxcar and longer than an eighteen-wheeler.

"We are," I answered, with more confidence than I felt.

"Wal, if y'all're still married at the end of it, that'll be a surprise."

That hit a nerve. Weeks before, in thrall to the notion of going it
alone, I'd worried about the effect a long separation might have on our
marriage. But now I wondered how well it would stand up to four months
in a space smaller than a walk-in closet. Leslie's friends had not exactly
encouraged her. "My husband and I would kill each other" was their
common refrain. "Two dogs and an impatient spouse, to boot," a boss
e-mailed. "Saint Leslie of the Highways." Her mother had given her a

book of "Tension-Taming Crosswords" to break out at the first sign of stress.

"Do you have any advice for staying married on trailer trips?" she asked Harry.

He thought for a moment. "Get a bigger trailer or take shorter trips."

Not through with cheering us up, he fetched a camera from his land-going cruise ship and took our picture.

"That's so we'll know what y'all looked like, case y'all disappear."

I went to the beach on Boca Chica channel, where tides from the Gulf of Mexico mingled with those from the Atlantic, and filled a third of a backpacker's water bottle. I intended to fill the next third at the Pacific, then top it off at the Arctic Ocean and shake it like a martini mixer, blending the waters that lapped all the coasts of America. A friend had suggested this ritual. He said it would symbolize the merging of races and nationalities. The notion charmed me.

As I walked back to the trailer, Harry Wade's warnings of severe marital thunderstorms preyed on my mind. I meant to ask people what they thought held the country together. Another riddle was: what held our marriage together?

Calling it a mixed marriage would be like calling gin and olive oil a mixed drink. Leslie was nervous before meeting me on a blind date in New York in 1985, but the minute she set eyes on me, she relaxed. *Phew,* she thought, *he's not my type.* For one thing, we're physically mismatched. Leslie is a slender, long-legged five-feet-nine. While I'm pretty well put together—I'll say that much in my favor—I'm not only almost thirteen years older but nearly three inches shorter. I'd wondered why she ever gave me a second glance, and she said that she liked my forearms.

The odd couple's differences extend to family backgrounds. Blue-blood girl meets blue-collar boy. My roots in America go back to a pater-nal great-grandfather, an illiterate Italian miner who emigrated in 1885. On her mother's side, Leslie's roots reach directly to two passengers on the *Mayflower,* and on her father's side to the Massachusetts Bay Colony through an early settler (1642). Add to her pedigree a roomful of illustri-ous ancestors and relatives: John Stevens, appointed by Theodore Roosevelt as chief engineer for the Panama Canal; Benjamin Seaver, mayor of Bos-ton under whose administration the Boston Public Library was built;

Henry Bryant, a renowned nineteenth-century surgeon and naturalist; and his grandson Henry Bryant Bigelow, founder of the Woods Hole Oceanographic Institute.

One day, when I discovered, in a genealogy in Leslie's parents' house, that she could trace her lineage to Charlemagne through a French nobleman, Count Sohier de Vermandois, I overcame my modesty about my own forebears and informed her that I was the great-nephew of Dominic Blasi, aka Nick Blaze, a high-ranking capo in the Chicago mob and the FBI's principal suspect in the assassination of its boss, Sam Giancana. Uncle Nicky, as he was known to his relations, was never charged. His highest achievement, a remarkable one considering his profession, was to die of natural causes at seventy-five.

Let's move on to matters of personality, temperament, outlook. Leslie was raised Presbyterian; I'm a practicing Roman Catholic. Leslie is a pacifist who'd marched in antiwar protests when she was in high school; I'm an ex-marine, Vietnam vet, and all that implies. Leslie was a diligent student in her youth; cum laude, St. Lawrence University; master's degree, University of North Carolina. I was a college dropout for a while but returned to school, barely graduating with a 2.2 grade-point average. Leslie never married before she married twice-divorced me. Leslie's steady, serene, quiet, self-effacing; I tend to be mercurial, moody, a motormouth never so animated as when I'm talking about myself.

So what has made this apparent *misalliance* work for twenty-three years? Our politics align, though she's more liberal on what are called social and cultural issues. We love dogs. We love literature and books and can talk endlessly about novels and poetry. We love travel, obviously. (Leslie climbed Mount Kilimanjaro when she was eighteen, rafted the Colorado through the Grand Canyon, and went to the Amazon on assignment with *Audubon* magazine.) We're both ardent conservationists with a passion for the outdoors and outdoor sports, though Leslie disapproves of my fondness for shooting animals large and small. She is reserved in public, playful and affectionate in private. She'll sneak up behind me as I'm shaving, stick her head on my shoulder and start talking about the morning's plans, then walk away with a faceful of shaving cream.

She has a tart tongue when called for, but there's always a wry humor in it. I like all that. I'm still not sure what she likes about me, beyond my forearms, that is.

In the end, it's best to look upon a successful marriage as the Lakota Sioux look upon any marvel beyond their understanding. They call such a thing *wakan*—mystery. Love, the deepest *wakan* of all, does not submit to rational analysis.

———

At a quarter past eleven on the morning of May 23 we headed north. U.S. 1 brought us to the Florida Turnpike and into metropolitan Miami's ghastly sprawl, a tide of asphalt and concrete that had been washing inland for a long time and now lapped the shores of the Everglades. That morning's *Miami Herald* reported that the Florida legislature, responding to calls from "the business community," had voted to dismantle the state's growth management laws because they were "unnecessarily inhibiting development." Well, whatever the growth management laws managed, growth wasn't it. Florida had about seven million people when I moved there in 1977; now, with a population edging toward eighteen million, it was the fourth-largest state in the union. It's always been a model of bipartisanship when it comes to making money off real estate. Democrat or Republican, from local zoning boards right up to the state senate and the governor's office, its officials seldom meet a developer they don't like, an instinctive affection nurtured by campaign contributions and more shadowy gratuities.

Comforted by the knowledge that tough times had not soured the legislature's love affair with developers, we swung off the turnpike in Sweetwater and went west on U.S. 41, aka the Tamiami Trail. It passes through Everglades National Park and Big Cypress National Preserve. The park's boundaries, south of the road, and the Miccosukee Indian reservation, to the north, serve as seawalls, halting the storm surge of strip malls and subdivisions. One minute we were surrounded by houses and IHOPs and gas stations, the next cruising through broad sawgrass prairies studded with islands of sabal palm.

In contrast to Florida politics, the Tamiami Trail is straight. As if on a runway, we sped across Shark River slough, the marshlands on both sides rolled flat to the horizons and mottled by the shadows of drifting stratocumulus. A flight of ibis, wedged like geese, flapped over a distant hummock, and egrets stalked in the grass with slow, patient motion, feathers so white they almost hurt the eye.

Past a cluster of Miccosukee houses with steep, thatched roofs, the road angled sharply northwest, then ran west again, direct as a rifle shot into Collier County and through Big Cypress. Leaving the Tamiami Trail, we followed State Route 29 toward Everglades City. If Key West had been Dodge City on the Gulf Stream, Everglades City had been Tombstone on the Gulf Coast in the drug-running days of the seventies and eighties. It faces the Ten Thousand Islands, which resemble pieces of a jigsaw puzzle dumped out of the box, forming a seascape-landscape that looks designed for illicit pursuits. Pirates lurked there in the eighteenth and nineteenth centuries, and it was a haven for bootleggers during Prohibition. A few decades later, the U.S. Interior Department banned commercial fishing in the Everglades and told the locals to find other ways to make a living. Fishermen, oystermen, and stone crabbers, each with a chart of the Ten Thousand Islands printed in his brain, took the department's advice and turned to marijuana smuggling. Pretty soon, half of Everglades City was in the trade. The money rolled in, good old boys exchanged their rattletrap pickups for new SUVs with smoked windows, their sluggish skiffs for fast fiberglass boats. It all ended in 1983, when two hundred federal agents swooped in and busted so many men that one female resident was heard to remark, "They've got all the men! This is gonna be a town of women!"

Actually, it became one more tourist town, though it still clung to its Wild West image. Crossing a bridge over the Barron River, we were greeted by a sign: WELCOME TO EVERGLADES CITY. WESTERN GATEWAY TO THE EVERGLADES AND THE LAST FRONTIER. In the twenties, it had bigger aspirations. A Gatsby-like entrepreneur, Barron Collier (his first name the eponym for the river, his last for the county), had visions of transforming what was then a decrepit fishing village into another Miami Beach. The Depression put an end to his dreams, and his half-finished resort city reverted to a backwater. These days, what was to have been a rival to Miami Beach has about five hundred residents. The Bank of Everglades Building and the city hall, both built by Collier in Classic Revival style, Doric columns and all, rise above crab shacks and clapboard cottages; the main street, a wide boulevard divided by a rank of stately royal palm, seems to cry out for upscale emporiums rather than the mom-and-pop stores lining it now.

A causeway carried us over Chokoloskee Bay to the island of the same name. We set up in a plush RV resort, as much for the dogs' sake as our own. They were gasping in the heat, though they had enough energy to chase the lizards skittering around. We had dinner in town, where Leslie picked up a glossy guidebook to the Gulf Coast. Sandwiched into the ads for airboat rides, Everglades tours, restaurants, and miniature golf courses was this sign of the times: "Foreclosure Tours! Free! Call Now! 239-443-3000."

A swollen sun hovered over the smoky horizon. It looked as cosmologists tell us it will look in its death throes four billion years from now: a red giant whose fires will incinerate whatever is left on Earth.

Varnished in insect repellent, we tried a morning walk with Sage and Sky, finishing up just as the mosquitoes and no-see-ums were stirring in the mangrove galleries alongside the causeway. How the pioneers lived in the Everglades without losing their minds was beyond me. You could make the argument that they were out of their minds to live there in the first place. The night we'd spent in the Everglades on the way to our start had already given us a small taste of what their existence had been like. Leslie had debuted one of my camping gear purchases, a mini–miner's light worn on an elastic headband. I wanted to sleep, she wanted to read, so I suggested she don the lamp. She did, then cracked open *The Innocents Abroad*—and in seconds she wore a veil of insects. Her curses and swats at the midges, mosquitoes, moths, and gnats woke me up, and as I laughed at her traffic-cop gyrations, she suggested that I try the miner's light, which she tossed helpfully at my head.

Now, in Chokoloskee, we sought directions from a guy in the campground office.

Leaning on a counter packed with fishing lures, Kenny Brown was deep in conversation with a rangy, saturnine man chewing tobacco.

"Come in here in the middle of the night and flattened that mound," the man said as he drew a diagram of a U-shaped ditch on scrap paper. "How d'yuh figure, bulldozes the mound flat without documentation from state archaeologists and closes off a public road with no permission from the county?"

Brown narrowed his gray-blue eyes. "Says he's well connected, and not here with the county." He waved a hand to indicate that whoever they were talking about had nothing but contempt for local officials. "Says he got connections in the state legi-slate-shur."

"Yuh know, the state archaeologist was all set to come down from

Tallahassee to see what was here, but somehow he didn't," the other man said. "So this fella hires his own private archaeologist, and of course he said there's nothing here."

He spit tobacco juice into a paper cup. Brown, silent, shook his head. Into the pause, I asked for directions to the Smallwood Trading Post, opened in 1906 by a pioneer couple and now a historic landmark.

"Mamie Street, named for Mamie Smallwood," the tobacco chewer said. "Closed off, all right. Developer blocked it off, a public road, like he owns it!"

I introduced myself. The man was Ken Smallwood, a descendant of the trading post's founders. That explained his outrage.

"What developer?" I asked.

A limited partnership called Florida-Georgia Grove had bought the shell mound and its adjoining property from the Seminole Indian tribe, he said. Now it was clearing land and dredging a boat basin for a marina.

"And no regard for what's here," said Brown. "Chokoloskee Island is one of the most significant archaeological sites in Florida."

"There's a lot here? Artifacts?"

"This whole island is one big shell mound," Brown said. "There's burial sites from the Calusas on through the Seminoles on through the early white settlers. After a rain, you can walk and look over there and see a deer bone and then a human bone. You can look a few feet away and see pottery shards."

"Or an arrowhead or a carved pipe," Smallwood interjected, to which Brown added, "There's no site like this in the whole world! Arrowheads made out of conch shells and Indian graves. Why, this place is huckle-buck full of stuff like that."

Kenny and Ken launched into a history lecture, displaying a passion for their heritage. Brown, a great-great-grandson of a Florida Indian agent, informed us that *Chokoloskee* meant "the old home" in the Semi-nole language. But the Seminoles were Johnny-come-latelies. The shell mounds had been built by their predecessors, the Calusas.

"They were on this island from the twelfth to the fourteenth centu-ries, not long before the Spaniards got here," Smallwood said.

"*Way* before that," Brown corrected. "The Smithsonian was down here years back and carbon-dated artifacts to 600 AD! The Calusas built canals. They built levees out of oyster and clam shells."

"Florida's first developers," I said.

He laughed and went on. At one time, the Calusas were the mightiest tribe in Florida, adept at war because they were fond of it. *Calusa* meant "the fierce people."

"When Ponce de León landed here in 1513, the Calusas met him with a whole bunch of war canoes and fought him off. Second time Ponce landed, 1521, the Calusas met him again. They wounded ole Ponce with a poison arrow, him and two other men. The Spaniards retreated, sailed away back to Havana, and Ponce took three days to die."

Smallwood replenished his wad of chew. "Their bows were powerful, and their arrowheads made from shell could penetrate the Spaniards' armor. Or they aimed for their knees, whatever wasn't protected. Yup, Calusas killed those Spaniards for their bad ways."

He and Brown seemed to draw inspiration from the tribe's resistance to Spanish conquest in their own fight against the bad ways of Florida-Georgia Grove LLP.

"This county is gonna make that man restore the road, " Smallwood predicted. "And when his investors find out all the trouble going on down here, they're gonna contact their lawyers, and you watch—one by one they'll drop out."

We wanted to see a shell mound, and where might we do that?

Brown grabbed a chart and a pencil. "You go across the bay to the mouth of the Turner River, then paddle upstream to here." On the chart he marked an *X* at a fork in the river. "You'll see it. Bigole midden, once covered half a square mile."

We rented a canoe and, with the dogs stowed in the trailer, set out across Chokoloskee Bay, cooled by a fresh southwesterly breeze. Schools of mullet creased the murky water, and an osprey circled above, seeking a meal with eyes that detect what the human eye can see only through binoculars. The canoe scraped a shoal entering the tidal river, coffee-brown, a quarter of a mile wide, shallow as spit, bordered by red mangrove whose roots looked like the legs of gigantic spiders. Young ibis waded nearby, scooping muck with their long, curved bills.

Near the fork, we spotted the midden. It resembled a rock pile, and it must have risen twenty feet above the shoreline. We turned toward it, passing a small blacktip shark cruising a bar, and a fine specimen of a tricolor heron—slate blue back, greenish head, a white stripe along its throat. It stood utterly motionless on spindly, crayon-yellow legs, its neck forming an *S*; then the neck straightened and snake-quick the long beak struck and came up with a minnow, shiny as a foil strip.

We beached the canoe. Wearing halos of mosquitoes, we climbed the mound and followed a path inland, above black, brackish ponds and snarled mangrove roots.

"How did he say this place was full of artifacts?" Leslie asked, looking at the ground.

"Hucklebuck full."

Heads down, we searched in vain for an arrowhead or pottery shard on this primitive landfill of oyster shells mortared with limestone marl. Enough oysters to keep a raw bar in business for a century, and there'd once been hundreds of these shell mounds in southwestern Florida.

And thousands of Calusas, reigning uncontested over the Gulf Coast until the Spanish arrived. Two centuries after they'd driven Ponce de León back to Cuba, the Calusas, decimated by wars and by European diseases, couldn't offer even token resistance to the Seminole Creeks migrating south from present-day Georgia. Soon afterward, they disappeared completely.

We boarded the canoe and paddled back across the bay. In the distance, the Smallwood Trading Post stood on its pilings above the muddy shore, no less than the Calusa middens a relic of a vanished culture. My heart was with Kenny Brown and Ken Smallwood, but I wasn't sure, if someone asked me to bet on them or the developer, where I'd put my money.

7.

THERE ARE MANY HIGHWAYS THAT COMBINE THE BANALITY OF
the interstate with the frustration of stoplights and heavy traffic,
and that describes U.S. 41 as it passes through the urbanized parts
of Florida's Gulf Coast: Naples, Cape Coral, Fort Myers. An hour of
stop-and-go persuaded me to temporarily lift the ban on interstates: we
turned onto I-75 and sped up to Tampa, where we violated another prohibition by staying at a motel. We were going to visit my son Geoff, and
there wasn't a trailer park within a reasonable distance of his house.

Geoff, a music teacher and jazz guitarist, was playing a gig that night
but promised to see us in the morning. He recommended that we kick
back at a downtown bar, the Hub, warning us not to order doubles.

The Hub, "established 1949," billed itself as Tampa's oldest continuously
operating bar, as if it were an English pub dating back to Henry VIII. It was
a time capsule of sorts: dimly lit, black-and-white checkered floor, and
some customers were smoking! Cigarettes! The reason for Geoff's
advice regarding doubles became apparent when Jamie, the bartender,
poured me a martini that could have accommodated a school of gin-
resistant goldfish.

She wore a ponytail, glasses, and a replica of the *Tampa Tribune* front
page from June 7, 2004, on her T-shirt. OURS, read the headline, set in a
font size usually reserved for declarations of war. "Ours" was the Stanley
Cup, won that year by the Tampa Bay Lightning.

What did you call citizens of Tampa? Tampanites sounded too much like an exotic mineral, and Tampons wouldn't do. Whatever the term, the whole city was hoping for a repeat, and all eyes in the Hub were on the TV, broadcasting the preliminaries to that night's playoff for the Eastern Conference championship. Game 6, and the Boston Bruins were leading the series, 3–2.

I asked Jamie why the team was called Lightning.

"You don't know?" growled a disreputable smoker sitting beside Leslie. He forgave my ignorance, then explained that Tampa Bay had an average of 874 lightning strikes per year, more than anywhere else in the world.

The martini was playing darts, and my cortex was the dartboard. I asked Leslie, sotto voce, if I was speaking clearly.

"You sound like a drunk trying to sound sober," she whispered.

I left it to her to carry the burden of conversation with Jamie, a pleasant woman who'd fled New Hampshire in 1995 to attend the University of Tampa.

"I hate the cold," she said. "Last winter, I visited my parents and I thought, *No human should live in cold like this.*"

However, Jamie's desire for warmth exacted its price. Her fine-arts degree cost $120,000 in student loans, and she'd been tending bar for years to pay them off.

"Sixty thousand so far," she said. "Sixty more to go. I'd really like to teach."

"My . . . sh . . . son told me," I ventured, "never order a double here."

Jamie's smile was kind but firm: she wasn't going to serve me another drink. "Good advice. Because a single is a double, a double a triple. Nope. You never have to order a double in the Hub."

———

We met Geoff for breakfast the next morning at La Teresita, a Cuban eatery where the waitresses called you "Hon" or its Spanish equivalent. We sat at the crowded counter, eating zingy three-egg omelets washed down with double espressos. While a video advertising bail bondsmen played on the TV overhead, Geoff regaled us with tales of the musician's perilous existence: moody vocalists who had to be humored, no-show sidemen. He had three bands: a bread-and-butter group for weddings and corporate events; a quartet called the Otha Brotha, because three are Filipino brothers, Geoff being the otha brotha; and the one dearest to his heart, the FLO—Fusion Liberation Organization.

He followed us back to the motel parking lot, where we gave him a tour of Ethel, accomplished in two nanoseconds. Glancing at the forward bunk, about five and half feet long by three wide, he asked, "Do you two lovebirds fit on *that*?" "No," I said, "that's mine"; out of my natural gallantry, and the fact that I'm more inseam-challenged than Leslie, I'd given the wider, longer bunk in the rear to her.

Once upon a time, Geoff lived the jazzman's life to the full. At thirty, he realized it was going to be a short life if he kept on, and he became a born-again Christian. Before we left, he put his arms around us and said a prayer for our safety and health. Though I suspected the divine intelligence of the universe had better things to do than watch out for us, I was touched.

8.

THE COASTLINE THAT RUNS NORTH FROM TAMPA TO THE WEST-ward hook of the Florida panhandle is referred to on splashy tourist maps as the "Nature Coast." It's as if some planning commission had zoned it for trees and grass and all the other coasts for parking lots and high-rises. My guess is that the absence of a main highway accounts for the Nature Coast's relatively untouched condition. It's not all that accessible. The nearest major road, U.S. 98, is a considerable distance inland and is a pleasure to drive, lightly trafficked and free of commercial glut in its passage through pine and palmetto forests and cattle ranches whose emerald pastures look as tended as park lawns.

Most people don't think "Florida" and "cowboy" go together, but the central part of the state has been cattle country since the days of the first Spanish settlers. The Anglo and Scots Irish cowhands who displaced the vaqueros pushed their livestock through the scrub with long drover's whips whose rifle-shot crack, some say, was the origin of *cracker* as a term for backcountry whites.

And there on the road map was Crackertown. Its derivation was obvious, but its immediate neighbor, Yankeetown, mystified us. Hoping for a colorful tale—maybe New England Puritans settled there after sinning, maybe Yankee carpetbaggers took it over after the Civil War—we were deflated when a gas station attendant told us that the town was named for northerner retirees who'd migrated to Florida.

State Highway 24 ran like a railroad track, which in fact it once had been, till it jogged to the right, bridged an estuary, and dropped us off in Cedar Key, a remote fishing village in danger of becoming self-consciously charming because it now depends more on tourism than fishing.

Downtown, patriotic bunting hung from the verandas of old-Florida inns and hotels, and workmen were putting flags on lampposts and telephone poles in preparation for Memorial Day. We found a seaside parking lot with sufficient shade to keep the dogs from dying of heat stroke and looked for a place to eat lunch. There were several on Dock Street, a street on a dock. The restaurant that caught our eye was a brightly painted shack boasting the best grouper sandwich on the island. It had a big deck and was called the Big Deck. Literal-mindedness appeared to be a town trait.

The waiter, a hefty kid who looked no older than sixteen, handed us a menu that featured a special—the Ripper, so named for the effect it would have on your digestive tract: a fried hot dog smothered in jalapeño peppers, banana peppers, cheese, tomato, sour cream, and salsa, and served with curly french fries. I opted for the grouper sandwich to test the Big Deck's truth-in-advertising. Leslie ordered crab cakes.

In answer to the waiter's query, I said that the grouper sandwich was good, though final judgment would have to wait till I sampled all the others on the island. He advised me to conduct my survey before the weekend; thousands were expected to descend on Cedar Key. Anyway, that was the hope. What with the plummeting economy, no one could be sure how many visitors would show up.

"You see, this side of the island survives on tourism. The other side on clamming," he said, motioning at broad-beamed dories in the harbor.

"To change the subject," I said, "we've got a couple of dogs in our truck. They're in the shade, but they might be happier if we could bring them here. Okay?"

"Don't think so, but let me check with Brian."

In a moment, he came back with a stocky man wearing a baseball cap and a stubble of beard. Brian Skarupski was the owner, also the cook, and he arrived at our table with a fellow restaurateur, Glenda Richburg, who ran a breakfast place, Annie's Café.

"I can't let you bring the dogs here," Brian said, apologetically. "I used to let my customers tie dogs up on the deck. Then the state health inspector told me I couldn't do that anymore. The state required city hall to pass an ordinance prohibiting pets in a restaurant unless the owner had a permit. To get the permit, I had to install doggy-doo stations and plastic bags on the deck. I wasn't going to. I thought, *Hey, if you see a dog on a restaurant deck and you don't like it, then you say, 'I'm not going to eat there.'* That's how America is supposed to work. You ask me, the whole thing is unraveling."

"America, you mean?"

"You ask me, it is. What brings you to Cedar Key? Memorial Day?"

I told him about our trip. We'd been on the road only a week, but I'd honed the speech to two or three sentences.

"The country unraveling, that's one of the things we want to ask people," I said. "If they think it is, or what they think holds it together."

"That's a hard question, the way things are going." Brian considered for a moment. "Take me for an example. I'm a small businessman. I own this place and a grocery in town. Found out the other day there's going to be a new regulation requiring scales to register not just the weight but the nutrient value in chicken, pork, and beef. So much of this, so much of that."

I asked how this instrument could distinguish a pork chop from a chicken breast, and then detect its content of protein, fat, vitamins.

"The scale has special software that calculates these nutrient levels," Brian replied. "So I asked a guy from a scale company what one would cost me. Thirty-four hundred bucks! He told me that he feels the same way I do about government meddling and regulations. Except in this case because now he gets to sell real expensive new scales."

"But aren't regulations necessary?"

"The big money they don't regulate," Brian scoffed. "Small money like mine they do."

Glenda jumped in. "Like the net fishing ban. All it did was put a lotta people outta work." She paused to drag on a Marlboro Light. Glenda had denim blue eyes, slightly tilted at the corners, and high, sharp cheekbones that gave her a kind of tough-cookie good looks. "Worked the net boats myself when I was a kid. They said we were killin' porpoise and crap like that. Well, we weren't. Hell, everybody loves frickin' porpoise."

"Has the clam industry made up for it?"

"Not much," she answered. Sure, at low tide you could see entire reefs of clams, but "big operators from up North came on down and bought up all the leases. The little guy doesn't have enough money to go out on his own. You asked what holds this country together. Well, I have no idea whatever holds it together."

9.

WHAT FINGER-SHAPED FLORIDA LACKS IN BREADTH IT makes up for in length; Tallahassee is 480 miles from Miami (farther than New York City is from Cleveland).

The two cities are separated by another, greater distance. Miami has become a Latin American capital, home to Cubans of course, but also Hondurans, Colombians, Brazilians. The city jumps to a salsa beat. You can drive the whole length of Eighth Street, Calle Ocho, and swear by the billboards and storefront signs that you're in Havana or Bogotá. Finding an English-language radio station is like an Easter-egg hunt with no egg at the end.

Country-and-western dominated the AM and FM bands when we got to Tallahassee, and the signs did not require translation. Magnolia and live oak bearded with Spanish moss shaded clapboard homes (in modest neighborhoods) and (in high-end precincts) the grounds of would-be Taras with white-pillared porticos.

We spent a day and a night with my son Marc and his wife, Erin, and babysat our three granddaughters. Although the guest room was no bigger than the trailer, Leslie was delighted to sleep on a real bed in a space that didn't rest on wheels. The two women in my life weren't getting along. Leslie is practical, down-to-earth, and low-maintenance, and she doesn't suffer high-maintenance girly-girls gladly. That described Ethel. Ethel was also unpredictable; the propane alarm had gone off again, for no apparent reason.

Now that I wasn't traveling alone, Marc's opinion of my sanity had moderated. He's a political reporter for the *Miami Herald* and helped me in my quest by arranging an interview with Dean Cannon, the Republican Speaker of the Florida House of Representatives.

I met Cannon at a Starbucks in a Tallahassee suburb. *Speaker of the House* evokes an image of a craggy-faced eminence like Tip O'Neill. Cannon, though forty-two, looked so young I wanted to ask him what he was going to do when he got out of college. As I approached seventy, almost everyone under forty-five looked eighteen. I sought Cannon's opinions about what keeps our monster, mongrel nation in one piece.

He replied with a lawyerly dissertation.

"The nation is held together for structural, cultural, and historical reasons. We have a federal, not a national, government. It's the difference between steel and Kevlar. The structure is flexible enough to respect differences in diverse peoples and diverse states, but strong enough to hold things together. It's the only form of government capable of sustaining such a diversity of geography and ethnicity without everything blowing apart.

"There is a universal yearning in the human soul to be free, to be unfettered, and the degree of personal freedom we have here is greater than in any other country. You can start a business in your backyard, you can own a gun, you can travel from Florida to Alabama or Georgia without showing your papers. The Bill of Rights is our shared cultural legacy.

"We were born out of a group of brave, original thinkers. We had an unbuilt continent, blessed by climate and soil, a country rich beyond compare, and at a key moment in history, they knew how to take the best of the best and build a new form of government."

There wasn't a word I disagreed with. But, I asked, if we had this wonderful system, why were so many people up in arms? Tea Partiers calling for secession, mainstream politicians hinting that armed revolt might be a viable option?

"You've got to distinguish. There are some Tea Party people who are angry, social misfits, they're just crazy jerks. But I think the vast majority of the Tea Party people I've spoken to aren't so much angry as they're afraid—afraid of the country, for the first time in its existence, losing sight of the fact that liberty and personal freedoms are the primary characteristics distinguishing us from every other country in the free world. The gravest threat to liberty is too strong a central government."

There I did partially disagree. As Justice Louis Brandeis said in 1941, we could have democracy in this country or we could have great wealth in the hands of the few, but we couldn't have both. Bigness was the gravest threat to liberty: big banks and big corporations in alliance with big government—an oligarchy, a corporatarchy, a plutocracy, call it anything you like. Maybe what had everybody, left, right, and center, so upset was the recognition that we were the suckers in a game of Texas hold 'em rigged by the Wall Street and K Street sharpies.

From reading too many newspapers and listening to too many news broadcasts and talk-radio ravings, I'd formed the impression that most Republicans were like the mad-as-hell character in the film *Network*. But Cannon, who described himself as a "William Buckley conservative," was so civil and reasonable that I left feeling better about Republicans all around. A lefty like me could talk politics with a righty like him without having a TV-style shout-fest.

10.

THE TWO HUMANS AND THEIR DOGS LEFT TALLAHASSEE ON Memorial Day and headed into the panhandle. A roadsign—TWO EGG—15 MI.—drew us off U.S. 90. Where better to have two eggs for breakfast? Fifteen miles on, another sign told us that we were in Two Egg, which appeared to exist in the sign maker's imagination. All we found were two farmhouses surrounded by peanut fields. We doubled back and asked a clerk at a convenience store if we'd missed the town. No, we hadn't. "Ain't much there," she told us.

"For sure," I said. "Why had it"—if there was an *it*—"been named Two Egg?"

"All sorts o' stories 'bout that," she answered. "Man named Cox wrote a book about town names in Florida. You'll find 'em in there, and the book in the bookstore in Marianna."

The bookstore was closed for the holiday, and none of the other businesses looked as if they would carry Mr. Cox's compendium of Florida place-names. It was hard to tell what kind of merchandise some of them stocked, like Bastion Piano and Christian Supply. Bullets and Bowls sold ammunition and either china or bowling equipment.

Marianna is a handsome town where the past is a presence. We drove by lovely antebellum mansions, the Confederate memorial—a white plinth like a miniature Washington Monument—and brass markers commemorating the Battle of Marianna, a fierce skirmish fought between a federal raiding party and the local garrison in 1864. In the cemetery of St.

Luke's Episcopal, we found the grave of John Milton—not the author of *Paradise Lost* but the Confederate governor of Florida, a fanatical secessionist who said he'd rather die than live in the United States. True to his word, he shot himself when the South surrendered. His grave, under a tombstone inscribed NON SIBI SED PATRIAE (not for self but country), lay under a huge old magnolia tree. I hoped he wasn't turning over down there. A small Confederate flag was planted on one side; on the other, the flag of the union he hated.

There is no memorial to a very dark chapter in Marianna's history. The tale of what happened to Claude Neal, a black man accused of raping a white woman in 1934, is *To Kill a Mockingbird* without the trial or Atticus Finch. A white lynch mob seized Neal from jail, mutilated him (I'll leave it to you to guess how), hanged him, stabbed him repeatedly with sharpened sticks, then dragged his corpse behind an automobile into Marianna, where it was strung up on the courthouse lawn. The atrocity made headlines all over the country and led to passage of the antilynching laws under Franklin Roosevelt's administration.

A long time ago, the city fathers say. Modern Marianna is progressive and diverse, a center of ecotourism with Florida Caverns State Park nearby. But that doesn't mean that racism is safely stored away in the reliquary of the Jim Crow past. During the 2008 presidential campaign, Marc covered a story about a Marianna middle school teacher who'd given his seventh-grade students an unusual civics lesson. Noting that Barack Obama's campaign theme was change, he wrote C-H-A-N-G-E on the blackboard and, with a laugh, told them that it stood for Come Help A Nigger Get Elected. The teacher was suspended for ten days, which represents progress of a sort in race relations.

Dwelling on this history, recent and remote, put me in a reflective mood as we rolled out of Florida and into Alabama. My body was in the New South, my head in the South I'd seen in 1961. Two college buddies and I were heading for the spring break bacchanal in Fort Lauderdale when we got lost somewhere in Georgia. We stopped at an all-night gas station to get directions. I was thirsty, and as I bent over the fountain on one side of the station, an attendant the size of a public monument tapped me on the shoulder with a wrench. "You don't look like no nigger to me, son," he said, and pointed at the sign I'd missed in the darkness: COLORED ONLY. I would like to report that I was outraged. What I did was apologize and go to the WHITES ONLY fountain on the other side.

I'm not dredging up this memory because I'm a snooty northerner who thinks Yankees are enlightened and southerners benighted; I grew up in Chicago, where the Klan could have taken lessons in bigotry. I dredge it up because in Alabama we found Old South and New South cohabiting.

A sign on a barn roof beckoned: HISTORIC CIVIL WAR BATTLE SITE. I'd no sooner glimpsed it than I saw another: TIN TOP CAFÉ. It was lunchtime, and we pulled off U.S. 231 onto a gravel drive and parked by an ancient tree, its branches casting shade for ten yards all around. Fred's thermometer read ninety-eight degrees. For the first month of our journey, we were seldom to experience a day under ninety, which led me to question the wisdom of traveling in the summer with two long-haired dogs. Their welfare was a constant concern. Dog wrangler Leslie let Sage and Sky out for a pee break, then leashed them to the shaded rear bumper and set a water dish on the ground so they would survive our lunch hour.

With a tin roof, junk-cluttered wood porch, old Coca-Cola signs, and logos of extinct oil companies tacked to its outer walls, the Tin Top looked as if it had been around since the days of Model Ts. (We found out later that it dated to the 1980s; the decor, like distress marks on modern furniture, was there to give it a homey, antique look.) Lunch was served cafeteria-style, in southern country abundance. Fried chicken, biscuits, green beans, and coleslaw heaped on our plates, we sat down, next to a wall covered with dated license plates and rodeo photographs.

"See that?" Leslie whispered, and cocked her head at a poster. COMING SOON TO A HOSPITAL NEAR YOU—OBAMACARE, it said. A photoshopped picture of the president's face, with a bone through his nose, was superimposed on the torso of an African witch doctor, clad in a leopard-skin loincloth.

"Guess they serve chicken here from the right wing only," Leslie observed.

But right wing and left wing were beside the point because Obama's health-care policies were beside the point. The photograph was the point. We were only a short drive from Montgomery, where in 1955 Rosa Parks changed a great deal by refusing to change her seat on a city bus. Segregated water fountains and lunch counters and bus seats were no more but, evidently, people like that gas station attendant were not yet an endangered species.

"Young man, have you had enough to eat? Enough to hold you till supper?" a man asked as we were leaving.

He was seated at a table near the door with two ladies of a certain age. Red suspenders held up his trousers, and pale eyes sparkled merrily behind his glasses. If he was older than I, it wasn't by much, and I thanked him for calling me young and said that I'd eaten so much I would probably skip supper.

This appeared to gratify him. He was the Tin Top's owner, Robert Messildine. He asked where we were from and where we were going, and after I answered he considered for a moment and said with a chuckle, "Alaska, huh? You'll find it uphill all the way."

Messildine exuded good humor and southern hospitality. I took an immediate liking to him and wasn't able to square my liking with the racist poster. But then, there are shadowy corners in my own soul that I can't reconcile with the brighter parts of myself.

"I'd like to see that Civil War battle site you've got advertised out there," I said.

Robert shook his head. "You cain't see it, cuz it ain't there. My nephew was a surveyor up in North Carolina, near to Nags Head, and he was cleanin' up after a hurricane and found that sign and brought it here. I got to take it down one of these days. How far you goin' today? Don't reckon you'll make Alaska by nightfall."

I said, "Tuscaloosa"—if the trailer parks and state campgrounds there had not all been blasted into oblivion. A month earlier, more than two hundred tornadoes had struck the Southeast in a single day, with the worst smashing through northern Alabama.

Robert spoke of million-dollar homes blown into a lake in Tuscaloosa, and of a Georgia woman who owned one of those homes. She was last seen fleeing in a red Jeep Cherokee, and most likely she and the car were at the bottom.

"If you want to help out in Tuscaloosa, there's plenty of work for you to do," he said. "They'll be cleanin' up for the next year."

As we rolled toward Montgomery, Leslie spoke into her Android smart phone, which we'd begun calling "Magic Droid," or "MD": "Tuscaloosa. Tornado. Volunteer relief work."

Allow me to digress. Though I'm not a Luddite, I have an ambivalent relationship with technology. It's made life much easier, saved me epochs of time, and yet I resent it. Every week, it seems, Apple or Microsoft rolls out some new, complicated, expensive device that I'm supposed to master or I'll get left behind in the digital dust. Even my flip-up cell phone, which doesn't do much more than make calls, came with an instruction manual half an inch thick. As chock-full of apps as Santa's bag, MD did everything but mix drinks and was to prove invaluable on the trip. Whenever we made a wrong turn, her GPS put us back on track. I use the feminine pronoun because MD gave driving directions in a female voice, a do-as-I-say voice—*In one hundred yards, turn left*—that reminded me of my eighth-grade teacher, Sister Joan Clare. And, like Sister Joan Clare, she was almost always right, which irritated the hell out of me.

I have navigated through wilderness with a map and compass, at sea with a sextant. Those instruments require skill and practice, and, accurate as they are, they're subject to error. That uncertainty creates a tingling tension; so when you arrive at your destination you feel not only relieved but gratified, because your own brain and abilities, mixed with a little luck, are what got you there.

When she was in GPS mode, MD removed the elements of unpredictability that make travel an adventure. I remember an old-world atlas that had belonged to my father in high school; it dated from the thirties, when some parts of the planet still appeared as white spots on the map. Oh, how I loved to stare at them and wonder, *What's there?* Even in my own youth, a few places, like the depths of the Brazilian Amazon or the interior of New Guinea, remained as uncharted as Mars. Now Mars itself has been partially mapped; as for our own planet, satellite technology has filled in every square mile. There were no mysterious, thrilling white spaces in MD. Communicating with those spinning satellites, she could take me down any road or street in America and deliver me to the exact spot I wanted to go. It was marvelous—and somehow depressing.

Leslie's relationship with MD was likewise complicated. Electronic devices *know* that she's nervous around them. "They react like a horse does around a tenderfoot," she told me. "They misbehave." For instance, she'd been typing a perfectly polite e-mail to a coworker when, in the middle of the message, MD somehow tossed in *fucked*. Leslie marveled at the Droid and needed it to stay in touch with the office, but she was frustrated when we entered gaps in Verizon's coverage, of which there were more than the company claims. "We're like idol worshippers with technology we don't understand," she said. "Punch this button because it worked last time. Like the ancients who sang up the sun because if they didn't, it wouldn't rise." Often, I'd see her holding one of her gizmos up to the sky at odd angles, as if offering a sacrifice. It didn't look too weird if the object was the phone or the little 4G device to connect to the Internet, but she made a peculiar sight when she walked around with the laptop hoisted over her head. As for me, I was delighted by those endlessly spinning "beachballs of death" or the message "No service."

There was service on the road to Tuscaloosa. Instantly, MD told us that the headquarters for Relief Work Volunteers was in the McAbee Center. Leslie phoned. Yes, volunteers were still needed. We were to show up at nine the next morning to register.

U.S. 82, a federal highway that had the charm of a county road, carried us through peach orchards and small towns and long stretches of pine and sweet gum into the fringes of Tuscaloosa.

We saw very little damage at first—a few boarded-up windows, a roof or two missing shingles—and then the destruction looked postapocalyptic. An entire shopping mall and a nearby residential neighborhood had been pulverized. All that remained of two houses were the foundation slabs, swept as clean as if newly laid; the tornado had sucked the plumbing out of the concrete. Severed tree trunks, branches amputated by chain-saw winds; the steel stanchions of a huge highway sign bent like straws; and everywhere, backhoes and bulldozers pushing rubble into mounds twenty feet high. Berms of dirt, brick, and concrete surrounded the lake Messildine had mentioned, and I pictured that Georgia woman at the bottom, trapped in her Cherokee. The twister had destroyed seven thousand homes and businesses and killed forty-three people. It was an EF4 in the weather bureau's parlance, the second most powerful category, internal winds of two hundred miles an hour, roaring and thundering, a furious choir singing its own "Dies Irae."

We found a functioning campground some twenty miles west of the city, in Lake Lurleen State Park, named for Lurleen Wallace, who married George and succeeded him as Alabama's governor. The next morning, on the way to the McAbee Center, we passed more evidence of the tornado's capricious rage: a sofa and TV set lay atop a pile of bricks and concrete blocks, the TV's screen without a crack in it; an American flag clung to its downed pole; one house stood almost intact; its neighbor had only one fractured wall standing, on which someone had painted "A Mighty Fortress Is Our God."

"Turn left on Fifteenth Street," MD commanded, and with annoying precision she guided us right to the volunteer center, a gym on the grounds of a Veterans Administration hospital. We signed in, were issued name tags, work gloves, and safety glasses, and received our assignment: the Phister Warehouse, across town.

Before leaving, we wandered over to two large, acetate-covered wall maps of the United States, on which volunteers had written their initials in their home states. Those in the South were so covered that there was no space left. We added *LW* and *PC* to the dozen or so entries in Connecticut. A relief coordinator, John Lambert, told me that fourteen thousand people had flocked to Tuscaloosa from every state in the union except Alaska. Some had come from abroad—from the United Kingdom, Germany and Switzerland, Jamaica. Lambert, a recent graduate of the University of Alabama, struggled to express his feelings.

"It is awesome . . . people wanting to come and help and saying, 'This is my neighbor, I want to reach out to them, I want to assist them.' It's kinda cool to see people from, like, Ohio coming down and saying, 'We've heard about this and we want to help y'all.'"

Dean Cannon's idea that what bonds Americans to their country is our form of government, combined with our shared history and culture, rings true; but evidence of something more fundamental was right in front of us, on the maps: a spirit of generosity arising from a recognition that we are not islands unto ourselves but parts of a greater whole. That spirit had compelled thousands of men and women to travel long distances to a place many had never seen and come to aid fellow citizens they'd never met. They'd disrupted their own lives to clear rubble, load trucks, deliver food and medicine, and comfort the afflicted.

At the Phister Warehouse, in a drab industrial district, I backed Fred into the shadiest spot I could find, under a mimosa whose pink flowers threw off an amazing scent. Leslie dropped the truck's tailgate, clipped Sage's and Sky's leashes to anchor points, and filled their water bowls to overflowing. The temperature had hit triple digits.

Fred shared the parking lot with a couple of rental trucks and several vans belonging to church groups.

The warehouse must have covered an acre. Boxes of supplies, number-coded to indicate clothes, towels, food, soap, shampoo, bottled water, and so on, were stacked on pallets or in bins from one end to the other. Supervising the volunteers were half a dozen women wearing yellow

T-shirts from Seventh-Day Adventist Disaster Relief. We reported to the lady-in-charge, who assigned us to Mary Rose.

We were to fill an order for the New Light Baptist Church in the town of Eutah, Mary Rose told us in a soft voice. A huge order for just about everything imaginable—Eutah had been devastated. She glanced at the clipboard in her hand. "It's so big, it's ridiculous," she said. "All right, first thing for you is to find four big pallets and bring 'em right here."

Mary Rose, who was about fifty, had doused herself in cologne. In a few minutes, after dragging two pallets down an aisle to the appointed place, I found out why. The warehouse, despite the whirring of giant exhaust fans, steamed like a greenhouse in Bangkok. I was dripping. We started with canned goods, which I was stacking neatly in a cardboard box until Mary Rose instructed me to not be so fussy.

"Just dump 'em in, baby," she said.

"Does the order ask for beans?" Leslie asked, holding two.

"Oh, just give 'em everything," Mary Rose answered. "And some tuna, and some peas, just throw 'em all in the box, yeah."

"We're going to give them a massive case of indigestion," Leslie muttered, and tossed in an ample supply of Imodium.

From foodstuffs, we moved on to toothpaste, toothbrushes, towels and washcloths, plastic tableware, paper plates, napkins, flashlights, batteries, with Mary Rose reading off the items on the order form.

After a lunch of chicken and dumplings, gratis from a local chain, she led us through the rest of her checklist.

"A generator!" she whooped. "The minister's got the nerve to ask for a generator? And look at this. TVs and a computer! What does he think we are?"

She handed us signs that read HOLD FOR NEW LIGHT B.C. and told us to tape them to the pallets we'd loaded. Then she walked off, maybe to look for a generator or computer. Nearby, a few high school kids and a couple of women were sorting clothes, and that's when I observed something I should have noticed earlier: all the volunteers were white, all the supervisors were black. This in Tuscaloosa, where on a sizzling June day in 1963, defying a federal court order to integrate state schools, Governor Wallace stood on the steps of Foster Auditorium at the University of Alabama to bar two black students from enrolling. The same George Wallace who'd vowed in his inauguration speech, "Segregation now, segregation tomorrow, segregation forever!" Forty-seven years, eleven months, and twenty days later, I was watching blacks and whites working side by side, and what was more astonishing, whites taking orders from blacks. It would have made a fine photo to post in the Tin Top Café.

The next day, it was 102 degrees, and the forecast promised three more scorchers. My aid-worker zeal beginning to wilt, I was pleased to hear from Mary Rose that most orders had been stacked and shipped.

"I'm trying to find something useful for you to do," she said as we traipsed after her down a corridor between bins of stuff. "But it looks like we've come to the end of the rope."

We ended up sorting clothes with a crowd of teenagers from various church youth groups—Methodists, Baptists, an Episcopalian or two, some in T-shirts bearing biblical quotations. Leslie asked one volunteer if nonchurch organizations like the Red Cross were involved. "Yes," he said, "everyone is here." But the religious current was stronger, for we were in the buckle of the Bible Belt. Southern religion is often the pulpit-thumping kind that favors judgment over mercy. I grew up with the Roman Catholic version but, it seemed to me, the relief effort was what Christianity should be all about. It was a time for mercy; for those who sought judgment, the tornadoes had rendered enough to last a long time.

We worked for an hour or so—men's shirts in this bin, children's shoes in that—and when it was all done, we hung around and tried to look busy. As always, that proved harder than work, so we chatted with a co-volunteer, a middle-aged woman named Carol. Like the Meyerses back in the Keys, she reminded us that we weren't quite as adventurous as we'd thought. Thirteen years ago, with her mother and her ten-year-old daughter, she'd driven from Tuscaloosa to the Arctic Circle and back, camping out in a tent every night but three for sixty-one days.

Mary Rose dismissed us, thanked us for our services, and we left, Leslie feeling that we hadn't done enough. I, on the other hand, felt virtuous and in need of a bath.

Lake Lurleen supplied it. We jumped in with Sage and Sky, only to find it nearly as hot as the air, more like a Jacuzzi absent the soothing jets.

That evening, I was grilling chicken breasts when Leslie, her face ashen, returned from a walk with Sage.

"Phil, she's peeing blood."

As if on command, Sage squatted, leaving drops of alarming red in the grass. She whined, twitched, and looked at us, with what I took to be a plea in her dark eyes. The dread that Sage might die on the trip had lurked in the back of my mind ever since leaving Connecticut.

We lifted her into the truck and drove through the darkening woods to the main highway, where we picked up a cell phone signal (for once, I was happy), called a local clinic, and then our friend Brad. Brad's a doctor for humans, but he's raised and trained many dogs, and knows more about them than most veterinarians. "Probably a UTI," he opined (medical jargon for urinary tract infection). "They'll give her . . ." He rattled off various "omycins" and warned us to avoid one omycin because "the vets love to give it, and it costs way too much."

The clinic was in a nondescript strip mall. Though never a candidate for a doggy Mensa society—whatever genius she had she showed in the field—Sage recognized a veterinarian's office when she smelled one. Knowing she was to be poked and prodded, she resisted when the vet, a large young woman with a raspy voice, led her to an examining room.

"It's okay, girl," I said, ruffling her ears.

We waited, anxiously, for twenty minutes or so, until the vet emerged with Sage, confirmed a UTI, and prescribed an omycin. We didn't care if it was the one Brad had advised us to avoid, and we paid the bill—$277—without a flinch.

We returned to carbonized chicken breasts on our little hibachi. In the morning, the puddle Sage left under an oak tree was pinkish, but she seemed to be on the mend. A brassy sun bobbed over the trees, forecasting another blazing day. We ate cold cereal, then sweated through the hitch-up drill. Leslie's iPod was playing "Sweet Home Alabama" as we pulled out, headed for Tupelo and the Natchez Trace.

11.

As we drove the road through Veterans Park in Tupelo, a band played "Stars and Stripes Forever" in my head. American flags picketed both sides almost all the way down to a placid lake dotted with Canada geese, mallards, and pintails. The flags might have been left over from Memorial Day and continued to flutter for the town's next big event: the eleventh annual Elvis Festival.

Leslie had talked me into visiting Elvis Presley's birthplace. Here was another of our differences. I am severely allergic to visiting iconic places where people gather in droves; Leslie's always up to try them. Years ago, she'd had to force me to go to the Grand Canyon. *A tourist trap,* I'd thought, determined to be unimpressed. She still likes to quote my reaction when I saw it: "Hoooollly *shit!*"

The basilica of Elvis worship is Graceland, in Memphis; the east side Tupelo neighborhood is the manger, dedicated to the first thirteen years of his life. It consists of his boyhood home, a clapboard shotgun house smaller than some of the travel trailers we'd seen on the road; the white frame Baptist church where he sang in the choir; a modern museum-cum-gift shop filled with memorabilia and kitsch; a fountain called the "Fountain of Life," inscribed with his dates of birth and death; a life-size bronze statue of thirteen-year-old Elvis in country-boy overalls, carrying an acoustic guitar; and all of this on fifteen manicured acres of a Tupelo city park bought with the proceeds from an Elvis homecoming concert in 1957.

Mississippi, touting its contributions to American music, has established a Blues Trail, a Gospel Trail, an R & B Trail, and a Country Music Trail. I learned from Dick Guyton, executive director of the Tupelo museum, that Elvis is the only entertainer with markers on all four.

"He took the black music, the gospel music, the rockabilly music, the rhythm and blues music and put 'em all together to make the Elvis sound," Guyton said.

Our first crossover star. Guyton's theory is that Elvis's church experiences, oddly enough, inspired his semiobscene stage style, those signature bumps and grinds. "The preacher in the church he attended as a little boy—that preacher played the guitar, he moved around on the platform, he made some moves, too, and Elvis picked that up from the preacher, thinking that if the preacher did it, it was okay."

Guyton, an affable man of seventy-two, is a Tupelo native who had seen Elvis in person in 1956 and 1957, when the King played concerts in his hometown.

I didn't dare confess to Guyton that I was never a fan of Elvis's music or his movies. That doesn't mean I think he lacked talent, even a genius of sorts. He reached the Mount Everest of fame for a reason; many stars today, however, are famous for being famous.

His legend has taken vicariousness to a whole new level, creating an entire subculture of Elvis impersonators who compete annually in Memphis for the title of Ultimate Elvis. (Incidentally, the current term is *tribute artist*, which I guess sounds tonier than impersonator.)

Tupelo's Elvis Festival is to this contest what a wild-card playoff is to the Super Bowl.

"We've got thirty-five guys performing this weekend for the opportunity to go to Memphis in August," Guyton told me. "Some of 'em are really good, some are questionable. But in the last four years, we've had two guys from the Tupelo competition win the Ultimate Elvis."

And the Ultimate isn't ultimate. There is an Elvis Extravaganza contest, an Images of the King contest, and, grandest of all, the Elvis Tribute Artist World Cup finals. All of which made me wonder: *Why no Ultimate Sinatra? No Images of Lennon contest?*

Guyton showed me a festival program with photos and biographical sketches of the tribute artists spread over three pages. There were fat Elvises, thin Elvises, and is-that-supposed-to-be Elvis? Elvises. Each, Guyton said, would be judged on the skill of his counterfeiting.

After fingering some Elvis dishtowels, Leslie paid her own tribute by buying a coffee mug. It pictured the King, in a blue turtleneck, hands clasped behind his head.

"It's not skinny Elvis," she said, studying his image. "It's not fat Elvis. It's androgynous Elvis. That pompadour is incredible! I look forward to my morning coffee."

12.

WE PICKED UP THE NATCHEZ TRACE PARKWAY NORTH OF Tupelo. Two asphalt lanes, smooth as tabletops, the shoulders speckled with wildflowers, unreeled through ancient woods broken here and there by farm fields where young corn sprouted in black soil. Tall pine, oak, and gum trees splintered the late afternoon sunlight, creating a hypnotic play of light and shadow. Many highways offer more spectacular views, but the Natchez Trace is the most enchanting road in America. It begins in Natchez, Mississippi, and ends in Nashville, Tennessee, and in all those 444 miles there are no cities, power lines, billboards, motels, big-box stores, or fast-food joints—and there's only one gas station. The absence of commercial enterprises is no happy accident; the highway, built in the late thirties on the remnants of a pioneer route, is administered by the National Park Service. It's a kind of elongated national park that carries motorized traffic.

And there wasn't much of that. On the Connecticut Turnpike, we could see ten times more cars and trucks in a one-second glance than we saw in an hour on the Trace. It bore us out of Mississippi, nipped off a corner of Alabama, crossed the Tennessee River, and entered the state of Tennessee, spooling past beds of bloodroot and clover bordering deep green forests. Cruising around the bends in a countryside spared from ruin, I thought, *This is what an American road should be—harmonious with the landscape.*

We left it, reluctantly, a little distance beyond Meriwether Lewis's

gravesite and found a charming mom-and-pop campground and adjoining roadhouse in a grassy spot on Swan Creek called Fall Hollow. Bill
Roper, a big, bearded guy who looked like Ernest Hemingway playing
Santa Claus, ran the place with his wife, Kathy. He came outside, brimming with an open-hearted, open-handed manner, and said, "You can
camp here under one condition: give me a tour of that bee-yew-tee-ful
ole Airstream." This was one of many compliments bestowed on Ethel,
and I worried that she was becoming vain.

We went to the roadhouse for dinner and found what we were to find
throughout the trip: there's amazing food in the most out-of-the-way
places. Roper's kitchen served huge slabs of deep-fried catfish with coleslaw and crispy dark brown hush puppies.

After dinner, Leslie found a new bone to pick with Ethel: the trailer's
gray tank (the one that held waste water) wasn't much bigger than a dish-
pan. Washing up the dinner plates had filled it to capacity. Dirty water
and greasy soap suds bubbled up the bathroom drain, turning the shower
stall into a disgusting wading pool. Fall Hollow lacked sewage hookups,
and I didn't feel like rehitching Ethel, pulling her a hundred yards to the
dump station, and then unhitching her all over again. We showered in
the campground's restrooms, located in a frame building atop a knoll.
While almost everything about Fall Hollow was lovely, the bathrooms
were anything but. Roaches flashed into hiding when the lights flicked
on; their dead brothers and sisters littered the floors; moths as big as
sparrows clung to the walls, along with insects only an entomologist
could have identified.

Leslie overcame her horror, showered, and then, queasiness giving
way to fascination, got her camera and took pictures of the lepidopteran
who would be her shower companion for the next couple of days: Mothra.
When she disrobed later, she was again horrified, discovering that five
ticks had hitched a ride on her.

As she plucked ticks, I sat outside for a while, listening to banjo frogs
twanging by the creek until the gnats and mosquitoes, which kept my
arms flapping like bird wings, drove me inside.

Breakfast at Fall Hollow was whatever Bill Roper felt like cooking, and
his mood that morning was eggs, waffles, and bacon. While he whipped

batter behind the counter, we sat drinking coffee with one of his regulars, Arlena Hochstetler, an auburn-haired woman of forty-eight. She was telling us how she and her husband had gone from living in a three-hundred-thousand-dollar Florida house with a swimming pool and a dock on a fishing canal to a camper on a wooded ridge in Tennessee without electricity or running water.

"We've got a generator for lights at night," she said. "Otherwise, we're completely off the grid. We bathe in the creeks."

And in the winter, they toted water to the camper and heated it in a big kettle. They'd been living like that for a year. It was the collapse of the housing bubble that set the couple on their journey from the twenty-first century to the nineteenth. The value of their house—it was in North Port, a Sarasota suburb—plummeted to eighty-nine thousand faster than an elevator on a broken cable.

"Things were real good there, but when they hit bottom, they hit real hard," she said. "We had to get away from it. John was in construction, and his job went kaput, there was just no work there, and our electric bills were getting real high, everything was changing. Nobody knew what was coming, and we didn't want to depend on them for everything." I took *them* to mean the institutions that provide our basic wants and needs: employers and banks, the water company, the power company.

With no hope of selling their Florida place, they rented it, then hit the road. They found seven hundred acres of semiwilderness for sale here in the Tennessee hills, bought sixty-one with their savings, and after clearing the brush moved in with their camper. They weren't alone. Five other families, all burst-bubble refugees from Florida, had established a settlement up on the ridge, a kind of fundamentalist Christian commune. "They have their own church back in there," Arlena said. "They have cabins. They want to be in a place where people can't rob 'em. It's hard to get where we're at, in the middle of a forest. Those people decided to do what we did—no electricity, no water—but they came here because they think it's the end times. We didn't do it for that reason."

Whatever the reasons, John and Arlena and their neighbors awaiting the Apocalypse were not like the Joads, forced to pull up stakes, load the jalopy, and seek a new life in the golden orchards of California. They had means and options and changed their lives as much from choice as from necessity.

"It's my husband's big dream," Arlena said, referring to their off-grid homestead. "He's up there all the time with his Bobcat, messin' around. He's happy as long as he's got diesel for his Cat."

They had been living the American dream, which has come to mean acquiring ever more stuff. It had failed them. As with the Meyerses back in Key West, the calamity of 2007 had brought the realization that the inner voice that cries *I want* can never be gratified; the fulfillment of one material desire only breeds desire for more; consumption, in the end, consumes the consumer. And so they'd taken to the woods to pursue Thoreau's vision of simplicity and self-sufficiency.

I was probably romanticizing when it came to Arlena. A camper without electricity or running water was John's "big dream," not hers. She'd had some experience with a stripped-down lifestyle during her first marriage, to a Mennonite farmer in Indiana. "I got used to it, but I didn't want to go back to it. I don't like living without air-conditioning when it's a hundred and three degrees."

She described herself today as a "Pretendenite" or, better yet, a "Don'twannabe-anite," and was looking forward to an upcoming move to Virginia, where she'd landed a job and her husband had found work with a company that manufactured conveyor belts.

At breakfast, we were joined by Ken and Patti Neider, her old friends from Florida. They were on vacation, helping the Hochstetlers make improvements, tasks to which Ken brought expertise. Wearing a Hawaiian shirt that looked as if it had been designed by Kandinsky and his dark hair long in back to compensate for its retreat in front, he'd been a contractor in North Port before the crash. Last year, he and his wife caravanned up to Fall Hollow with John and Arlena. They, too, were looking to make a change. Sarasota County had gone from building forty-five hundred homes a year to twenty, Ken said, and his contracting business was on life support.

They stayed in the Ropers' campground for six weeks. After the Hochstetlers bought their property, Ken lent a hand at brush clearing. But when John said that he was moving his trailer into the wilderness where there would be no showers and no power, Ken replied, "Well, you might as well add 'No Kenny' to that list." He and his wife headed back to Florida to try to revive their fortunes.

"We saw that everyone is struggling everywhere. It's everywhere, it's not just regional," Ken told us.

Arlena nodded. Not long ago, she'd gone to visit family in Elkhart, [I]iana, which at one time had been the Detroit of RV manufacturing. She found rust-belt desolation, almost every plant shut down, the gates padlocked, weeds and grass taking over vacant parking lots.

"Lived in Indiana and things went bad," she said. "Lived in Florida and Florida went bad, and decided to come up here. This place is already bad, so I don't think I'll have any problems. The people are great, nicest people you'll ever meet, but that doesn't make up for it."

Optimism is the quintessential American trait, for America has ever been the province of the future, the hope and promise shimmering yonder on the western horizon. Ken was as American as they come, and as if to buff up Arlena's bleak picture, he exclaimed, "Florida is resilient! Florida is comin' back, and when it does, nobody'll want to be the last in line!"

This miracle, he predicted, would happen by the end of the year. Ken had no evidence to support his fair-weather forecast. Indeed, all the evidence pointed to the contrary, but the thing that distinguishes American optimism from other kinds is its faith that tomorrow will be brighter than today, no matter what the facts. It's a peculiar form of magical thinking, and what makes it peculiar is its power to make the magic happen, to transform illusion into reality. Americans see the world as it is, imagine it as it could be, and make it so. I thought of the pioneers in their westering wagons, convinced for no sensible reason that their lives would be better in Oregon or California, and their children's lives better still. I thought of my own ancestors, crossing the Atlantic aboard teeming immigrant ships with the same fantasy in their heads, and in the land Fitzgerald described as "commensurate with man's capacity for wonder" the fantasy came true. I thought of Ronald Reagan declaring during the last recession, "It's morning in America." A realist would have looked at the country then—suffering from double-digit unemployment and double-digit inflation, still embittered by its first lost war, humiliated by the hostage crisis and the disastrous rescue attempt in Iran—and scoffed. Jimmy Carter, the nuclear engineer, had spoken truth when he said that America was gripped by a "profound malaise." But his successor wasn't selling truth; he was selling illusion. Americans bought it because that's what they wanted to believe. If you believe it, it will happen, and lo, it did.

Ken Neider was cut from the same cloth as Reagan. He, too, had once been an entertainer, albeit on a considerably lower rung of the ladder. He was a certified clown, having graduated from clown school in his teens. He made more money in one weekend clown gig than his classmates earned all week at their part-time and summer jobs. After high school, he applied to Ringling Brothers Circus but turned them down when he learned that he would have to take whatever job they offered. "You could sign up as a clown and come out as an elephant shoveler," he said with a chuckle.

He taught himself to juggle and to ride a unicycle, and did stand-up comedy in Sarasota, but "there was no money in it, so I decided to get serious and went into construction and got my contractor's license."

His timing was perfect. Florida was booming. Ken grew up in North Port (that rare creature, a native Floridian!), a town then so small its phone directory consisted of three typewritten pages. When the good times began to roll, eight hundred contractors were building houses and subdivisions in the Sarasota area, and all were prospering.

"We were self-employed in construction for seventeen years, without having to worry. When the crash came, we took two years off, and I did security work."

From builder of minimansions to security guard. Even that comedown did not discourage him or Patti.

"He got tickets to the Super Bowl for that," she said, parting the cloud to show its silver lining.

"The New Orleans Saints and the Indianapolis Colts," Ken elaborated. "I was in charge of the roving camera. When the camera moved, I went ahead and got everyone out of the way—in my clown suit! I scared 'em out of the way!"

He roared with laughter, and so did we. When it died down, he told us that his newest venture was roofing. "We have a situation with roofs in Florida. All those roofs built in the nineteen eighties weren't to modern specs. Roofing is the coming thing in Florida, and we're working on becoming roofing contractors. We're movin' on up the food chain."

If that didn't work out, would he fall back on clowning for a living? Leslie asked, provoking more laughter. He shook his head. It was too undignified for a man his age (forty-seven). "The worst part of it is driving to the show, because you can't go dressed like this. You have to show up as a clown, and there you are, drivin' down the street with your big red nose on."

He turned abruptly and said he would put on a show for us. His juggling balls were in the car. "Brought 'em along in case I ran out of gas money."

We watched his performance for a few minutes. Ken Neider knew how to keep several balls in the air at once. It didn't surprise me that he dropped only one.

———

Meriwether Lewis has been a hero of mine since boyhood. Sunlight striped the parkway as we drove to the park where his bones lie under a stone block pedestal ten feet high and topped by a broken column to symbolize a life cut short, at thirty-five. Eighty thousand people a year flock to Elvis's birthplace. Pulling into the empty parking lot, I doubted if even a tiny fraction of that many visit the grave of the man who, with William Clark, accomplished one of the greatest feats of exploration in history. (To test their iconic status, I later googled their names. Elvis Presley yielded 11.5 million results, Meriwether Lewis slightly more than one million.)

We had a look at a replica of Grinder's Stand, a log cabin on a lawn surrounded by split-rail fences. ("Stand" was the name given to the rough lodges that serviced travelers on the Natchez Trace two centuries ago. Bill Roper described them as "the Holiday Inn Express of their day.") Grinder's was where, a marker said, Lewis's "life of romantic endeavor and lasting achievement came tragically to a close on the night of October 11, 1809." (In fact, one of the few facts known about Lewis's death: he died on the *morning* of October 11.)

The phrase "came tragically to a close" elides the murky circumstances of Lewis's final hours.

He put up at Grinder's on the night of October 10, 1809, three years after his epic expedition and six weeks into a journey to Washington, D.C., from St. Louis, where he'd been serving as governor of the vast Upper Louisiana Territory. According to most accounts, he was on his way to the nation's capital to answer allegations that he'd embezzled government funds.

That evening, Priscilla Grinder, the innkeeper's wife, observed Lewis behaving irrationally. He paced around, at times raving, at times talking to himself "like he was talking to a lawyer," she'd told a friend of Lewis's more than a year later. After she'd gone to bed, she was awakened by gunshots. Looking into Lewis's room through a chink in the log wall, she saw him bleeding profusely as he crawled across the floor. He cried out for water but, claiming that she was terrified, she did not go to his aid until the next morning. She found Lewis clinging to life, with two bullet wounds, one to his head, the other to his chest. Shortly after sunrise, he died.

When the news reached them, the two men who knew him best, William Clark and Thomas Jefferson, concluded that he'd taken his own life. "I fear O! I fear the weight of his mind has overcome him," Clark wrote to his brother. Lewis was known to suffer from melancholia, as clinical depression was called in those times. In a letter, Jefferson offered an astute analysis of how the disease led Lewis to do what he did: "During his western expedition the constant exertion which that required of all the faculties of body & mind, suspended these distressing affections; but after his establishment in St. Louis in sedentary occupations they returned upon him with redoubled vigor, and began seriously to alarm his friends. He was in a paroxysm of one of these when his affairs rendered it necessary for him to go to Washington."

But tales that he'd been murdered started almost immediately, based on discrepancies in Priscilla's story—she changed it several times—and on a couple of questions. Lewis was armed with two fifty-caliber muzzle-loading pistols. A fifty-caliber ball causes tremendous damage at point-blank range. How could Lewis, having shot himself once, had the strength to fire the second pistol? And, more cogently, how could an ex–army officer and crack marksman bungle his own suicide? The debate continues today, with multiple theories ranging from the plausible to the outlandish.

Some proponents of homicide make a good case, but if we apply the principle of Occam's razor—among competing hypotheses, the one that's simplest and makes the fewest assumptions is correct until disproven—suicide seems the more likely to me. I've never led an expedition, but as an infantry officer in Vietnam, I've known what it's like to be consumed by a mission requiring "all the faculties of body & mind" and the profound letdown, beset by the trivial demands of ordinary life, that follows such an intense experience.

I pictured Lewis as we hiked a section of the Old Trace, a preserved stretch of the original route. Sage and Sky, delighted to be off lead, quartered out ahead of us. There are few sights I love more than watching them running stretched out through rough country. Yet Lewis haunted me, as I walked the same road he'd ridden two hundred years ago.

Tragedy is a word that's lost its meaning through overuse and misuse. But Lewis was a tragic figure in the classical sense; he'd fallen from a high place, though not because of a fatal flaw in his character. The weight of his mind, in Clark's phrase, had brought him down.

The Old Trace, no wider than a jeep trail, snaked along a low, gently sloping ridge, crowded by oak and pine casting deep shadows. The shade was welcome; the day was hot, as usual—ninety-seven. Mosquitoes whined. The weather would have been crisp that October evening in 1809 as Lewis approached Grinder's Stand. The insects would have been dormant, the trees arrayed in autumn colors. Did he notice their beauty, or was he too preoccupied with the blot on his name? Had his mind already entered the dark house? On those and many other questions, the woods were silent.

13.

WE WOULD NOT HAVE THOUGHT THE FORESTED TENNESSEE highlands congenial to the growing of grapes; nor that they would shelter a hippie commune. It was June 4, our twenty-third anniversary, and we were looking for a place to celebrate. Roper suggested the Amber Falls Winery. A winery? Here? "Sure," he said, and gave us directions as they're given in the backcountry. Once we'd sorted out the natural and man-made landmarks, we found the winery three miles up a one-lane asphalted trail with more twists than a pretzel. We expected something on the rough-hewn side, and so were surprised to come upon an establishment that would not have embarrassed itself in Sonoma County: ruler-straight vineyard rows, each labeled with its varietal; a winery resembling an upscale lodge, with a broad patio and a gazebo, beneath which customers sipped Amber Falls's offerings while listening to a jazz ensemble play old standards.

We joined the audience for a while, sampled a crisp chardonnay, the big-city strains of Gershwin tunes transporting us back to our first year together in Manhattan, when we frequented the jazz clubs in the Village and midtown.

The cellar tasting room was attended by a middle-aged man and his young apprentice, a local boy happy to have landed a job that didn't require operating tractors or chain saws. I will resist the temptation to lapse into vino-patois about nose and texture and a finish with hints of blackberry, and simply state that the reds and whites we sampled were quite good. We settled on a blended white (called a "Chardonel") and a blended red (cabernet-merlot-syrah, labeled "Meriwether Lewis" and bottled in 2009 to mark the bicentennial of his death).

As for our wedding anniversary, I'd made it a practice to present Leslie with a dozen yellow roses each year—part of my effort to ensure that my third marriage would be my last. There being no florist in the vicinity, I stopped at the roadside on our way back to the campground and plucked a bunch of black-eyed Susans, which brought a smile and a kiss.

———

Bud Runyon remembers the day, four decades ago, when the caravan of school buses passed through the town of Columbia, Tennessee. He'd just finished his shift at the Phelps Dodge aluminum plant, where he worked in the coiling (pronounced *cawlin*) department, which milled thirty-foot aluminum bars into wire (pronounced *wor*). He pulled out of the parking lot and drove to an intersection, where a red light and a city policeman had stopped traffic.

"Man, I tell you what, we were hot and sweaty and ready to go home," he recollected. "And there we were, settin' at that red light, and here they come, all in a line, seventy, eighty school buses all painted in funny colors, with stovepipes stickin' out the winders, and we wondered, *What in the world*? We didn't know what was goin' on. We thought somebody was invadin' us."

It wasn't an invasion. Bud was witnessing, that afternoon in 1971, the end of a cross-country odyssey of 320 hippies disillusioned with the self-indulgent scene in San Francisco. Led by Stephen Gaskin, a balding, bearded ex-marine who preached a fusion of Christianity and Eastern religions, the pilgrims had searched the nation for a place to establish a settlement based on the principles of nonviolence, respect for the earth, and communal living. They'd found it in Lewis County, Tennessee, purchasing eighteen hundred acres of woodland for seventy dollars an acre. They named their property "the Farm" and soon went to work turning it into one.

Lewis County was, and is, perhaps more tolerant than others of non-mainstream ideas and ways of life; Mennonites and Amish have made homes there, alongside conventional families whose roots go back to the days of Andrew Jackson and Davy Crockett. Not that residents rolled out the welcome wagon when Gaskin's tie-dyed followers arrived. As Bud

Runyon remembers it, there was "talk about runnin' them off with guns," but the general reaction was bewilderment mixed with wariness. "When we heard the caravan was hippies, we didn't know if to think the worst or what. People were wonderin', *Are they gonna be enemies or friends?*" (pronounced *frinz*).

Those who thought the worst imagined freaks on acid and free-love orgies. It turned out that most of the commune's values were traditional, even conservative—with one exception. Alcohol, tobacco, and psychedelic drugs were prohibited; likewise sex outside of marriage, artificial birth control, and abortion. The exception was smoking marijuana, considered a sacred ritual. In 1974, Gaskin was arrested for growing weed. Otherwise, there was no trouble. The Farm came to be accepted by its neighbors, and in Runyon's words "for forty years they've been friends."

The Farm is like an amalgam of an American small town, an Israeli kibbutz, and the Oneida Community. It's said to be the oldest hippie commune in the United States, but that isn't quite accurate; it's no longer a commune in the pure sense of the term. Members aren't required to take vows of poverty and surrender their personal property, as in the beginning. They form an *intentional community*, meaning one where everyone lives together with common purposes. Those are written in a lengthy statement of "Basic Beliefs and Agreements," a kind of charter. ("We agree to be respectful of the forests, fields, and wildlife under our care . . . We believe in nonviolence and pacifism . . . We believe that vegetarianism is the most ecologically sound and humane lifestyle for the planet.")

The Farm generates electricity with solar panels and has its own water supply. Its residents, now numbering 175 (some are grandchildren of the founders), own homes and small businesses, provide midwife services, grow crops for personal consumption as well as for sale. They trade and barter with neighbors. Pregnant Amish women, who choose not to go to hospitals, use its midwife clinic; in exchange, the Farm obtains Amish timber and wood products. It's about as self-sufficient as any community can be in this century. If ever the American economy goes over the cliff, the commune may have to arm itself against desperate hordes trying to get in.

Bill Roper, our font of local lore, had said that we *had* to visit the Farm.

Tennessee Route 20 brought us there. Amish and Mennonite farms lent the countryside a quaint charm, but the pastoral landscape was deceptive: in the distance, a paper-company clear-cut looked like a bombing range, littered with stumps and slash piles and felled trees. No hippie-dippy funny stuff about the sacred earth up there, the chain saws ripping into the raw material for all those useless catalogs that pile up every Christmas season.

At the entrance to the Farm, we met a band of conservationists preparing a sortie to document endangered species (like the snaketail dragonfly). The loggers, they said, weren't reforesting but selling off the cleared land to developers. I wondered if there was one square mile of America, outside national and state parks, that was safe from Yankee Doodle rapacity.

The Farm appeared to be. A narrow road wound past vegetable gardens and pastures, silos and cottages painted in recall of the psychedelic artwork of Haight-Ashbury. People waved and called out hellos. I confess I didn't know how to react to such friendliness. We stopped off at the general store, crammed with organic condiments; also lots of tofu, soy, and rice milk. The clerk, Kathleen, a soft-spoken fifty-year-old with teeth as straight as a CNN anchorwoman's, was another Sunshine State refugee and a new resident. Her sister, a commune member since 1975, owned the store. "There are three generations living here, and I love it for the sense of community," said Kathleen, who had waitressed in Daytona for thirty years.

Leslie stocked up on vegan commodities, albeit the least healthful she could find, then had a look at books stacked up beside a railing outside. They were there for the taking, an eclectic assortment: *Strumpet City*; *Alternative Dispute Resolution in Business*; *The First Wives Club*; *Healing AIDS Naturally*.

The Dome, a kind of community center next to the store, was a lofty hexagon of parabolic arches built from scrap I-beams meeting at the apex. That's where we ran into two third-generation Farmites, Noah ("like the Ark," he said) and Cedar ("like the tree"), respectively eighteen and nineteen. Both were college students home for summer vacation. Noah wore a faint beard and a tie-dyed baseball cap flipped backward, with Grateful Dead wings pinned to the back, Cedar a long braid and khaki shorts and a black T-shirt so perforated with tiny holes I would have thought it had been used for shotgun practice if guns were allowed on the Farm, which they most certainly are not. In our travels thus far, we'd observed that the Land of the Free is becoming the Land of the Flabby and that the obesity epidemic is most severe among the great republic's youth, not a surprising development: TV, computer games, and Facebook bind them to their chairs; their supersize-me diets ensure massive ingestion of empty calories. Noah and Cedar, both six-footers and lifeguards at the Farm's riverine swimming hole, looked the way young American males used to look: lean as saplings, doubtless because junk food and fatty meats are forbidden fare and because life on the commune involves planting and harvesting, hauling and splitting wood.

Noah was the talkative one, speaking in a voice edged with irony; Cedar was quieter but occasionally tossed out a wry comment. A music major at Middle Tennessee State University in nearby Murfreesboro, he said that he had a backup plan. "I'm thinking of minoring in philosophy so I'll be employable."

Noah was enrolled at a community college in Eugene, Oregon—"to get some outside perspective," he said. "Murfreesboro is too close."

"Yeah, but Murfreesboro is a lot different than here," Cedar interjected. "It's dirty, it's filthy, there's crime and only one or two parks, and forty thousand college students into drinking and electronica."

Their roots in the "intentional community" are deep. Cedar grew up there from infancy; his grandfather Rob had arrived on the caravan; his mother was in the first class to graduate from the Farm's high school. Noah's uncle was also an original settler, but Noah's immediate family arrived more recently. His parents, both PhDs from the heartland of the counterculture, the University of California at Berkeley, had moved to New Jersey, where they "stuck out like sore thumbs."

"When I went to public school, I wasn't a normal kid. I got made fun of a lot. My dad worked for the New York City school system. He was the science director in District Two. When No Child Left Behind got pushed through, he saw everything he'd worked for obliterated by that seemingly useless piece of legislation, and we moved here, in 2003."

And how did he find it? Wasn't it a bit insular and claustrophobic?

He shook his head. "I love it here. You feel safe, knowing that all these people are there for you. That's what community is all about. There are no age distinctions. I can hang around with twelve-year-olds in the day and party with my parents at night. As a whole, we're greater than the sum of our parts. It's what I loved about growing up here—you're not locked into your own mind."

He said he intended to come back and start a family of his own when he finished college.

"Me, too," Cedar said. "Not right now, but that's my American dream."

I couldn't recall meeting teenage boys who actually *liked* living with their families. I wondered if Noah and Cedar were painting an idealized picture for a stranger. It didn't seem so.

They laughed at the myths outsiders once had about the Farm: that its residents swam naked in the swimming hole, that they grew fields of pot, that they didn't know the first thing about real farming. Noah recalled meeting Lincoln Davis, their congressional representative.

"He said, 'So you're from that farm? Okay, what's the one thing a potato has got to have before you plant it in the ground to grow?' And I said, 'An eye.' And he said, 'Okay! You're good by me.'"

Noah and Cedar were about to leave when a man who looked like a bearded Benjamin Franklin and spoke in a hill-country twang showed up. This was James "Bud" Runyon, the same who'd watched the school buses roll in forty years earlier. Bud could not have known it then, but he was looking at his future employers. He lost his job in 1982, when the Phelps Dodge plant shut down. Soon afterward, he was working at the Farm, first as a woodcutter, later as supervisor of the water company. Now, at sixty-four, he had a contract to haul trash.

Bud is a natural-born storyteller, a man who harks back to a time when the oral narrative was an art form. His tale about the caravan's arrival, which I abridged considerably, rambled on for about twenty minutes. When I remarked on his luxuriant beard, he asked, "You know why that beard's there?" and proceeded to answer with another long tale. The condensed version: he'd had a heart attack the previous New Year's Eve, received stents in two coronary arteries, and was put on blood thinners, his doctor advising him not to put a razor to his face. So he stopped shaving.

I then popped the question I'd been asking almost everyone we met.

Noah's response: "I think it's greed and the quest for material possessions that holds the country together. What our leaders want is us to be good little consumers and keep buying, buying, buying."

Cedar's: "One of the big things is complacency . . . We're used to it this way, the quote free market unquote. What people need to do is wake up and say, 'As a nation we're not happy. We don't love each other.'"

Bud disagreed. "I know there's a lotta violence in this country, but I believe it's gotta be love holds us together, and our faith, and wantin' to get along with people all over the world. There's people all over the world I never met, but I love 'em, and I pray for 'em."

In Arizona, the Yaqui Indians believe there are two kinds of people in the world, those with magic in their hearts and those with disturbances in their hearts. Bud Runyon belonged to the former tribe. In all the miles we traveled, we wouldn't meet anyone with a better heart or more generous spirit. Not that he was unaware of the other tribe. As we parted company, he said, "Y'all be careful. Lotta crazy people out on that road."

14.

W E'D BEEN ON THE ROAD FOR THREE WEEKS AND HAD SET-
tled into a routine. I woke up first, usually while it was still
dark, made coffee, walked the dogs for about twenty minutes,
then did calisthenics and stretching exercises outside the trailer for
another twenty. Occasionally, I threw in a headstand. Leslie made breakfast and took care of the dogs the rest of the day when we were in camp.
On the road, while I drove, she worked in her virtual, mobile office, muttering expletives when her 4G connection or Magic Droid entered gaps in
coverage (three bars on the screen prompted her to whoop like a gambler
hitting a winner at the slots). Setting up and breaking camp was a joint
effort, though it was mostly my responsibility, and it was sweaty, dirty
work in that equatorial weather.

At night, one of us cooked, but not always. We often opened a can or
two and concocted some peculiar cold dinners. "How about beets, brown
bread, and canned peaches?" Leslie would say. "Fine," I'd answer. And,
mirabile dictu, it would be fine—or fine enough. These meals reminded
Leslie-the-WASP of family dinners when she was growing up. (Her
mother—this is true—has praised hospital fare.) When we did cook, it was
usually the three S's: spaghetti, sausage, and sauce, washed down with
cheap wine in our plastic crystalware. Whoever didn't cook was the
dishwasher. These domestic assignments weren't as formalized as the
household chores at home. If something needed doing, one of us did it
without asking, "Isn't it your turn to . . . ?"

There was, too, a certain separateness to our lives back in Connecticut. Leslie commuted to her office, I went to my writing studio behind the house, each of us in different worlds until evening. On the road, we were together *all the time*, and we pulled together to accomplish each day's simple, shared mission: to start at Point A and arrive at Point B. We'd been married for twenty-three years and lovers for longer than that; now we were closer than ever, an intentional community of two. We'd become road buddies.

On the morning of June 6, I was up at a quarter to six. Walking Sage and Sky along Swan Creek, I watched a turtle making slow progress toward an egg-laying spot and heard wild turkeys clucking in the twilit woods. The temperature had fallen to a frigid seventy-five, and I was hoping that the heat wave had finally crested.

Hopes thwarted. It was back into the nineties by the time we were hitched up and rolling westward on U.S. 412.

We stopped at a veterinary clinic in Hohenwald for tick meds for the dogs—they were peppered with those loathsome things. Spotting the Airstream through a window, the vet asked where we were going. "Did you get lost?" he said after I told him. "Alaska!" the receptionist exclaimed. Then, in a wistful voice: "I've always wanted to go there. Can I stow away with you?"

We'd heard words like those from family and friends before we set out. *Take me with you.* The longing to be somewhere other than where you are, to just *go*, is as American as the World Series. Or at any rate used to be. In *Travels with Charley*, Steinbeck records this exchange with a Connecticut store owner who'd asked him the same question the vet asked us.

STEINBECK: All over.
STORE OWNER: Lord! I wish I could go.
STEINBECK: Don't you like it here?
STORE OWNER: Sure. It's all right, but I wish I could go.
STEINBECK: You don't even know where I'm going.
STORE OWNER: I don't care. I'd like to go anywhere.

Writing more than a century earlier, in *The Oregon Trail* (which may be considered the first American road book), Francis Parkman observed that not all the emigrants were making the hard, dangerous trek west to better their prospects. He was amazed to find a man of seventy-one leading a train of government provision wagons. The old man couldn't explain why, at his age, he was chasing the sunset across the Great Plains. Parkman concluded that "some restless American devil had driven him into the wilderness at a time of life when he should have been seated at the fireside with his grandchildren on his knees."

Back on 412, with Leslie busy editing an article on bottled water, I fell into idle reflections, asking myself if Parkman's restless American devil was easing into retirement. Considering all the travelers filling up trailer parks, even in these times of economic woe and high gas prices, it would seem not. But most were either retirees or families on vacation. I was looking for but not finding a different breed of wanderer: the college kid taking the summer off to thumb across the country; the young adventurer driven to see what lies beyond the beyond; the rebel nomad with a wayward wind blowing in his soul—Jack Kerouac and Neal Cassady, delirious with white-line fever; Tod Stiles and Buz Murdock, blasting down Route 66 in their Corvette convertible.*

I was looking for a reincarnation of myself as I was half a century ago, a college dropout under Kerouac's spell. I'd landed a job as a railroad brakeman. Later, with the money earned, I hitchhiked, hopped freights, and rode buses from Chicago to southern Mexico and back—eight thousand miles in four months. Compared to the hobos set loose in the Great Depression, the high-iron riders of whom Woody Guthrie sang, I was a middle-class, dilettante bum, but I wouldn't trade those four months for anything. I can still summon up images from a mental photo album: hitchhiking to Laredo through the chalky mesquite plains in south Texas and eating roadhouse eggs with two cowboys; the Milky Way spilling across the skies of Sonora; the Mexican truck driver who'd given me a ride—and nips from his mescal jug—declaring, "Tu y mi, somos amigos de la carretera" (You and me, we are friends of the highway).

There'd been rough patches. On my way back to the States, two braceros picked me up in Guerrero, and one flicked a switchblade and said, "Somos dos pobres hombres" (We are two poor men), so I flicked mine and said, "Yo tambien" (Me, too), but when their 1941 Plymouth broke down, I ended up paying for the repairs, my companions claiming they

---

* The characters portrayed by Martin Milner and George Maharis in the TV series *Route 66*. It aired from 1960 to 1964.

didn't have a peso, the mechanic calling a cop who said we were all three going to jail if the gringo didn't fork over. With my last ten dollars, I made it to Nogales, Arizona, shelled out two bucks for a flop, where I had my first bath in two weeks, and the next morning an old rod rider led me to a Southern Pacific freight, northward bound.

There were a lot of other young men out on the road with me, under the same spell. But where were they now, the Cassadys and the Kerouacs? The Woody Guthries rambling the sparkling sands of diamond deserts? Maybe they were out there somewhere; maybe, with my wife and dogs, staying in Triple A–approved campgrounds, I was traveling in the wrong circles and simply didn't see them.

On the other hand, maybe the Internet and satellite and cable TV have quieted the restless demon. If you want to see the world, why risk flipping a boxcar, why stand at a windswept roadside with your thumb out, when in the climate-controlled safety of your room you can make the world come to you with the click of a mouse or a remote?

However, the Internet and TV—the talking heads on cable speaking in perfectly modulated, generic American—have not dulled the regional accent. At a diner where we stopped for lunch, Leslie cocked an ear, and when I realized she'd stopped listening to my no-doubt fascinating conversation, I asked what she was doing. Turns out she was listening raptly to snatches of local speech: *She dint wawnta go inta the hawspitul for her whiz-dum teeth.* And: *He cunnit rize his awrms.* And, the talk turning to computers, *WiFi* came out *Wah-fah.*

Nor has electronica entirely obliterated regional differences. Judging by the billboards and churches on our route, the South remains the most religious part of the country, with the rural Midwest a close second. In some towns, there was a house of worship on almost every corner; in Linden, Tennessee, population one thousand, we passed three on a single block, United Methodist, Church of Christ, and First Baptist.

"The churches here are like Starbucks back East," Leslie marveled.

We also observed, in a very unofficial census, that the number of adult superstores in the South was directly proportional to the number of churches. Drive outside town past the steeples and you'd be sure to see a windowless, block-brick building luring customers with billboards featuring hot babes and lists of X-rated videos, lingerie, sex toys. Because there can be no redemption without sin, ample opportunities for both are offered.

The character of the landscape was changing, hills shrinking, horizons widening—the South easing into the lower Middle West. We crossed the Mississippi west of Dyersburg. A sign on the bridge welcomed us to Missouri. I planned to join the Lewis and Clark National Historic Trail, a network of highways and byways that trace their journey to the Pacific, at the state capital, Jefferson City.

Broad cornfields in the bottomlands lay under sheets of shallow water, sandbags lined the roadway against a slow-moving disaster. Record snowfalls melting in the Rocky Mountains, a thousand miles away, were pouring into the whole vast watershed east of the Continental Divide, swelling the Missouri, the Platte, the Arkansas, and the Mississippi. Farms were inundated, towns and cities threatened, and in the west of the state, a tornado had annihilated much of Joplin. Wind and flood—a season of natural catastrophes.

Leslie had never been to Missouri, had, in fact, chosen North Carolina's journalism school over the University of Missouri's in part because *Chapel Hill* sounded, well, more peaceful and bucolic. But she fell for the Ozarks. "Have you noticed how every square inch is covered in green?" she asked. Of course I had. State Route 19, a scenic road that, for a change, really was, whipped northward through the lush hills like a carnival ride, all steep ups and downs and hairpin twists. Jade-colored rivers tumbled under narrow bridges. Towns were few and too small to support the usual Walmart/McDonald's/Holiday Inn barnacles. Canoe rentals and rafting outfitters appeared to be the main industries. Between the towns, we'd sometimes see a house as grand as any on a southern plantation, and then a shack that looked abandoned but wasn't, the yard decorated with cast-off appliances, a derelict pickup on blocks. The rural scenery, however, wasn't as tranquil as it looked. The Ozarks were once moonshine country; now, way back in there at the ends of the logging roads, meth labs have replaced the whiskey stills.

Weary of crowded campgrounds, needing to give the dogs a break from the cramped truck bed and ourselves from Ethel's coffin-size bunks, we rented a cabin on Meramec Farm, which Leslie had found in one of the growing number of brochures that were now sliding around Fred's interior.

The cabin was small but well fixed with a refrigerator, an air conditioner, and—this drew a gasp of delight from Leslie—a real bed, mattress, box spring, and all.

We parked Ethel atop a rise near the main farmhouse. I backed her in with more skill than I'd previously shown, and was feeling proud of myself. Pride, as we know, goeth before the fall. As Leslie cranked the jackpost to unhitch the trailer, I noticed that Fred was slightly downhill of Ethel, causing the hitch assembly to form a shallow *V.*

"Wait till I block . . ."

Focused on her task, Leslie kept on cranking, and before I could finish the sentence—"the trailer's wheels"—Ethel's hitch sprang loose from Fred's hitch ball with such force that she jumped backward and the jackpost leaped off the wood blocks. With a sickening *bang,* the trailer pitched forward, the jackpost plowing into the ground. Ethel now looked like a boat sinking by the bow.

Leslie stared in silence, first at Ethel, then at me. Three marriages and a few relationships in between qualify me to make this observation about *Homo sapiens femalis*, subspecies *Americanus*: they are congenitally incapable of apologizing for a mistake because they're incapable of admitting they've made one. It's always the guy's fault. Number two son Marc, married for a decade, has likewise noticed this trait and has revised the old riddle about the falling tree not making a sound: "If a man were all alone in a forest with no woman there, would he still be wrong?"

I did two things: kept my temper and devised a solution. With the truck jack under one side of the A-frame and the hydraulic jack under the other, we would right the trailer—and hope the jackpost wasn't bent. This we did, wringing wet in ninety-five-degree heat.

The jackpost was fine. Leslie murmured to the effect that she was glad I'd figured out what to do. I replied that we'd solved the problem together (gallantly, I thought), but added, "If you mention this in your blog, I wouldn't mind your saying that I'm your hero."

I knew that would be difficult, but I credit her for trying. This is what she wrote: "Phil asks that I write he's my hero. Here you go, Phil! I make a delicious spaghetti dinner to celebrate."

Mists thicker than a New England fog cloaked the Meramec Valley in the morning. When the sun burned them off, we rode the farm with its owner, Carol Harrison Springer, a fifty-nine-year-old woman whom it's easy to misjudge because she stands only five-four, is cordial and hospi-table, and speaks mildly, often finishing her remarks with a self-deprecating laugh.

The farm has been in her family since 1811, established by Springer's great-great-great-grandfather on a land grant issued by President James Madison. She is the sixth generation to run the place, and when she retires, her son, Andy, will take over. Right now, they're partners. Andy is in charge of the farm's cattle operations, Springer tends to its herd of gaited horses and to urban visitors seeking a taste of rural life. As she put it, "You don't live on a farm for two hundred years if you don't adapt. Darwin was right about that. If you don't adapt, you don't last."

After you've been around her for a while, you realize that her amiable manner and moderate tone of voice are, well, call them adaptations to her role as guest wrangler. They soften her natural feistiness and tenacity—not always successfully.

We experienced a failure in that regard on the ride. At the barn, a tall blonde young woman led our mounts into a corral. Leslie's was a Mis-souri Foxtrotter named Penny, mine a Tennessee Walker called Beauty. We offered to saddle and bridle, assuring Springer that we knew how.

"Sofia will do that. By the time you got it done, it would be too hot to ride."

She spoke with a firmness that foreclosed on any discussion. Sofia was from Sweden. Springer runs a "work-away" program, hiring young people from abroad to help out each summer.

"The reason I hire European kids is that they work harder than Americans," she explained, showing some more of her no-nonsense side. "I've hired Americans, these young men who come out here in their cut-off T-shirts with muscles created in a gym. They're beautiful to look at, but after a couple of hours stacking hay bales in the heat they suddenly remember they have to drive Mom to the store."

Joined by Springer's friend Laura, we set off, the horses' legs swish-ing in the stirrup-high grass carpeting the Meramec River bottom-lands. Leslie and I ride gaited horses quite a lot in Arizona. It's something of an art. The object is to get the animal into its distinctive, four-beat amble and keep it there. A slow walk is okay, but pacing, trotting, or loping are discouraged. Correctly managed, a gaited horse offers a ride so smooth that, in the words of an Arizona rancher we know, "it makes your ass laugh."

As for mine, it chuckled once or twice, now and then gave out a guffaw; otherwise, it lost its sense of humor as Beauty broke into high lopes or slowed into jack-hammer trots. All the while, exasperated as a gym teacher coaching a klutzy kid, Springer threw out instructions: "Don't kick her! Just squeeze with your legs! No, *no!* That's not a gait, it's a pace!" I can't speak for the mood of Leslie's derriere; it seemed happy on board Penny. She's a fairly accomplished equestrienne; still, Springer wasn't pleased with her performance. "You said a friend taught you to ride gaited horses? She didn't teach you that you don't just let the horse gait whenever she feels like it? You have to *make* her gait." I decided to divert her attention from our horsemanship.

"How many acres is your farm?" I asked. "How many head of cattle and horses do you run here?" Springer winced. I'd spent enough time in the West to know that such questions are tantamount to asking how much money someone earns or has in the bank. "Sorry, Carol. But I've got to ask that. I'm a journalist."

"Well, that's your problem, not mine."

Then, confessing that she had a degree in journalism (though she'd never practiced that dark art), she relented. If I had to know, Meramec Farm covered 475 acres and supported twenty-five horses and a hundred head of cattle.

Turning out of the pastures, we followed a trail into woods of oak, poplar, and shagbark hickory, then topped out on a rise above rolling green hills specked with black cattle and horses of every color: white, pinto, brown. But for Springer and a resolute band of citizens, Laura pointed out, we now would be gazing at an inland sea plied by water skiers and fishermen.

"Flat water recreation—that's what it was all about," Springer said, not without an undertone of scorn.

"It" was an Army Corps of Engineers project to dam the Meramec River and its tributaries to create an artificial lake that would have drowned Springer's farm and the entire Meramec Valley. At the time— the midseventies—Springer was putting her journalism degree to good use managing the pack string for the Outdoor Leadership School in the Montana Rockies. She returned to Missouri to save the family farm and for another reason: "I was tired of looking at evergreens. I decided that I was a deciduous person."

She and her cohort—sometimes called the Meramec Valley

Irregulars—filed suit to stop the project in 1974. The guerrillas faced long odds against the conventional forces, a triumvirate of the Corps, the U.S. Congress, and local chambers of commerce, who saw tourist dollars flowing in place of the rivers.

"People thought we were crazy," Springer told us. "You can't fight the U.S. Army and the federal government, they said. You can't, you can't, you can't. But a lot of farmers had already lost their land to eminent domain. We were going to lose ours, and we had to make a last-ditch effort."

They waged a prolonged battle in the law courts and in the court of public opinion. In 1981, President Reagan signed a bill deauthorizing the dams—the first time in history that a federal water project had been scrapped. We understood Springer a little better. You don't win victories like that if you're made of cotton candy.

As we halted at the clear-running river to let the horses drink, Springer and Laura harmonized on an old bluegrass tune.

> *She walks through the corn leading down to the river*
> *Her hair shone like gold in the hot morning sun*
> *She took all the love that a poor boy could give her*
> *And left me to die like a fox on the run*
> *Like a fox, like a fox, like a fox on the run.*

Cicadas, waking up in the midmorning heat, sang a different tune in the trees, a million-voiced whine that rose and fell at regular intervals. On the high note, the sound created a pressure in your ears, as if a wind were blowing right through them. The noise was almost frightening, and we were to find cicadas, with their weird orange eyes, crawling, flying, and belly-up all over the farm.

Taking a dirt road on our way back, we ran into Dell, a retired hospital administrator wearing denim coveralls, high rubber boots, and an Old West sheriff's mustache. Dell was working in his garden, where he grew okra, kale, onions, carrots. Behind him stood a handsome dark-wood house and barn he'd built with his own hands in two years. He had a distinguished air—take off the overalls and put him in pinstripes and you'd think he was a diplomat. He, Springer, and Laura talked horseflesh for a while. Dell bred and trained gaited horses and mules and sold them to buyers all over the world.

"He might look like a farmer, but he's got some brains in his head,"

Springer said to us in an aside. "Dell trained a world-champion Tennessee Walker."

He acknowledged the slightly backhanded compliment with a scuff of his boots.

"Wouldn't mind travelin' the country myself," he drawled when told about us.

But he didn't mean it. With a gesture that took in the house, the barn, and the tidy rows of vegetables, he said, "This place is as close to heaven as you'll ever get."

"Say hello to Norma for us," Springer called as we rode away.

Once upon a time it was like this everywhere in rural America, I thought—people riding up a dusty road to exchange small talk with a neighbor, cultivating his garden.

The three-hour ride left the horses lathered in sweat. At the corral, a man garbed in a royal-blue jumpsuit removed their saddles and blankets and began to hose them down. Springer introduced us to Jerry Woods, a handsome man of seventy-two, with hazel eyes, strong, straight teeth, and wings of gray hair sprouting from under his baseball cap.

"Jerry is my horse trainer, best there is," Springer said.

In a near-whisper, Woods told us that the relationship wasn't strictly employer and employee: "Carol's my sweetie pie."

With her sharp critiques of my riding skills fresh in mind, I admit that while I found it easy to admire her, imagining her as a sweetie pie wasn't so easy. I asked Woods for some horsemanship advice, and he gave it, tacking on a brief treatise on his training methods.

"My dad was in the U.S. mounted cavalry, and he could ride the hair off a horse," he said, starting to brush Beauty's flanks. "But he was tough on them, and on men. I knew from an early age that I wanted to train horses, and I decided that that wouldn't be my way. I'm half Indian, and the Indians were the finest light cavalry in the world, horsemen extraordinaire. But they had a gentle way with horses. You won't see me wearing spurs all the time, only when I need to, cuz all it takes to get the horse into a gait is to give him a little nudge, check, and release. You keep that up for four hours, you'll never have a problem."

Like Bud Runyon back in Tennessee, Jerry Woods was a born yarn spinner, and in due course he spun the yarn of his life. As he did, we realized he was a breed of American that will, when his generation passes on, become as extinct as the mountain man and the open-range cowboy.

His father—not his grandfather—was born in 1896. After serving in World War I (Woods showed us a brass U.S. cavalry rosette worn on his father's bridle), he returned to the Ozarks, a sharecropper who owned nothing, had no education, and raised whatever crop landowners wanted. He also raised ten children, five girls, five boys, of whom Jerry was the eighth in line.

"We didn't have no electricity and no running water," Woods said. "People usta call us hillbillies. We didn't mind that. We wore it like a badge, but that's not politically correct anymore, so now we call ourselves"—he grinned—"Ozark Americans."

In the category of traditional values, you could do far worse than those that Oren Woods instilled in his brood: "My dad said you need to be honest and truthful. If you tell somebody you're gonna do something, you do it till you die. Give a man, for a day's pay, a day and a quarter of work, and you'll always be needed."

For their mother's health, the family moved from the Ozarks to Arizona, but Woods didn't care for it—too many cacti, lizards, rattlesnakes. "Hell, the grass out there would bite you." At thirteen, he left home and thumbed his way back to Missouri, going to work at an uncle's sawmill from daybreak till dark. Five years later, he enlisted in the navy, and the horse soldier's son soon found himself patrolling the Mekong Delta's treacherous labyrinth in a swift boat. On his first action, the boats were strung out to prevent an ambush from getting them all at once. But the sailors, he said, had miscalculated "how conniving the Vietcong were. Just as we turned to head back, Charlie gave us hell. Twenty-five boats went up, thirteen come back."

Done brushing, Woods bent down with a pick, lifted one of Beauty's forefeet, and scraped the mud caked in her hoof. I admired the economy of his war story. He'd produced a full-length documentary with that last sentence.

He planned to make a career of the service and did three tours in Vietnam. When he got orders for a fourth, he concluded that the navy was trying to kill him and got out, after ten years in uniform. He has no regrets. "I was ornery as a kid, bad ornery, even mean. Vietnam took all that out of me, it changed me for the better."

He paused in the hoof picking and turned philosophical. "I've figured out by livin', and it took me years to learn this, that you can't control nobody in this world but you, and that's a full-time job. Because if you lose control and get mad and angry—which I usta get bad mad—you've lost control of the only thing in this world you can control. You can't control what people say to you or do to you or how they act toward you, but you can control how you take it. Like an old boy told me one day that I was ugly, and I said, 'Well, I didn't realize that but I'll work on it.'"

"But you're not, Jerry," I interrupted, laughing as I pictured him consulting a cosmetic surgeon.

"It's all in your perspective," he went on, over the neighing horses, the screeching cicadas. "Like the little boy whose daddy come inta the house and asked, 'Son, did you roll the outhouse off the hill?' And the little boy said, 'Dad, just like George Washington, I cannot tell a lie. Yes, I did.' And his dad beat the shit out of him. When he got done cryin', he said, 'Dad, when George Washington's dad asked him if he cut down the cherry tree and George said I cannot tell a lie, yes, I did, George's dad didn't whip him.' And the little boy's dad said, 'Yes, son, but George's dad wasn't *in* that cherry tree, was he?' Like I said, it's all in your perspective."

After his discharge, Woods went to work for the federal government as a mechanic in a warehouse in California. Like his father before him, he was drawn back to the Ozarks when he retired. Unlike his father, he didn't have to sharecrop for a living. With his government and military pensions, he had the means to buy a place of his own, on land Oren Woods had tilled behind a mule-drawn plow. And there, Woods fulfilled his boyhood dream to raise and train horses.

"It's up there on the hill past the graveyard. The house that's there now ain't the house that usta be there—an old sharecropper's shack. I've got pasture for my mares. Hadn't been for Miss Carol, it would all be under water now." He choked up, his eyes growing damp. "I just love it here, the hills and the rivers. Wouldn't trade places with anyone."

Leslie and I walked back to our cabin, talking about Woods's hard-won philosophy.

"That man," she observed, "has saved himself a hundred thousand dollars in psychiatrist's bills."

Later on, after lunch, I met the kinder, gentler Carol Springer. She served me ice-cold lemonade in her kitchen and reminisced about the Meramec Valley Irregulars' fight against the Corps of Engineers—a good time to be green in America, she said, the days of Ed Abbey and his Monkey Wrench Gang.

She seemed, this petite midwestern farm woman, aware that she sometimes came off as edgy; though she didn't apologize, she did point out that she came from a long line of spirited, independent women who broke convention or picked fights with formidable adversaries. A great-aunt graduated in journalism from Columbia University in 1904, when *journalist* was synonymous with *newspaperman*. Another female relative, as Springer would do decades later, locked horns with Washington in the thirties, stopping a federal road-paving project because it would have required felling a treasured grove of trees on her land. As for herself, Springer "never wanted to be someone who said, 'Yes, sir!' If you're not uppity, you get stepped on."

I'd put a thousand dollars on the Chicago Cubs winning the World Series before betting on the chance of anyone stepping on her. She refilled my glass and expanded on her theory of survival through adaptation.

"Take me. I'm bilingual. I learned to speak urban. I can speak to city people in a way my kinfolk couldn't. That's how we stopped the dam. We got a referendum of the people because I and other people could speak urban."

And then came her complicated laugh—self-deprecating but tinged with a sarcasm that said she didn't think highly of the urban tongue.

The campaign against the dam was long ago. What about today? How had the Great Recession affected life on Meramec Farm? It hadn't. Cattle prices had hit a high, and there were more cattle than people in Crawford County. It was good to be a minority, Springer wisecracked. Fewer car wrecks, no crime, quiet neighbors that do nothing all day but munch grass.

She and Andy and Jerry were another kind of minority—rural Americans, who now accounted for, at most, 17 percent of the population, a statistic she lamented. When she was a kid, her elementary school classmates knew what a cow was and what was done on a farm even if they weren't from farm families. Folks these days seemed to think their supermarket vegetables and chickens and beef came into existence wrapped in plastic.

"It's not a great evolutionary thing to be so distant from where your food comes from," she said.

Everyone else upon whom I'd sprung my Big Question had to ponder before answering. Springer didn't hesitate a beat, as if she'd already given it considerable thought.

"I think the glue is a belief, that's not clearly defined, that we have more in common than not, that we're more alike than we're different. I'm not sure it's true, but the important thing is that we believe it is."

In other words, the perception becomes the reality?

She shrugged. "I've been known to believe I'll get home in the dark in the rain. I'm not convinced, but I believe I will, and I get there."

15.

NEXT DAY, WANTING TO TRY OUT SPRINGER'S BARTER arrangement—she will trade a night in a cabin for work on the farm—I offered my services. When it came to agricultural work, my résumé was pretty skimpy. I could operate a chain saw, but she didn't need any wood cut; I could muck out the horse stalls, but that was Sofia's job.

"Can you drive a tractor-mower?"

Yes!

"Then you can mow my lawn."

I'd never driven a tractor-mower but reckoned that it didn't require a license. Andy, a muscular man of twenty-two, led me to a shed where the machine resided, showed me the starter button, the gearshift, and the lever for raising and lowering the rotary blade. I took my seat and sputtered off. The lawn covered close to an acre; it was littered with sticks, broken up by trees and bushes, and had many dips and embankments, but I was determined to make it look like a Pebble Beach fairway. It came to me that I wanted to please Carol Springer; at least I didn't want her telling some future guest that she had this writer who claimed he could drive a tractor-mower and made such a mess of her lawn that she had to call in a landscape crew to resod the whole thing.

When my labors were done, I took the absence of criticism as praise. Inspired, I decided to give Andy a hand mowing a hay meadow. That notion dissolved as soon as I saw him, in a straw cowboy hat and wrap-around sunglasses, mounted atop a much larger, more complicated tractor pulling a disk-mower, an expensive piece of machinery prone to breakage if it was run over rocks. I contented myself with listening to a tutorial on the fine points of making hay. The stuff in this field was inferior because there were too many weeds; it would be baled by a round baler for cattle feed. The higher-quality hay in an upper field would be baled by a square baler for horse feed or for sale.

Levelheaded, clear-sighted, serious without being a bore, Andy was a senior at the University of Missouri, where he majored in animal science with minors in business administration and English (there appeared to be a literary strain in the family). His ambition was to go on to veterinary school, then establish a practice and manage the farm.

He was working his way through college in untypical fashion, paying for tuition and expenses with profits from his cattle business. He'd been in it since he was fourteen, when he'd inherited the Meramec Farm's herd and seventy more head on another farm from his grandfather. There seemed to be little he didn't know about breeding and the nuances of the market; he kept an eye out for fluctuations in the price of feed-corn, which dictated at what weight he would sell his steers and heifers. Sometimes he had to leave the campus in Columbia and come home, a two-and-a-half-hour drive, to deal with a cow with a prolapsed uterus, to treat a sick calf, or, as happened once, to repair a quarter mile of fence ripped apart by a tornado. Doing all that while carrying a full load at school, crewing on the rowing team, and maintaining a relationship with his girlfriend left little time for trivialities like, say, social networking.

The one sure sign that you've entered geezerdom isn't gray hair, wrinkles, wattles, or waning physical powers; it's the conviction that the younger generation is going to hell and taking everyone with it. I guess it's ever been so. Geriatric Cro-Magnons, huddled in their drafty caves, probably moaned that the tribe was done for because their kids were too lazy or inept to kill mastodons. Listening to Andy, I felt that the country's future was in good hands, or at least in hands no worse than those of earlier generations. But he was a rarity in twenty-first-century America, rooted in the soil. He'd inherited a herd of cattle and with it the responsibility to care for it and the land that had sustained his family. His work as husbandman (now there's a word you never hear anymore) had hastened him into maturity. He had a seriousness I've seen in young war veterans—without the nervous tics, the jumpiness, and all the dark legacies that war confers. Life isn't a joke, time is too precious to waste texting inanities to your friends for hours on end. His mother had been onto something when she said that it's good to know where your food comes from.

Andy knew where his came from. He looked it in the eye, there on the pastures trod by his forebears for two hundred years.

———

In the afternoon, at an outfitter called Ozark Outdoors, Leslie and I rented a canoe for a firsthand look at the waterways saved by Springer and the Irregulars. The white-haired, white-bearded man who drove us in a van to the launch point wore a LIVE FREE OR DIE tattoo on his forearm. That being New Hampshire's state motto, I asked if he was from there. Nope, he answered in a clearly non-Yankee accent. Missouri born and bred. Worked as a welder in the Chrysler plant and made good money till it shut down and moved to Mexico. He'd taken a buyout, spent most of it on home improvements and big-game hunting trips all over North America, and had to go back to work. Now he welded for Ozark Outdoors but occasionally transported canoes and canoeists to the rivers. He complained that the United Auto Workers union (to which he'd belonged) and government regulations were responsible for the Chrysler factory's migration to Mexico.

"In a plant that big, you need unions," he said. "You need government regs like OSHA, but they didn't know where or when to stop. The company couldn't afford it and the corporate taxes we've got in this country."

As the son of a union man and a former union man myself, I thought he was being too kind to the Chrysler Corporation. Sure, if bigness was the font of the nation's economic sorrows, Big Labor would not have been guiltless if it was still big. But it wasn't. Like Chrysler's muscle cars, it had been scaled down, stripped of its (figurative) fins and chrome and V-8 engines.

We put in at a landing on the Huzzah, a tributary of the Courtois (pronounced, in a corruption that would horrify a Parisian, *Coataway*), which spills into the Meramec. Gliding over gravel shoals and through dancing riffles in our metal canoe, I reflected on the odd consequences of history. The end of the Vietnam War, no less than the efforts of conservationists, brought salvation to the Meramec River valley. Grumman, which had been building warplanes, found itself with immense stockpiles of surplus aluminum and began turning out canoes. Disdained by purists, the aluminum canoe was popular with weekend duffers and outfitters because it's rustproof, weatherproof, and laughs at the rocks that can rip out the bottoms of the wood-and-canvas vessels. In a short time, the Meramec and its sister streams were busy with canoeists, and, as their numbers grew, landowners fighting the dam project gained an army of allies, without whose support the battle might have been lost.

The waters of the Huzzah and Courtois ran clear and golden brown, and in the deeper pools we saw garfish, like silver spears, and smallmouth bass finning against the current. I am a passionate fly fisherman, and I love rivers and creeks more than I do lakes. Rivers take you places; lakes confine you. Rivers change, channels flowing into oxbows, rapids tumbling into flat water, pools tailing out into riffles; lakes stay the same. We coasted through the mouth of the Courtois into the broader Meramec, rounded a bend, and passed other canoeists, rafters, tubers, and picnickers, who waved and called out things like, "Hi, y'all havin' a good time? Pretty day to be on the river."

I dislike crowds, but on that sparkling June afternoon it gave me pleasure to see so many people enjoying themselves on a river running free. Its liberty, its very existence, was Carol Springer's legacy, and a good one.

She saw us off the next morning with a lovely phrase: "You should come back in the fall. When the light falls on the trees, it's like looking through a stained-glass window." Though I'm a chronic wanderer, a part of me envied her, Jerry, Andy, and Dell, fixed to one place and content to be there.

———

It was a Saturday, June 10, my seventieth birthday. I'd reached the life span allotted by the Bible,* a milestone I marked rather than celebrated

---

* Psalm 90, verse 10: "The days of our years are threescore years and ten; and if by reason of strength they be fourscore years, yet is their strength labor and sorrow; for it is soon cut off, and we fly away."

on several roads: Interstate 44, Missouri Routes 19, 94, and 63; I-70 (to make better time, I'd again broken my no-interstate vow). What I remember of this itinerary was the forlorn charm of Route 94, winding alongside the swollen Missouri, and the sudden, dramatic appearance of the capitol building dome, bulging from out of distant trees as we approached Jefferson City. The building itself lived up to the grandeur promised by its dome, an imposing, many-pillared structure that looked as if it aspired to surpass the nation's capitol. We parked and walked across the street to a memorial plaza dedicated to Lewis and Clark.

On its twenty-second day out from the confluence of the Missouri and Mississippi Rivers, the Corps of Discovery—about three dozen men plus Lewis's Newfoundland hound, Seaman—stopped at what's now Jefferson City to repair a broken mast on their keelboat. An ensemble of bronze statues dominated the plaza: Meriwether Lewis, with Seaman at his feet, peering through a telescope; George Drouillard, a trapper clad in buckskins, standing with a flintlock resting against his shoulder; York, William Clark's black slave, sitting beside a hatless Clark, who takes a sight with a sextant. The genial, redheaded Clark was the expedition's cartographer. In sunlight and rain, in mosquito-ridden heat and blizzard, he noted compass bearings, mileages, and sextant readings in a leather-bound journal with quill and ink several times a day every day for the eighteen months it took the corps to reach the Pacific. He estimated that they had covered 4,162 miles. He was off by forty miles.

———

We overnighted in a Kampground of America outside Independence, a country town when Harry Truman was born there, now welded in asphalt and concrete to Kansas City. Leslie had noticed on our many KOA stays that the letter *c* was prohibited at the KOA. Guests bought food and supplies at the Kampground Store; those unequipped with trailers could rent a Kozy Kabin.

For my birthday, my lady treated me to dinner at Hereford House, a landmark eatery noted for—surprise!—beef. She ordered pork ribs, served in such abundance that she took half a hog's worth home in a doggie bag. I had a Kansas City strip, the finest steak I'd eaten anywhere, including Gene and Georgetti's in Chicago. We ferried the rib scraps and steak fat back to the dogs at the kampground.

It struck at eleven that night, a storm such as only the prairies can dish out, a gale-force wind shaking Ethel, rain and hail clattering against her roof. I ran outside in my underwear to close the hardtop's windows. I was soaked in seconds and pelted by hailstones. As the dogs would have no fresh air, I coaxed them out of the truck and led them into the trailer, where they shook themselves dry, licked my legs in gratitude, and promptly went to sleep on the floor. Leslie looked at them and drew in the perfume of wet gundog.

I took a towel to myself and went back to bed, and that was how I spent the first night of my seventy-first year.

The "lean and slippered pantaloon" is the sixth of the seven ages of man recited by Jaques in *As You Like It*. Now that I'd begun my journey to the seventh and the extended care facility awaiting my arrival there ("Mere oblivion," saith Jaques. "Sans teeth, sans eyes, sans taste, sans everything"); now that I turned to the obituary before the sports page, spirits rising when I read of the passage of nonagenarians, tumbling when the deceased were in their seventies; now that I was forced to listen to my peers narrate sagas about surgeries and infirmities, I reflected on Jaques's soliloquy. The pantaloon refers to the snug, youthful hosiery worn by rusted-out Elizabethan males trying to look young.

I vowed never to make myself ridiculous by adopting the dress, mannerisms, and slang of twenty-, thirty-, or even forty-somethings. I would not rinse what was left of my hair in Grecian Formula or address my male friends as "dude" or say things like "cool app." The sixth-ager's task is not to preserve the illusion of youth; it is to avoid nostalgia and remain relevant for as long as possible—tricky in an era when just about everything becomes obsolete in six months.

How to stay current without latching onto every trend, how to age without growing into a cranky old fart mired in the past—those were my questions. I drew inspiration from my grandparents' generation, because it, more than my parents', lived through a time of dizzying technological change, radical upheavals in society. My paternal grandmother, Rose, born in Chicago in 1894, married in 1913 wearing a whalebone corset, was twenty-six before women won the right to vote. She lived well into the era of miniskirts and the feminist movement. She remembered horse-drawn fire engines, gaslight, wooden sidewalks, and hearing about the Wright Brothers' first flight. At seventy-five, in my parents' family room, she sat beside me watching Neil Armstrong set foot on the moon, shaking her head in disbelief.

———

The storm had broken the heat, this time for real. I actually felt goose bumps in the morning air as I spread my exercise mat on the gravel, did my stretches, push-ups, and sit-ups, then took a fifteen-minute walk in a broad meadow, where Sage and Sky gamboled off lead.

Leslie could not celebrate our passage from Kansas City, Missouri, to Kansas City, Kansas, with an iPod blast of KC and the Sunshine Band, since her selections left out most everything from 1975 to 1990, so she picked up Magic Droid for amusement and edification. MD informed us that K.C.K., which we'd thought was the larger of the two, was actually the smaller and considered a suburb of K.C.M. West of the city, where the Missouri bends northwestward for hundreds of miles almost to the Canadian line, we left I-70 for Kansas Route 73/7, another road on the Lewis and Clark Trail, so indicated by triangular markers showing the silhouettes of one man standing as he points forward, another kneeling with a musket in hand. The plan was to follow the river all the way to its headwaters in Montana. It's a military axiom that no plan survives contact with the enemy. That morning's *Kansas City Star* warned in bold type of our enemy's approach—**"Road, rail closures are possible as the swollen Missouri River moves south"**— and we met it at a lonesome junction north of Atchison. Barricades had been flung across Route 73/7 with a sign: ROAD CLOSED DUE TO FLOODING.

Leslie has noted a certain rigidity in my nature—anal retention, she diagnoses, looking into my face and puckering her mouth. Flummoxed, I stared at my Rand McNally atlas, the planned route marked in yellow highlighter. I'd been so dead set on following it that I hadn't considered any alternatives. Now, I couldn't think of one. Leslie took the atlas and studied it for a minute or two.

She laid a finger on the town of Lebanon, far out on the Kansas plains. Just above it was a red dot. "There's where we need to go," she said. Next to the dot were the words *Center of the Conterminous United States.*

THE THINGS WE CARRIED

As on a long voyage in a sailboat, we had to be as self-contained as possible, with a place for everything and everything in its place. At least once a day, one of us would forget in which place a particular thing resided, leading to the cry of "Where's my stuff?" Here's a partial list of what got stowed on the roof rack, in the truck's bed and backseat, and in the trailer's cupboards and compartments.

Phil's clothes: 10 pr underwear and socks; 2 pr shorts; 2 pr jeans; 4 T-shirts; 2 lightweight long-sleeve shirts; 2 heavyweight long-sleeve shirts; 2 sweatshirts; 1 sweater; 1 rain jacket; 1 fleece jacket; 1 pr each, cowboy boots, hiking boots, walking shoes, sandals; 2 belts; 2 baseball caps; 1 wide-brimmed "packer's hat"; sunglasses. Also, over Leslie's objections, a .357 magnum revolver.

Leslie's clothes: Pretty much as above but multiply by three. Also her paints and canvases and, over my objections, a bright-red folding bike.

Dog stuff: 1 4-by-6-foot dog bed; metal dog dishes; chest harnesses; leashes; brushes, clippers, antitick medicine; 40-pound bag dry dog food (replenished en route as needed).

Cooking and eating equipment: 1 4-place setting of Corel dishware; 2 metal cups; 1 package of plastic cups; 4 ea., knives, forks, spoons; 2 kitchen knives; 1 small cutting board; 1 large frypan; 1 small frypan; 2 pots, 1 large, 1 small; 1 hibachi; 1 camp-style coffeepot; 2 butane lighters; dishtowels, dishwashing soap, aluminum foil, freezer bags.

Truck, trailer equipment: Complete tool kit; 15-, 20-, and 30-amp fuses; 1 truck jack w/ lugwrench, 1 hydraulic jack; spare lug nuts; 1 30-amp power cord; 1 water hose; 1 sewer hose; 4 stabilizer jacks; duct tape (for redneck repair work); electrical tape; 2 spare tires for truck, 2 for trailer; 2 5-gallon gasoline jerry cans; 1 7-gallon jerry can for water; extra cans of motor oil and brake fluid; WD-40 and other lubricants; emergency flares; tow strap. Also, 2 pr canvas work gloves; rope; bungee cords.

Camping gear: 2 lightweight sleeping bags; 2 small backpacks; 1 GPS; 1 orienteering compass; Swiss Army knife; Leatherman tool;

first-aid kit; 1 lantern; 2 camp chairs; 1 camp table; 2 headlamps w/ spare batteries; 2 mag lights; 2 fishing rods and reels, flies, hooks, etc.; 2 pr chest waders; 1 pr hip boots.

Electronica: 2 laptops; 1 Android smart phone (for Leslie); 1 dumb phone (for Phil); 1 digital voice recorder; 1 Nikon digital camera; 1 4G wireless connector; 1 Kindle e-reader; a bag full of wires, rechargers, and spare batteries.

Misc.: Books (the printed kind): *The Innocents Abroad, On the Road, The Oregon Trail, The Journals of Lewis and Clark*, others; road atlases, maps, guidebooks; spare sunglasses and reading glasses; journals, notebooks, pens; passports; towels, soap, pillows.

PART TWO

In the Heart of the Heartland

At the geographic center of the United States.

16.

THE MIDWESTERN WOODLANDS AND SAVANNAHS SURRENDERED grudgingly to the central Great Plains. We saw fewer and fewer trees, and then none, except for the cottonwoods fringing the creeks and rivers: the Delaware, the Vermillion, the Big Blue. It was possible to think of our rig as a small ship; under a cloud-tiled sky, the land rose and fell, rose and fell, like green sea swells in arrested motion. A sea of corn and wheat, but mostly corn—this was Kansas—the row-crop monotony sometimes relieved by vestiges of the original tallgrass prairie that had sustained the buffalo and were now cattle ranges, bounded by barbed-wire fences.

U.S. 36 was called the "Pony Express Highway"; its asphalt covered the trail ridden by the jockey-size couriers who had carried the mail between St. Joseph, Missouri, and San Francisco. In case the traveler forgot this fact, every gas station and convenience store was themed to the Pony Express, and markers occasionally appeared at the roadside displaying the emblem of a rider at full gallop.

Ahead, for as far as we could see, the highway lay upon the undulating land like a broad, black cable reeling off the stern of a ship sailing a perfectly straight course. Accustomed to the foreshortened horizons east of the Mississippi, we had to get used to distances, immense distances, and emptiness. Many of the towns we passed through had a forsaken look—abandoned gas stations, shuttered shops, hardly a soul to be seen on the streets, and no lack of parking places if you cared to stop, but there was no reason to.

In the late 1880s, a Paiute mystic, Wovoka, began to preach a hybridized religion combining Christianity with Native American spiritual beliefs. It spread like a prairie fire among the remnant plains tribes, penned up on reservations and desperate for anything that promised to restore their nomadic way of life. The central rite was the Ghost Dance. In a version of the Rapture, Wovoka prophesied that Indians who performed the Ghost Dance would be taken to safety high in the sky while a great flood drowned the white man and all his works. When the waters receded, fresh grass would grow over the whites' farms and roads and towns; the buffalo and herds of wild horses would return in their former numbers; then the Indians suspended in the heavens would descend to a renewed land, there to meet the risen spirits of their ancestors and live again as they had from time immemorial.

The Wounded Knee massacre in 1890 ended Wovoka's millennialist dream but, as we drove on through the dying towns, I wondered if it was coming to pass, not through Ghost Dance magic but as a result of free-market efficiency. The family farm, that much-revered but largely fictitious institution, isn't efficient; the megafarm is. Only the large-scale farmer can afford the equipment and machinery needed to wrest a reliable income from the land. "Get big or get out" has been the catchphrase on the Great Plains for years, and most small farmers have gotten out. Zeke and Maude and their towheaded kids working their quarter and half sections have been replaced by agribusiness giants owning immense acreages, sprayed with chemicals and plowed fence line to fence line by GPS-guided tractors. That's the main reason why the region is emptier today than it was in 1920, when the tide of white settlement that began in the 1840s reached its high-water mark. Thousands of square miles have fewer than six people per square mile—the benchmark density historian Frederick Jackson Turner adopted to distinguish a frontier from a settled area.

The slow, steady exodus has inspired a vision akin to Wovoka's, minus the mysticism. Two geographers who teach at Rutgers and Princeton, Frank and Deborah Popper, have studied the Great Plains and concluded that the present level of corporate agriculture isn't sustainable. It depends on underground aquifers and on billions of dollars in subsidies to remain viable; but even the big farms will probably go bust as water runs out.

The huge Ogallala aquifer, the principal source of water for most plains farms and ranches, is emptying at the rate of four feet a year and is predicted to go dry in another twenty years. In 1987, almost exactly a century after the Paiute messiah began his ministry, the Poppers proposed creating the "Buffalo Commons," an enormous (half the size of Texas) natural park sprawling across parts of ten western and midwestern states. It would be restored to native prairie and repopulated with bison, elk, wolves, and grizzly bears. Like the game reserves in East Africa, it would draw ecotourists from the world over and revive the declining economies in the heartland.

For nearly two decades, the Poppers have traveled the plains, promoting the Buffalo Commons. Although they've sold a few people on their idea, I doubt its chances of becoming a reality are much greater than Wovoka's vision. Most prairie citizens haven't warmed to the picture of themselves playing host to safari parties and of their land as a game park. It's one thing in America to preserve wilderness, altogether another to reverse our concept of progress by turning once-productive land back into wilderness.

Maybe because it was more cow town than farm town, Washington, Kansas, was a lively place. A rodeo was to be held that evening in the county fairgrounds, and a dozen trailers occupied the town park where we camped for the night. Families sat around in tight little circles, waiting for the contest to get under way. Pickup trucks and gooseneck stock trailers filled the fairgrounds; cows, calves, horses, and bulls with mayhem in their eyes milled in pens, raising dust; young cowboys in straw hats wandered about with girlfriends in tight jeans. Some were spectators, some contestants, the female barrel racers and the male bronc and bull riders wearing numbers on the backs of their shirts. Almost all were thin, a few downright skinny. Cattle country has been spared the plague of obesity; ranching still requires hard physical work, and rodeo cowboys are athletes.

After buying tickets, we discovered that we had only eight dollars between us, and as we waited in the food line, Leslie calculated what combo would be most filling on our limited funds. Two brats, two sodas, and two bags of chips left us with a dollar. We took our seats in the rusting steel bleachers, packed to capacity. The rodeo got under way as a red prairie sun hovered over a horizon twenty miles away. It was, this rodeo, the equivalent of a minor-league baseball game. The contestants were either up-and-comers or aging journeymen. Not one bull rider made it to the eight-second buzzer. A team of young men in purple silk shirts—El Latigos del Diablo (the Whips of the Devil)—did tricks with bullwhips, like popping balloons and snuffing out rolled-up burning newspaper. Impromptu entertainment was staged in the bull pen, where a huge, tumescent brindle kept trying to mount his pen mates.

Another plains storm rolled in that night, with long, sublime rolls of thunder. This time it was Leslie's turn to close the truck's windows and bring the dogs inside. In the morning, I walked my ambassadors around the campground, hoping to find out what the rodeo stars and their families thought about the Buffalo Commons and other matters. Attempting to blend in, I'd donned a wide-brimmed hat, put on a snap-button shirt, and exchanged my hiking boots for a beat-up pair of Tony Lamas. Sage and Sky failed in their mission, and so did my disguise. You can dress up in pinstripes and suspenders and pass yourself off as a stockbroker, but even the most careful attention to details of proper western attire will not fool anyone. There is something in the way a real cowboy carries himself that defies imitation.

In quest of an ATM and someone to talk to, we moved on to Belleville, around ten miles west on U.S. 36, a brown sign directing us to the "historic business district." Almost all the towns had historic business districts, and they truly are historic in the sense that they are history. Very little business is done in them these days, and the attractive but vacant brick buildings lining Belleville's center looked like an Edward Hopper painting. It did, however, have a functional ATM and a diner with food, Big Foot Freddy's. Its founder, one Fred Zimmerman, stood six-feet-five in his size-fifteen shoes. A worn, wooden bar, counter stools, and blue-and-white checkered cloths covering the tables completed the image of a small-town restaurant circa 1950. Most of the patrons met the age qualification for Medicare. The two youngest people in the place were the waitresses, Laura, about thirty, and Paula, about forty.

In my journalism career, I'd interviewed everyone from mob hit men to prime ministers, from Saudi Arabian princes to Israeli cabdrivers. I was confident in my ability to get just about anyone to talk on just about any subject, but I couldn't milk a word beyond *hello* out of the customers in Big Foot Freddy's. Laura and Paula were civil enough, but too absorbed in watching *The Voice* on the TV above the bar to chat about the weather, much less the Buffalo Commons.

Frustrated, we took a detour after lunch to the Pawnee Indian Village, a museum-cum-archaeological dig on a hill overlooking the Republican River. Surely the curator would talk to me, and she did. She had no choice; we were the sole visitors. Betty Bouray, an attractive woman in her thirties, with a winning smile and brown hair that threw off reddish glints, was the assistant curator. I thought she had the loneliest job in Kansas. The museum, a circular structure built around the excavation of a Pawnee earth lodge, stood all by itself out there on the rolling expanses, at the end of a country lane eight miles off the highway.

Betty and her husband had lived in Belleville for six years before moving to their present home near the museum. Without my asking for one, she supplied an explanation as to why its citizens were so close-mouthed.

"People are very cliquish in Belleville—it's like high school. We didn't care for it. Belleville is a melting pot—Czechs, Swedes mostly—and the nationalities tend to stick together. They don't bring in strangers very well. They're not downright rude, just not very welcoming." It pleased me to hear that. I wasn't losing my touch; I'd simply bumbled into that rare thing in the Middle West—an unfriendly town.

Of course, Betty had a lot to say about the Pawnee, long ago the dominant power on the Great Plains: they lived in villages of earth-and-log lodges fortified by palisades to protect them from the Sioux, Cheyenne, and Arapaho; they were fastidious, bathing several times a day, and considered whites to be a filthy race; and they were known as "the astronomers of the plains," though astrologers would be more accurate. They believed that the stars were responsible for the creation of the universe, influenced weather, crops, and hunting, and guided men's lives. On display, among other artifacts, was a three-hundred-year-old star chart, painted on a buffalo hide.

We were getting set to leave when a tall, wiry man walked in with a portfolio under his arm. His name was Duane Guile, a retired agricultural chemical salesman of sixty-one. He approached Betty with a request: could the museum display a painting he'd commissioned? He opened the portfolio, which contained several prints of *Dog Soldier Raid at New*

Scandinavia—1869, based on an actual incident in which a boy settler was killed by the Cheyenne. Betty looked at the raw, gory picture and offered a cordial, noncommittal smile.

We lingered for a while, talking to Duane and Betty about their lives and the state of the country. Out where they lived, distance and isolation bred self-reliance (or the illusion of it) and a suspicion of centralized power. They felt that there was too much government intrusion into private lives. For example, she said, a bill pending in Congress would prohibit people from growing backyard vegetable gardens like hers.

(A parenthetical note: One of the things we learned on the trip was that the age of instant communications has not slowed but accelerated the spread of myth and rumor. The bill, known as the Food Safety Modernization Act, was intended to tighten safety regulations in industrial food processing plants, not to criminalize home gardeners. It had, however, ignited hysteria in cyberspace. Bloggers and gardening and farming Web sites, from one end of the political rainbow to the other, howled. "Giant chemical companies are conspiring with Congress to ban organic farms and gardens!" screamed lefty greens. "The bill is a Stalinist plot to collectivize American agriculture!" libertarians cried. Because the strands of truth and baloney are seamlessly woven into the Web, it's very difficult to figure out which is which. Betty couldn't be blamed for fearing that she was going to be turned into an outlaw for growing tomatoes and cucumbers.)

Meanwhile, Duane moaned that too many taxes were "going to things the people who pay them don't believe in."

"Don't get me on my soapbox," he pleaded, so I asked how he occupied himself, now that he was retired.

He raised cattle on a small pasture. It was more or less a hobby. One thing was certain: Duane wasn't going to move into a Sunbelt retirement community. He would cling to the Great Plains like the big bluestem grasses carpeting the ranges. His great-grandfather had settled in the town of Skandia in 1874, and his grandchildren were the sixth generation to live there, in the American Outback. The people of the plains are what mattered, he said. They took care of each other.

"It's easy to see what binds us together," he said. "When someone gets into trouble, neighbors jump in and help. That's always been the case out here."

Driving away, I asked myself if that sense of community would survive the depopulation of the Great Plains and all the places like it. I had my own vision of the America my grandchildren might inherit: huge, sprawling megalopolises with nothing in between, galaxies dense with humanity separated by vast reaches of empty space. People would be connected by social media, or whatever their equivalent will be at mid-century, but could the impersonality of electronic links ever replace the intimacy of a few words exchanged over a fence, the joys or sorrows or needs revealed in the expressions on someone's face, in a tone of voice, a touch? Would neighbors jump in to help someone in trouble; would they pull together or pull apart?

At Lovewell State Park, I nudged Ethel into a space above a reservoir created by a dam on the Republican. (The river, incidentally, hadn't been named by political partisans, but by early French fur traders who'd mistaken the Pawnees' form of tribal government for a republic.) After we set up, Leslie went off to exercise the dogs. Dead tired, I broke out a camp chair, splashed a double shot of Johnny Walker into a tin cup, and sat down, my mind as blank as the prairie sky.

Leslie and the dogs returned early from their excursion, her left wrist swollen, her forearms bruised. She tossed the leashes my way.

"I'm through as dog wrangler."

She glared at Sage and Sky, a look of caninicide in her green eyes.

"What happened?"

She'd been walking them, in her flip-flops, when they scented something interesting, lunged, and yanked her off her feet onto the gravel path. She broke her fall with her arms. We still had no ice—the mini-fridge's tiny freezer couldn't seem to keep anything frozen—but a chilled bottle of vodka served well to reduce the swelling in her wrist.

It was still puffed up and sore in the morning, when, filling in as dog wrangler, I took the miscreants for a stroll along the river. They pulled like sled dogs and nearly tripped me as they crisscrossed in front of me, tangling the leashes around my ankles. There was bird scent all over the place; swallows were nesting. In unison, Sage and Sky froze on point, straining forward, their eyes and noses fixed on something in the grass. It was a newborn swallow, smaller than an egg, covered in fuzz. Its mother dive-bombed me and the dogs. I saw by the trembling in their muscles that their instinct to pounce was about to overcome their training to hold fast, and I practically tore a rotator cuff pulling them away.

We hiked back to the trailer, man and dog seasoned with ticks. As I plucked them off with tweezers, I explained to Leslie the reason for the dogs' behavior. It did not mollify her. The one-woman Union of Dog Wranglers would be on strike till further notice. Her wrist remained swollen and painful. Treatment took us to the nearest hospital, across the state line in Superior, Nebraska, for an X-ray. A kindly nurse proclaimed a sprain, applied a Velcro splint, and gave Leslie a mild painkiller. Then we left for the middle of the middle of the country.

17.

I N 1940, TWO SURVEYORS, L. T. HAGADORN AND L. A. BEARDSLEE, determined that the exact geographic center of the contiguous United States was at 39 degrees, 50 minutes north latitude, 98 degrees, 35 minutes west longitude. Its location was inglorious—a hog pen on a farm owned by one Johnny Grieb. A monument was to be erected, but farmer Grieb did not want tourists tramping over his land, so another site was chosen half a mile away. The marker stands there today, at the junction of County Road AA and Kansas Route 191. Thus it only purports to be at the middle of the nation. As a matter of fact, it's a fiction of a fiction; there is no such thing as an *exact* geographic center. Here's why: if the continental United States were as flat as a playing card and each square mile of uniform weight, the precise center would be its balance point. But because coastlines are ever shifting, reaching out here, shrinking back there, that point keeps moving, even if by only a yard or two.

Anyway, for the sake of convenience, let's say we arrived at the exact center, 2,582 miles from Key West, including detours and side trips. We were the only sentient beings out there, besides two horses grazing nearby. A low, lead-colored sky and a high prairie wind heightened the feeling of desolation. A tourist publication we'd picked up at the campground advised that "there really isn't very much to see and do at the geographical center of the United States." That was a half-truth. Yes, there wasn't much to see, but there was absolutely nothing to do except to stand there so you could later tell your friends that you'd been there. Leslie videoed the scene. Sound: complete silence except for the whoosh of a buffeting wind. Picture: a small park with a covered picnic table; a tiny frame chapel; a defunct motel that a rich Texan had converted into a hunting camp; a stone pyramid with an American flag snapping from a pole embedded in its top; an age-greened plaque with a sketch of survey lines and the inscription:

THE GEOGRAPHICAL CENTER OF THE UNITED STATES.

And one other thing: a glassed-in display of press clippings and a copy of the remarks delivered by State Supreme Court Justice Hugo T. Wedell when the marker was dedicated on April 25, 1941. He said: "We have here in Kansas something distinctive which should be preserved at any cost. It is the spirit of the pioneer who settled in the center of this great nation. That spirit is worthy of its definite and distinct qualities. That spirit is neither radical nor ultra-conservative. The spirit of the Kansas pioneer of necessity possessed the rare combination of idealism and realism."

Lebanon, two straight-line miles from the marker, also claims to be "the Center of the U.S.A." Or, as a resident once put it, "Lebanon isn't in the middle of nowhere, it is the middle of everywhere." Huddled on the horizon-to-horizon expanses of wind-ruffled wheat, it didn't look like the middle of anywhere. On both sides of one street boarded windows stared from derelict houses, porches sagging, paint peeling like skin from a sunburned back, NO TRESPASSING signs tilting in neglected yards. The siding on one place appeared to have been sandblasted by someone who'd quit with the job half done. In the business district—"historic," of course— overlooked by grain elevators and storage bins, rubble lay in vacant lots where buildings had once stood. Stores had CLOSED signs pasted to their locked doors. A fair-sized redbrick church was in good shape, as were a few residences nearby, but all in all Lebanon was a wreck.

"What happened here?" Leslie asked. "It looks like it was hit by a tornado."

To find out, I went to city hall, only to discover that it, too, was defunct. The municipal offices were now in a steel-sided box that looked like a construction-site trailer. There I met Sondra Kennedy, a blonde, solidly built woman who wore several hats: town treasurer, town clerk, mayor's assistant. After I explained what I was up to, I remarked, as gently as I could, that Lebanon looked in rough shape.

She bit her lip. She'd lived in Lebanon all her sixty-one years and in that time had seen its population fall from almost a thousand in the fifties to three hundred at the turn of the century. Today it was—she flipped through some papers on her desk—218. The school closed years ago—there were so few young people left, no jobs to hold them here. The pharmacy was gone, the hardware store, the grocery store. The bank had shut its doors, the building condemned and demolished.

"The bank was the hardest for me," Kennedy said. "I worked there for twenty-one years." She choked back tears. "It's hard, so hard to see this happening to your hometown."

The same slow death we'd seen elsewhere, but in Lebanon the condition had progressed. Present trends continuing, the town would be uninhabited in less than twenty years. I felt as if we were touring a kind of demographic ICU ward and had come upon a patient with no hope of recovery.

Were there any plans to bring new life to the town? I asked. Tourism? Light industry? None that Kennedy knew of. She suggested I talk to the mayor, Duane Ream.

I found his place, a neat, modest yellow clapboard on U.S. 281, across from Lebanon's last remaining gas station. He lives there with his wife, Joan—pronounced *Jo-anne*—a lively woman with short, silver hair whose hobby is making porcelain dolls.

Ream and I spoke in the den, where a grandfather clock ticked over our voices. Outdoor scenes hung on the wood-paneled walls; photos of children, grandchildren, and great-grandchildren stood in easel frames on bookshelves. Ream's thick, dark hair took a decade off his eighty-six years. The only sign of advanced age was the quivering in his hands. Dressed in a maroon shirt and jeans held up by blue suspenders, his accent pure country, he looked and sounded like a son of the prairies, but he was no provincial with a narrow view of life. He'd studied photography at the Yale University School of Art when he was young, had traveled all over the country with Joan, and he read three newspapers a day and kept abreast of events on CNN and the Internet.

"This is a farming community, ever'thing is tied to the farm, there is absolutely no industry," he said, sitting in a lounge chair. "And the farms got big, there was nothing for anybody to do, the young people go to college and head for somewhere else. I read somewhere that the average age of a Kansas farmer is fifty-eight."

He paused, plucking at his jeans. The clock's ticking seemed to deepen the silence.

"When I was a kid—that's quite a while ago—there was at least one family living on each quarter section, so there was at least four families on each square mile.* Well, I have a nephew out here who farms *six thousand* acres. Wheat, corn, soybeans, milo. He owns some, leases some from retired farmers and farm widows who can't work the land themselves."

Ream remembered the day when farmers like his father plowed with horses and considered a yield of twenty to twenty-five bushels per acre a good harvest. Now, mechanical marvels like giant combines and GPS-guided tractors that plow furrows as straight as yardsticks allowed one man, like his nephew, to cultivate huge tracts of land and bring in sixty to eighty bushels an acre.

Technology had likewise shrunk the need for human labor at the grain storage facility at the north end of town. It handled a million bushels each harvest but employed only three people full-time, a few more to operate the scales and keep books during the season.

"Downtown Lebanon at one time had a business on every lot on both sides of the street for two blocks," Ream said "We had six grocery stores, we had hardware stores, we had ever'thing. But then farmers started to retire and there was no one to replace them. Well, you can't have a grocery store if there's no one to buy anything."

And so, he went on, Lebanon was fading away "a little bit at time."

How did he feel about that?

"Ever'body here is happy," he answered.

Happy? I was thinking of Sondra Kennedy, stifling a sob.

"If they need something, they drive fifteen miles to Smith Center or two hours to Salina or Grand Island in Nebraska. Nobody minds that."

Was it difficult to be the mayor of a disappearing town?

He shook his head. All he had to do was maintain the streets, keep the sewers working and the water running. Periodically, he organized clean-up campaigns, hauling junk from abandoned houses or from houses occupied by people too old to do the heavy work themselves. And, no, there were no plans to rebuild the bank or put new businesses

---

*A section—640 acres—equals a square mile. Kansas is laid out on a grid of townships, each consisting of thirty-six sections.

on the vacant lots, some of which out-of-state buyers had bought on the Internet, sight unseen.

He gave the impression that he was resigned to Lebanon's plight; it was a natural process, and he couldn't do anything more about it than he could about the weather. He'd lived a long time, and some of it had been tough, and maybe that's what made him so placid. He remembered how, during the Depression, farmers never went hungry but they never made a nickel, either, bartering surplus eggs for groceries, a bushel of wheat for flour. He remembered the Dust Bowl, when clouds of dirt blackened the sky.

"I'd seen my dad scoop dirt off the floor in the house with a scoop shovel that blowed in from a dust storm. I had to go out and dig a trench around the pig pen. The dirt had come up over the top of the fence, and the pigs could walk over it. You left your machinery out, the dirt would bury it. It was bad, it really was. We raised very little in those years."

To him, the Great Recession wasn't even an inconvenience. "We didn't know it happened," he said. "Nobody here has any money to lose. What they have got is invested in machinery. A tractor costs twenty to thirty thousand, a combine two hundred thousand. People out here were madder'n hell when they read about what the big banks and the mortgage lenders were doin'. All that was caused by people stealin' money. They wanted to loan money and get that interest. They didn't care if you went broke."

The clock ticked on, gonged the hour, and then Ream threw out a question: "Why do we have to have a four percent increase in the gross domestic product every year? We're gonna die if we don't get the prices raised four percent every year? I don't know who dreamed that up. The workin' guys in a factory have to get a raise. So the guy makin' the stuff they buy has to give his workers a raise, and prices go up, so they have to get another raise. Why can't we just live the same?"

Although he was one of those Kansans whom Justice Wedell described as "neither radical nor ultra-conservative," this was a radical proposition. I'm not sure he realized how radical it was; were it put into practice, it would subvert the consumer society top to bottom. We would have to redefine the cherished belief that our children *must* live better than we, even when we're living pretty damn well.

He didn't expect an answer, which was good because I didn't have one.

"Thanks for giving me your time," I said.

"That's okay," he replied with a wry grin. "My time isn't worth much."

Wondering if Ream's comment that everybody was happy might have been mayoral propaganda, I returned to Lebanon the next day with Leslie to snoop around. In the post office, next to an empty lot once occupied by a hardware store, we found the postmaster, Debbie Whitman, waxing floors. A slim, strawberry blonde, Whitman was as open as the plains, as cheerful as a sunnyside-up egg. She'd been the town's postmaster since 2003.

"This is a manual station," she said. "No automation. I sort the mail, stamp everything by hand."

Often, letters arrive with just a name, no address, but Lebanon is now so small she has no trouble getting mail into the right hands.

"There used to be five rural routes here. Now we're down to two, and they're not big routes. Lebanon was a booming town then. It held celebrations that drew people from all over. It had a bar, the Wagon Wheel, restaurants. A lot different now. The old bank building had to be torn down because bricks were falling off it during harvest, from the big semis driving past. Overall, it's kind of sad."

Was she sad? She was not. She had only two complaints: one, everybody knew everybody else's business, and two, Lebanon was too big for her and her husband, a retired Kansas state trooper.

"*This* is too big?"

She nodded. They lived on the edge of town, and sometimes she curtained off the windows facing other houses to create the illusion that she was out in the country.

"We're rural people. When we get into Omaha or even Salina, it's too fast-paced. I wouldn't mind living someplace where we'd get into town once a month. That would be awesome."

It turned out that Lebanon did have a grocery; also a hardware store, a variety store, and a café. All were consolidated under one roof, in a two-story brick building beside the American Legion Hall, Post 185. This was Ladow's Supermarket, and the whole of it would have fit into one department in a Walmart superstore. The second-floor windows were boarded, but the café downstairs was bustling with some twenty customers while the owner, Randall Ladow, cut and packaged pork chops and breakfast sausage at the meat counter. The noon siren moaned, a sound I hadn't heard since I was a kid in those small Wisconsin towns where my father serviced the canneries. We had lunch: my cheeseburger cost a buck fifty; Leslie's pulled pork sandwich was two dollars. I couldn't find a soul as sorrowful as Sondra Kennedy. They weren't in denial, and all pointed to Big Ag as the drum major on Lebanon's march toward ghost-town status, but, like their mayor, they'd adopted an attitude of jaunty stoicism.

"I suppose we don't like it," Ladow told me, wrapping sausage in plastic, pasting price stickers to the package. "But we don't know how to draw young people back."

At fifty-four, he was one of the kids in town. He'd lived in Lebanon since he was four and, except for a year attending a technical school, had never been anywhere else. Talk about roots! He didn't have time to mourn what was happening. Running a market, a hardware-variety store, and a café all at once kept him and his wife busy twelve hours a day.

"And there's always something to do if you want to get involved."

Like the musical review advertised on a poster in the market's window: *Give Our Regards to Broadway.* It promised "songs, skits, fun." Another announced a July Fourth fireworks display. A town spirit wasn't dead yet, and if everyone wasn't happy, most were. I might have been the most melancholy person in Lebanon, aware that I'd been talking to people who were the last of their kind. The adagio to Dvořák's *New World Symphony*, wistful, solemn, played in my mind, and I felt as I imagined Edward Curtis did when he photographed Sioux and Apache and Hopi early in the previous century.

18.

I T SURPASSES STRANGE THAT THE WHITE RACE ETHNICALLY
cleansed North America of its aboriginal inhabitants and then proceeded to name just about anything that could be named for them.
Sioux City, Iowa. Cheyenne, Wyoming. Cochise County, Arizona. Pontiac.
Mohawk. The Atlanta Braves. Red Cloud, Nebraska, is the eponym for the
Oglala Sioux war leader who waged a textbook guerrilla campaign that
stopped settlement in traditional Sioux lands for a decade.

Red Cloud is renowned, however, as the hometown of Willa Cather,
whose lifetime (1873–1947) spanned the passage from the frontier to the
modern era. No one before or since has written better about the West as
it was experienced by ordinary people. In *My Antonia*, the final book of
her Prairie Trilogy, she wrote one of the most moving passages in American literature. It comes in the voice of the novel's narrator, Jim Burden,
as he reflects on the grave of Antonia Shimerda's father, a Czech immigrant who found only misery in his pioneer life on the Great Plains and
committed suicide. Denied burial in consecrated ground, Mr. Shimerda
was interred out on the prairie.

> Years afterward, when the open-grazing days were over, and the
> red grass had been ploughed under and under until it had
> almost disappeared from the prairie; when all the fields were
> under fence, and roads no longer ran about like wild things, but

followed surveyed section lines, Mr. Shimerda's grave was still there, with a sagging wire fence around it, and an unpainted wooden cross. As grandfather had predicted, Mrs. Shimerda never saw the roads go over his head. The road from the north curved a little to the east just there, and the road from the west swung out a little to the south; so that the grave, with its tall red grass that was never mowed, was like a little island; and at twilight, under a new moon or the clear evening star, the dusty roads used to look like soft gray rivers flowing past it. I never came upon the place without emotion, and in all that country it was the spot most dear to me. I loved the dim superstition, the propitiatory intent, that had put the grave there; and still more I loved the spirit that could not carry out the sentence—the error from the surveyed lines, the clemency of the soft earth roads along which the home-coming wagons rumbled after sunset. Never a tired driver passed the wooden cross, I am sure, without wishing well to the sleeper.

That paragraph is highlighted and underlined in my beat-up copy of the novel. I suppose I've reread it a dozen times, often aloud; it's as if I'm reciting an incantation to summon the angels who sang to Cather. No response as yet.

Red Cloud is a handsome old town, and with its streets paved in brick and its brick and sandstone buildings, most definitely red. *It* is definite—no accretions on its fringes, there is the country and then there is the town—and I liked that. As the model for the town of Black Hawk in *My Antonia*, Red Cloud had become a destination for literary-minded tourists and scholars. Willa Cather is almost a cottage industry. The Willa Cather museum is housed in a three-story brownstone on the main street; the Willa Cather home, a beige frame with picket fence and historical marker, is less than a block away; the Willa Cather Foundation has offices in the restored opera house. Five miles outside of town lies the six-hundred-acre Willa Cather Memorial Prairie, and the area all around is known as Cather Country. No surprise—commerce has claimed her name, and Leslie chuckled as she took a picture of a license plate holder advertising Cather Country Auto Sales.

The museum and the Cather home were closed for the afternoon. We drove out past the Memorial Prairie, its tall red grasses speckled with primrose and aster, as all the wide land looked before it was plowed under and fenced.

"Let's give three cheers for Red Cloud," I said.

"Definitely," Leslie said. "But why in particular?"

"For giving Willa Cather the Elvis treatment."

An hour of meandering took us through places where time seemed to have stopped, then brought us to I-80 and back into the present. Cars racing east and west, semis blasting by at eighty miles an hour, buffeting Fred and Ethel. A line from Cather's *Death Comes for the Archbishop* seemed appropriate. *Men travel faster now, but I do not know if they go to better things.*

In Doniphan, a few miles south of Grand Island, Nebraska, we rented space at another kampground, this one nestled in a shady grove of locust and poplar wedged between a corn field and a wheat field.

A Canadian cold front invaded. Thunderheads scalloped the level horizon, loomed higher, then rumbled overhead, lightning flashing inside as from gigantic welding torches. The wind howled up to forty miles an hour, with nothing between it and the campground but a few barbed-wire fences. Streamers of dust flew from the prairie like spume from the waves of an unquiet sea. No rain fell, so I managed to barbecue pork chops bought from Ladow's market, and we managed to eat them at a picnic table under a trembling poplar, though the gusts nearly blew the plates away. The sunset was a spectacle; the great clouds racing overhead, colored by its light, looked like billowing fires in the heavens as spears of lightning shot horizontally across the seam of land and sky.

19.

I HAD PLANNED TO PUSH ON FROM GRAND ISLAND THROUGH THE Nebraska sandhills into South Dakota. A couple of chance encounters changed my mind.

To kill time while Fred was getting his oil changed and tires rotated, I walked Sage and Sky in a park across from the garage. I noticed two black men on a bench. I'd been to Sudan twice in the past, on assignments, and recognized them as Sudanese by their Nilotic features, their great height, obvious even though they were seated, and the Arabic they were speaking. It was fairly unusual to see Africans and hear Arabic in Nebraska. What could have brought those two to Grand Island?

An answer of sorts came later, when I went to the post office to pick up forwarded mail. I was standing in a long line behind a thirtyish white guy wearing a tank top, his neck and arms wallpapered in tattoos, when a man in a straw cowboy hat asked me, "Spick Spanich?"

"Un poco. Muy poco. Que quieres?"

I guess my accent discouraged him. He turned away.

"Spick Spanich," snorted Tattoo-man. "He asked me the same thing. Too goddamn many Mexicans in this town. I remember when there was one black family and one Mexican family in Grand Island. Now we got a million of 'em, and Somalis and Sudanese comin' in, and bringin' bed-bugs with 'em."

"Why are they coming here?"

"To work at the Swift meatpacking plant," he said. "It's here in town, it's big. You can't miss it by the smell. They come directly here. They give 'em money, give 'em a car, give 'em a house, give 'em a job, and they get to work tax free. You wonder where our tax dollars go."

"Who gives them all that? The company?"

"The government! Nebraska! The only state I know more screwed up than California."

I said I'd never heard of any government buying houses and cars for immigrants, much less assuring them of work in private industry.

Tattoo-man swore it was true. The Africans, he said, "need to go home." He didn't say what the Mexicans should do.

I asked, "They're causing problems?"

"Oh, yeah. That's why half the nightclubs are shut down. They come in there, and all they want to do is fight. Fight, fight, fight."

Back in the truck, I told Leslie about the encounter and she consulted our oracle, Magic Droid. It turned out that Tattoo-man had purveyed yet another myth. Neither the federal government nor the state of Nebraska provided the Somalis and Sudanese with houses and cars; they'd found work at the meatpacking plant because Swift had recruited them.

The Law of Unintended Consequences may not be as immutable as Newton's First Law of Motion, but it runs a close second. A few years ago, in response to the outcry about illegal immigration, the Department of Homeland Security began raiding meatpacking plants throughout the Midwest, found hundreds of undocumented workers, and deported them. Half a dozen Swift factories from Colorado to Iowa lost almost thirteen hundred employes. To replace them, the company sent recruiters all over the farm belt and Great Plains states to hire foreign workers who were in the United States legally. Sudanese and Somalis, who had refugee status because of civil strife in their homelands, formed a natural labor pool, and that was how they arrived in Grand Island.

The unintended consequence was to turn the city of some forty-eight thousand into a melting pot where little was melting and much was on high simmer. It boiled over in 2008, when more than two hundred Somali workers walked off the job, demanding that Swift give them special breaks to observe daily Muslim prayers. Management decided to cut the workday—and the pay—of its other employees to allow the Somalis time for evening prayers. That set off days of strikes and protests by Latino workers, and the company scrapped the plan.

I held a number of dirty, backbreaking jobs when I was young, but I never worked in a meatpacking house. The closest I came to being in one was when I was eight or nine and my father took me to the Union Stockyards, on Chicago's South Side. I don't remember much about the visit except the commingled reek of raw meat, blood, guts, manure, urine, and the pungent smoke from the rendering factories nearby.

I picked up that same stench on the northeast side of Grand Island and followed my nose to the JBS Swift plant. Tattoo-man, wrong about some things, had been right about the smell. Also about the size of the place. The steel and concrete structure, almost windowless, with venting stacks poking through its roof, covered several acres. JBS was devoted to the disassembly of hogs and cattle, two thousand head a day, seven days a week. They were herded off cattle cars and livestock trucks into the slaughterhouse to be killed instantly by pneumatic darts to the brain, then stripped of their hides, decapitated, dehorned, dismembered, and carved into quarters, into rib eyes, sirloins, flank steaks, and pork chops by three thousand people laboring amid mounds of bloody offal.

Looking at that huge abattoir, I pondered the commonplace that immigrants do the grueling, dangerous work Americans aren't willing to do. The reality is that immigrants, the illegal kind in particular, are more willing to tolerate long hours, faster line speeds, and pay much lower than it was three decades ago, when meatpacking jobs were prized by people born in the United States.* The physical stress causes injuries and chronic disabilities. It also exacts an emotional price. As we drove away, Leslie asked me to stop so she could photograph a peculiar pairing of highway billboards. The one on top, in red, white, and blue, proclaimed JBS—GREAT JOB OPPORTUNITIES. Then came a list: STARTING WAGE—$12.95 AN HOUR . . . EARN UP TO $18.60 AN HOUR IN PRODUCTION . . . Right below it was a sign showing a young, disconsolate Latino man sitting with his head in a hand. SUICIDIO, said the headline, NO ES LA SOLUCION. A panel alongside identified, in Spanish and English, the Hall County Suicide Prevention Project and gave a number to call.

———

Singing the song of These, my ever-united lands—my body no more inevitably united, part to part, and made out of a thousand

———

* In 1980, the average hourly wage in the industry, measured in today's dollars, was $21.75; by 2007, it had fallen to $12.03.

diverse contributions one identity, any more than my hands are
inevitably united and made ONE IDENTITY... Nativities,
climates, the grass of the great pastoral Plains... These affording,
in all their particulars, the old feuillage to me and to America...
How can I but as here chanting, invite you for yourself to collect
bouquets of the incomparable feuillage of these States?
—WALT WHITMAN, *Leaves of Grass*

We drove into Grand Island on the Henry Fonda Highway (the actor was born in Grand Island in 1905). Mexican restaurants spiced up the Locust Street commercial strip; American eateries appeared to be in a cuisine minority. Locust led downtown, past a concert hall with the word *Liederkrantz* chiseled in stone above its front door. (Grand Island was founded in 1867 by mostly German immigrants.) In the Salvation Army thrift store, beside the Union Pacific tracks and a grain elevator, every tag and sign was in Spanish and English, and Latinos and whites shopped together for bargains. A few blocks away, in Mickleson's, an old movie theater converted into a bar, restaurant, and pool hall, Anglo retirees gathered to eat lunch and shoot eight ball with custom-built sticks carried in fine leather cases. Not far from there, around East Fourth Street, was Grand Island's old business district, and it wasn't historic; nor was it a museum of preciously restored buildings with nobody in them. It was a little worn around the edges, a little run-down here and there, but in the way of a house that looks lived in rather than like a subject for *Better Homes and Gardens*. Once again, the Latino influence dominated—Mexican restaurants, bodegas, laundromats, but we spotted two places offering African food, another serving Laotian.

I'd grown up in a city that was home to people from half the world: Irish, Poles, Italians, Germans, African Americans, Chinese, Swedes, Norwegians, Mexicans, Czechs, Jews, Serbs, Croatians, and Greeks, among others, dwelled in ethnic and racial enclaves. Up through the fifties, Chicagoans identified themselves by their national origins. I recalled a conversation I'd had with Mike Royko, the great *Chicago Daily News* columnist, in the Billy Goat Tavern (owned by a Greek, Billy Sianis). Royko (Polish) had taken his family to visit friends in California. Royko's kids had reported disturbing news. "Dad, they aren't anything," they said of the friends' kids. "What do you mean, they're not anything?" Royko asked.

"We asked them what nationality they were, and they said they were American!"

It's not that everyone got along. In my father's time, neighborhood borders were as hard and fast and as zealously guarded as those in the old country. My father was around ten when he strayed out of Little Italy into an Irish precinct across Blue Island Avenue. A woman leaned out of a tenement window, and spotting the olive-complected boy with jet-black hair and a distinctly Roman nose she yelled, "Get outta here, ya dirty little Wop!" and to encourage his exit dumped a pan of hot water on his head.

The American blender did not work its homogenizing magic until after World War II, when the children and grandchildren of the immigrant generations began an exodus to the suburbs. They had to get along because now they lived next door to each other, and they made the astonishing discovery that they had more in common than not. They all wanted the same things: fresh air, a house to call their own, a car, decent schools for their kids.

When my parents moved out to Westchester, Illinois, into a new house that stood by itself on an as yet unpaved street cut through a fallow cornfield, my best friend was Bob Stloukal, half Czech, half Irish. We played sandlot ball and hunted rabbits and went skinny-dipping in Salt Creek and ran around the woods of the Cook County Forest Preserve, digging up Pottawatomie and Sauk-Fox arrowheads. We'd become leaves in Whitman's feuillage, as American as Huck Finn and Tom Sawyer.

Was it possible that twenty-five years from now the sons and daughters of Grand Island's Mexicans, Africans, and Asians would be speaking with midwestern twangs and rooting for the Cornhuskers?

Maybe.

———

The three men, all white, asked me not to use their names or identify them in any other way, so I'll call them Jim, Joe, and John, and describe them as prominent opinion makers in Grand Island. Not that they said anything controversial, but the immigration question had become so sensitive that even an innocuous comment could be taken the wrong way by some folks in town.

Jim offered a few statistics to show me how recently, and how quickly, Grand Island's complexion had changed. Minority enrollment in the city's schools had more than doubled, from 20 percent in 1999 to 44 percent in 2010. The number of Latino students had tripled in the same period, from 1,139 to 3,357. Whites were projected to become a minority between 2020 and 2030.

But without immigration, Joe pointed out, Grand Island would have lost population in the past ten years. He praised Latinos. They were the most acculturated group in the city and were "terrific entrepreneurs. They've branched out into fields like construction. The guy who reroofed my house was named Lopez."

Outlooks like Tattoo-man's were not rare but were confined to a "vocal minority" of the white population.

"We see somebody who doesn't look, dress, eat, or worship like we do, and we resent it," said John. "But if today we brought over a bunch of people from the Black Forest, nobody would think twice about it."

He found it ironic that the people from the Black Forest who settled in Grand Island had once been victims of nativist fervor. The Know-Nothing Party was formed in the 1850s by American-born citizens furious about the rising tide of Irish and German immigration.* During World War I, as anti-German sentiment washed over the land, the Ku Klux Klan raided a social center in Grand Island and burned all of its German-language books.

Now sentiment had turned against those whose skin was brown and black, and who spoke strange tongues. But racial animosity didn't come from whites alone. The 2008 labor strife lifted the lid on a stewpot of ethnic bitterness—the dark side of diversity. Latinos were pissed off at Somalis for demanding special privileges. One Mexican described workers like himself as "humble" and Somalis as "arrogant." The Sudanese, mostly Christian, were suspicious of the Muslim Somalis, who returned the feeling. The handful of Asians in the city, Burmese and Laotians for the most part, cast wary eyes at one another. Listening to all this, I thought the volatile mix could update a verse from the old Kingston Trio tune "The Merry Minuet":

The whole world is festering with unhappy souls
The French hate the Germans,
The Germans hate the Poles.

---

* Official name, the American Party. Its members were called "Know-nothings" because their leaders had instructed them, if they were asked about the secret organization, to answer, "I know nothing."

Italians hate Yugoslavs.
South Africans hate the Dutch,
And I don't like anybody very much.

Was the center holding here in the center of the United States? I asked. All three were at once hopeful and skeptical.

"I think that whatever governors we used to have on what we say and how we behave are gone," John said, weighing in on the skeptical side. "What's happened to our manners? To our civility? Maybe it's because of the anonymity of the Internet. It lets people feel free to say whatever they want, and it becomes legitimized because it's on the Internet."

Donald Anderson and Sandra Towne were sitting on a bench outside a community center, waiting for the doors to open for a meeting of Parents Without Partners. They were quite civil and reasonable. Maybe it was the influence of the Great Plains, whose level spaciousness fosters levelheadedness. Sandra harbored no ill feelings toward immigrants, so long as they were here legally. Her next-door neighbors were Mexican— "good, decent people," she said, but lamented the lack of neighborly conversation. "They don't speak English, and I don't speak Spanish, and we never say a word to each other."

Anderson, a squarely built man of seventy-three, with hands that testified to a life of hard work, was a retired farmer. He'd also done a stint in a meatpacking factory in Omaha and believed that Americans had become too soft, leaving immigrants to take on the tough, dirty jobs.

"They come here to work, and they're welcome to come here to fill in for the people who won't do the jobs. If they [Americans, he meant] want the jobs, they should accept the wages." Anderson spoke in full, concise sentences, with never an *ah* or *uh* or silent pause between them—the emphatic voice of a man whose convictions had been won through experience, not learned from an editorial or a blog. "I farmed, and every year we hired Mexicans to pick our sugar beet crop. But people got after us. 'Why don't you hire locals?' they said. So one year we did, and they destroyed about one fourth of the crop, didn't care if they worked well or not. So the next year we hired our old crew back."

He thought that the friction between the native-born and immigrants was worse now than in the past, and he wasn't confident that everyone would eventually get along. Not only were there more foreigners; they were more assertive.

"The outsiders were kept back in the past, but now they're setting their foot forward and saying they want equal opportunities, and there are some here who are against that, them stepping up, saying, 'What're you doing, saying that you're the same as us?'"

Returning to my car, I passed St. Stephen's Episcopal Church. Kids from a Christian youth group, some white, some black—children of Sudanese refugees—were skipping rope, supervised by a young man and a woman. The kids lined up and took turns at jumping the rope, twirled to a sung cadence by a white girl holding one end, an African girl, her hair wound in tight braids, the other. There was much laughter and chatter, and the whole scene was so heartwarming I could have believed it was staged to show that harmony between native and newcomer was possible. Still, I was careful not to make too much of it. Maybe these kids were new blooms of the "old feuillage"; but in the current atmosphere, it wasn't certain that the African children would be allowed to graft themselves onto the American tree. I hoped they would be, as my forefathers were, even as I was, but if they and the other seedlings blown here from far away had to sprout up separately, I wasn't sure what would happen to Whitman's cry, "My ever-united lands."

The following day I had lunch at Sanchez Plaza, a restaurant, grocery store, and bakery. I might have been in Nogales instead of the heart of Nebraska: coral-colored walls outside, terra-cotta tiles inside, mariachis trilling on the sound system, shelves crammed with red beans and black beans, poblano and serrano and jalapeño peppers, piquant sauces, many varieties of rice, and a bakery case with Spanish breads and thickly sugared pastries.

This establishment was the creation of Filemon Sanchez, short, muscular, forty-six years old, with restless eyes deep set in a strong, square face. As I talked to him, I entertained a fantasy that he could change Tattoo-man's ideas about Mexicans.

You could think of Sanchez as ordinary—a small businessman in a small city in a sparsely populated state. But the obstacles he had to overcome to get where he was from where he'd been made him remarkable. He was born in southern Mexico, in the state of Michoacán, one of eight children, his father a subsistence farmer.

"Our life was very poor," he said. "I wanted an education. I told my father that I wanted to stay in school, but he couldn't help me out. When I saw there was no way out, I decided to come to the U.S."

In 1986, through a family connection, he signed up with a crew of migratory field hands bound for the citrus groves of Florida. He picked oranges and grapefruits from sunrise to sunset, moved on to North Carolina to harvest cucumbers and tomatoes, making forty cents a bucket. The more he picked, the more he earned, but it was hard to earn much.

"We were on our knees all day, and sometimes you couldn't take it anymore and had to stop."

From North Carolina, the crew headed west to Nebraska's soybean fields, and there Sanchez underwent a kind of conversion experience.

"My idea was that I would stay here for two years and save twenty thousand dollars and go back to school in Mexico," he said over a love ballad's brassy riff, his quick, dark eyes darting side to side. "But after a couple of months in this country, I saw that there were more opportunities here, and that I could do better here, and I decided I didn't want to go back."

He threw a fleeting, economical smile across the table while I ate my chicken fajita and marveled at America's power to beguile and bedazzle. The only opportunity it had given him was the opportunity to break his back in the dirt twelve hours a day for pocket change; yet he saw a possibility to better himself. I couldn't think of a sensible reason how or why that vision popped into his head. I can't now. It's as if a magical pollen swirls in the air of this country, summoning up dreams in the waking mind.

Sanchez landed a job with a roofing contractor, worked at that for a year and a half, then hired on at Swift, pulling down seven-fifty an hour cleaning hog bellies in the tripe room. He had to quit four years later, disabled by injuries to his neck and shoulders. He found less arduous employment with a program to educate Grand Island's Latino community about HIV-AIDS. A turning point came when Swift offered a settlement for his injuries.

"I had to start something with that money. You know how it is when you get money: you spend it and don't know where it goes." He flicked another spare smile. "A friend of mine out of Chicago taught me how to bake Spanish breads and pastries. I started doing baking in my house. Eighty bags a day. I knew the Latino community from working with the program. I knew the market and went door to door, and I made maybe forty bucks a day."

Business grew, he rented space in his present location, and opened a bakery and, eventually, this restaurant.

I looked around the busy place and asked, Was this what he'd dreamed of the moment he'd decided he wasn't going back to Mexico?

"No," he said. "This came up . . ." Sanchez hesitated, his pupils slipping right to left, left to right. "I don't know how it came up . . ." He paused again. "I think this came up thanks to the guy who showed me how to make pastries . . . And that guy told me, 'You gotta open a business.' That's what motivated me."

He was drilling the value of education and of a dollar into the heads of his children, three girls and a boy. His eldest daughter was going to college in the fall; she and her sisters have jobs in the business, waitressing, working the register; his four-year-old son sits beside him when he's behind the counter.

"A lot of kids, you know, they say, 'Poppy will buy it.' I tell mine, that's not how it works. You have to earn it, you have to do something. I don't want you at home, watching TV or playing silly games on the computer."

He dismissed the tensions in Grand Island. Yes, Latinos had marched in the streets for immigration reform; yes, there'd been attempts to pass anti-immigrant laws; but no, Sanchez himself had seldom gotten a hostile look or any other indication that he wasn't welcome.

"Maybe sometimes I say hi to someone and they don't answer. I'm the kind of guy who smiles a lot—it's my way of saying hi—and maybe someone doesn't smile back at me or say hi, but that doesn't stop me."

I'd seen the walls and barriers rising on the Mexican line, the glass eyes of the surveillance cameras peering into the desert at night. Three thousand Border Patrol agents are stationed in Arizona alone, ten for every mile of its border with Mexico. Keep out, you huddled masses yearning to make our motel beds, butcher our hogs, build our houses, harvest our crops, landscape our yards. This is nothing new. The Chinese Exclusion Act in the 1880s aimed to block Chinese from landing on our shores; as late as the early twentieth century, certain East Coast ports prohibited Irish immigrants from disembarking. (New York was an exception. That's why so many Irish had bought steerage tickets on the *Titanic*.) Now we've transformed the Mexican border into a semblance of an eastern European frontier during the Cold War. We've chosen to arrest and deport those already here (giving the businesses that hired them a scolding at the worst). How many Filemon Sanchezes have been cuffed, jailed, and sent home, and are we really the better for it?

20.

THE MODEL NAMES OF THE TWO RVS THAT PULLED IN BESIDE US were an omen. Storm and Hurricane. At one in the morning, barefoot and naked except for a pair of boxer shorts, I dashed outside into a Niagara of rainfall, slipped on the trailer step, and jammed my toes into the ground. I then limped to the truck, shut the hardtop windows, and herded the dogs into the trailer.

Leslie took the wheel for the next day's drive, west on U.S. 30, the Lincoln Highway. I sat with the passenger seat pushed all the way back, my throbbing right foot propped on the dash. I was positive I'd broken my big toe and had said so on a cell phone call to a friend. Maybe I went a little overboard.

"If you're going to say you *fractured* your toe," the dog wrangler quipped, "then I'm going to start saying I *shattered* my wrist."

Nevertheless, she took me a couple of days later to the Great Plains hospital in North Platte to find out if I had indeed broken bones. A tall, crew-cut doctor named Ben examined me; a charming blonde, Collette, took an X-ray. Both flinched when they looked at it.

"You've had an awful lot of work done on this foot," Dr. Ben observed. "What happened to it?"

Putting on my best laconic Clint Eastwood imitation, I said, "Old war wound."

"Vietnam?"

I shook my head and gave the abbreviated version: I'd been covering the Lebanese Civil War in 1975 when I was ambushed and shot in the right foot and left ankle with an AK-47.

"Well, a lot of that shrapnel is still in there," said Dr. Ben.

"Yeah, it is," I said, trying to impress Collette with my stoic bravery, though to what end I can't say.

Turning to present injuries, Dr. Ben told me that I hadn't fractured a thing and gave me a prescription for hydrocodone.

Steinbeck called Route 66 the "Mother Road." The Lincoln, then, is the Father Road, the first transcontinental automobile highway in the United States, opened to traffic in 1913. Jumping off from Times Square, it spanned thirty-four hundred miles to its finish in San Francisco's Lincoln Park. Early guidebooks cautioned that the monthlong trip was "something of a sporting proposition," and advised adventurous motorists to carry camping equipment and all necessary tools and not to wear new shoes because they would have to wade rivers and streams to test their depths before crossing.

The idea to build a coast-to-coast motor road sprang from the fertile brain of Carl Fisher, the automotive entrepreneur who also built the Indianapolis Speedway and developed Miami Beach. He may have been inspired by Horatio Jackson, the first person to cross the continent by automobile. Jackson and his mechanic Sewell Crocker accomplished the feat in an open-top Winston touring car in 1903, exactly one hundred years—by a wonderful coincidence—after Thomas Jefferson assigned Meriwether Lewis the mission of exploring the Louisiana Territory. Someone had bet Jackson that no one could make the trip in less than three months; he and Crocker did it in two.

With machinery primitive by modern standards, and with a lot of human muscle wielding picks, shovels, and sledgehammers, construction of the Lincoln was finished in just two years. Aside from the fact that it was built in an era when Americans did big things rather than argue about doing them, it was completed quickly because it was laid down on existing routes, some of which had been in use for centuries: a Dutch colonial road in New Jersey from 1675; the Lancaster Turnpike in Pennsylvania dating to 1796; a Sauk-Fox Indian trail in Ohio.

The five-hundred-mile stretch between Omaha and the Wyoming uplands followed the Platte River valley, which had been carrying human beings from one place to another for a thousand years. The valley's flatness (*plat* is French for flat, and the Otoe Indian word *Nebrathka* means "flat water") and the plentiful water and lush grass it provided for game as well as livestock made it an ideal corridor for travel.

You could make an argument that if it weren't for the river, there never would have been a Lincoln Highway. Its genealogy would go something like this: the Platte begat the Great Medicine Road, a web of paths beaten along the riversides by migrating buffalo and the plains tribes that tracked them; the Great Medicine Road begat the Platte River Trace, a caravan route for pack trains hauling supplies to Rocky Mountain fur trappers in the 1820s; the trace begat the Oregon and Mormon Trails, and they begat the Pony Express, which begat the Union Pacific, the first transcontinental railroad, its storied golden spike banged down in 1869; the Union Pacific begat the Lincoln, and it U.S. 30, which today flanks the north side of the river. Hugging the south side is the youngest member of the lineage, Interstate 80.

Traveling the Lincoln, I felt connected to that past, to the history of America and its ceaseless comings and goings. Here and there we saw markers that would have been familiar to motorists nearly a century ago. The emblem—a white square with an *L* in the middle, bordered by a red stripe above, a blue stripe below—appeared on the original road's mileposts. Fred rolled on pavement covering the tire tracks of automobiles with extinct brand names; those had bumped along crushed rock laid over the wheel ruts of prairie schooners and freight wagons trundling beaver pelts out of the Rockies; over the bootprints of pioneers, forty-niners, and mountain men, the moccasin prints of Kanza, Otoe, Arapaho, Pawnee, and Cheyenne.

Early pioneers had joked that the Platte was "a mile wide and an inch deep, too thick to drink, too thin to plow." They would not have recognized the modern river, considerably less than a mile wide (irrigation dams on its north branch have strangled its flow), or the modern landscape: corn, soybean and wheat fields, pivots, grain elevators tall as NASA rockets. Gun barrel straight, the Lincoln shot from one small town to another, each with its civic-booster slogan. Wood River proclaimed possession of "a Proud Past and a Promising Future." Shelton boasted that it provided "a Slice of the Good Life." Gibbon announced, "Welcome to Gibbon—Smile City." A sign across the highway as it passed through Cozad (whence that name?) declared that the town was split by the hundredth meridian. A milestone on our journey—from the Texas hill country well into Canada, one hundred degrees west longitude marks the approximate boundary between the moist forests and prairies of eastern North America and the semiarid climate of the western. We were on the high plains, the True West.

For a while, we paced a Union Pacific freight train, its boxcars canvases for graffiti artists. The statue of a zebra stood on a farmhouse lawn; beside it a (real) polka-dot horse grazed. We flipped off the Lincoln onto Nebraska 47 for a look at the Platte. Swollen from the snowpack melting in the Colorado Rockies, it roiled along between corridors of cottonwood and pale green Russian olive.

We pressed on toward Ogallala. A wall of bruise-colored cloud blotting out half the sky persuaded us to end the day's travels there. We found space at a family-owned place called Area's Best Campground—best, apparently, because it was the only. A biker club rumbled in, rolled their Harleys under a ramada, threw covers over them, and huddled together to wait out the advancing storm. It came on with a menacing beauty. Thin, white clouds scudded past the blue-black thunderheads; rain curtains dropped, edged in pink at top and bottom. Then thunder that made us think we were under bombardment, lightning bolts rocketing at the vertical, at the horizontal, at crazy angles, at times lighting up the entire sky. There seemed no end to these Great Plains storms, and we were getting sick of them.

After unhitching the trailer in a torrential downpour, we went to the faux-frontier Front Street Steakhouse and Crystal Palace Saloon for dinner and to catch its weekend Wild West show. One hundred and twenty years ago, when Texas trail drives ended at the Union Pacific railhead, Ogallala was a rowdy place. Though it's still something of a cow town, the only gunfights now are blank-cartridge duels fought by waiters in cowboy getups. The waitresses dress as dance-hall girls and kick up their heels on the same stage where the make-believe gunslingers die make-believe deaths while a piano player in period costume plinks old-timey tunes. Chewing on a so-so prime rib, I thought it would be interesting if towns like Ogallala staged the West as It Really Was shows. The dance-hall girls would exchange their cute outfits for smudged calico shifts and go without bathing for a couple of weeks; the men wouldn't die in thrilling shoot-outs but of cholera—the big killer on the Oregon Trail, accounting for a hundred times more victims than all the outlaws and Indians combined. Clearly, I'll never land a job in Hollywood or the tourist industry. To paraphrase a line from the film *The Man Who Shot Liberty Valance*: This is the West, sir. If it's a choice between legend and fact, you'll never make a dime going with the fact.

Fred's trip odometer read 2,930.6 miles. I was anxious to head north, back to the Missouri and the Lewis and Clark Trail. Leslie found the route on our atlas: Nebraska 61, a skinny red line wiggling 140 miles into South Dakota. Entranced by the blank spaces through which it passed, she dubbed it "the road to nowhere"; there were only three towns on it: Arthur (pop. 117), Merriman (pop. 128), and, between them, Hyannis (pop. 182). Old photos of the Kennedys playing touch football on Cape Cod flickered in my mind's eye. How did a village way out here come to be called Hyannis? That's what drew me. And the white spaces.

Becoming more adept at hitching up, we got off earlier than our usual 9:45 a.m. In need of groceries, we then tried stocking up at the local Save-A-Lot, where we saved quite a lot because we hardly bought anything. Leslie noticed that the signs above the aisles that usually said CEREAL or CANNED FRUIT directed shoppers to Pop-Tarts, Kool-Aid, and beef jerky. "The three basic food groups," she said.

The road to nowhere actually led into somewhere: the Nebraska Sandhills, one of the lonesomest regions in the country. An expanse of virgin mixed-grass prairie and cactus-specked dunes more than two-thirds the size of Maine, with fewer people than you'd find on a single block in New York City, it's no place for the agoraphobic. I'd been to the Sandhills before, in 1997, the year of the Hale-Bopp comet, and remembered standing in a lunar silence outside the town of Valentine, the vagabond comet a brilliant streak among stars so numerous there seemed as much white as black in the night sky.

The hand of man lay lightly on the Sandhills. Plows had never scarred them—the arid soil guaranteed that a farm would fail—and the threat of erosion checked cattlemen from overgrazing. A reincarnated Francis Parkman could have stood in those spaces and, if he were out of sight of the road and its file of telephone poles, gazed at a landscape almost unchanged from the one he'd seen more than a century and a half ago.

Yellow-head crows clung to barbed-wire fences. A lone buck antelope stood atop a hill, as if posing for a calendar photograph. In the hollow below, a pond glittered, fed by springs bubbling up from the Ogallala aquifer, an underground sea bigger than Lake Huron. The scenery was grand, but living in the Sandhills wasn't easy. I recalled another picture from my first trip: a ranch family driving their cattle to new pasture, the father riding point, sons on the flank, hunched in their saddles against snow flurries whipped by a raw March wind, their mother at drag in a dirt-caked pickup truck. If I'd had any romantic illusions about the cowboy life, they would have dissolved right then.

At thirty-five miles an hour, it took about five seconds to drive through Arthur, shut down for the holiday. Beyond, white birds rose off a pond, flew to another, and settled. Snow geese?

"Pelicans!" Leslie said as we drew closer.

Pelicans, fifteen hundred miles from the nearest ocean? I thought we were hallucinating. The sighting was confirmed at That Stop gas station and café outside Hyannis by the woman who ran the place. She was seconded by Troy Debbs, a broad-chested rancher who looked as if he'd been a steer wrestler in his younger days. He was eating a Father's Day dinner with his wife and two sons.

"Migrate here every year from the Pacific," Troy said. "I don't know why they come here. Never seen them breeding, never seen any young pelicans. We get seagulls, too. We love the seagulls. They eat the grasshoppers."

He seemed up on local lore, so I asked how the town got to be named Hyannis. Troy gave a brief nod that said he'd heard the question before.

"There's only two Hyannises in the country: this one and the one back East where the Kennedys lived. When the Burlington Northern was being built in the early nineteen hundreds, most of the section hands came from New England. You go up to Route Two—the railroad runs along it—you'll see a lot of the towns are named after the towns they came from."

In Cherry County, bigger than Connecticut and Rhode Island put together, almost as vacant as the Mohave Desert—one person per square mile—there was nothing but static on the radio, and our cell phones were as useless as semaphores. We were, for the moment anyway, disconnected from the world, and I was happy. *Disconnected.*

Most state boundaries are arbitrary, but the landscape told us when we'd entered South Dakota. North of the line, the heave and toss of the Sandhills leveled off into a broad, gently rolling plateau, and the virgin grasslands became hay meadows, mown in stripes of green and brown.

We made our way to the Pine Ridge Reservation, home of the Oglala Lakota (the tribes we call Sioux call themselves Lakota, meaning "friend" or "ally") and scene of the 1890 Wounded Knee massacre and the militant uprising in 1973. Looking for the massacre site, we got marooned on a muddy road that dead-ended in a church parking lot near Wounded Knee Creek. A skinny Lakota man with crooked teeth materialized from out of nowhere and asked if we were lost. After introducing himself as John High Hawk and showing us where we could turn truck and trailer around without running into a ditch, he presented a business card: "Wounded Knee Lakota Youth Organization," it read. "Promoting wellness through a healthy environment. Dakota High Hawk, Executive Director." John motioned toward an SUV parked nearby, with a young man inside. That was Dakota, his son. John produced a plastic bag containing dream catchers—rings of fine beadwork hanging from rawhide loops. I sensed a sales pitch coming and wasn't disappointed. Proceeds from the sale of dream catchers helped fund his son's organization, which ran programs to keep Lakota kids off drugs and booze. The asking price was exorbitant. I bargained without much seriousness and managed to chip off a buck or two before succumbing. There were two reasons for this capitulation: I was eager to pull the rig out of the muddy cul-de-sac and find a campground before nightfall; and it seemed fitting, sort of evening things out, for a white guy to buy a trinket from an Indian. I hung the green-and-white dream catcher from the rearview mirror. John didn't say what dreams it would catch, but he offered to show us around the reservation the next day, promising a tour of "poverty areas."

21.

WE CAMPED UNDER WILLOWS BESIDE THE WHITE RIVER. THE nearby town of Interior consisted of a gas station, a grocery store, two bars, and sixty-seven inhabitants. The Horseshoe Bar issued a mandate on its highway sign: BIKERS MUST STOP. Harleys parked outside indicated that the summons had been obeyed. A poster on the grocery's front door advertised the upcoming Interior Frontier Days rodeo, noting that it was voted the second-best rodeo in the United States in 1920. It's rare to see second best as a boast, rarer if the honor was conferred ninety years ago. The campground restaurant dished out fry bread tacos for dinner. Fry bread—flat dough deep fried in oil or lard and leavened with yeast—is a staple in Indian country. It's very bad for you and therefore very good to eat. I ordered a plateful, adding a new item to my diet to horrify Leslie.

The fry bread taco had been invented, said Steve, our chef, by a Lakota entrepreneur, Ansel Woodenknife. He'd owned a restaurant serving his mother's recipe, got discovered, appeared on the Food Channel, franchised his specialty, and then retired.

"You should meet him. He's quite a guy."

I found Woodenknife's house in the morning, next door to the Wooden Knife Café at a crossroad in Interior. His wife, Teresa, answered the door, then summoned him from inside. Out came a broadly built, broad-faced man with cropped black hair and black-rimmed glasses. I explained what I was up to and told him I was curious about his journey from the reservation to the Food Channel. For some reason, I expected him to be a little guarded, but he was warm and engaging and responded enthusiastically. He, too, was amazed by the size and diversity of the country and that it all somehow held together.

"It's because of change," he said. "This is the only country where everything changes *all the time*. People come here expecting change, and if they're going to survive, if they're going to be successful, they've got to learn to adapt to change, to different people from different races. I'd like to talk to you more about this stuff."

But he couldn't at the moment; he was a volunteer firefighter and was studying for an EMT test. Maybe he'd drop by our trailer that night the or next. As I was to learn, Ansel Woodenknife had a PhD in adaptation, and he hadn't acquired it in a classroom.

A steady rain scotched our plans to hike in the Badlands. Leslie attempted to e-mail her office, perfectly routine in civilization but in those parts an adventure. She drove up a slippery mud road, where, a campground brochure promised, she would be sure to get a signal. But the gaily colored wheel on her laptop spun as Fred's wheels had in the mud. She parked in the middle of the road and with the wipers and flashers on held the connection device out the window in the rain, waiting for its little green 4G light to glow. The little blue wireless light flickered, telling her that it was trying. But not hard enough. After half an hour, she gave up, muttering that Verizon's vaunted coverage was like a cheese grater.

We headed south, returning to the Pine Ridge Reservation to try again to find the spot where the last battle of the Indian wars was fought. I use the word *battle* loosely; most of the twenty-five cavalry troopers killed at Wounded Knee were victims of friendly fire; more than half the 350 Lakota involved, including old men, women, and children, were slaughtered in a maelstrom of bullets and shrapnel.

One of the largest Indian reservations in the United States (almost twice the size of Delaware), Pine Ridge is also one of the poorest. The "poverty areas" John High Hawk mentioned covered nearly all of it, and it wasn't romantic poverty, no, it was dire, here-to-stay poverty. Tumbledown houses and battered double-wides, each with its collection of rusting automobiles, cast-off appliances, and bits of scrap that didn't look as if they had ever served a useful purpose, reeled by like footage from a grim documentary. Tiny settlements—Potato Creek, Sharps Corner, Kyle—clung to a precarious existence out on the grasslands. The few bright spots, a well-maintained home here or there, or the groomed campus of the Oglala Lakota College, did more to accentuate than to relieve the surrounding wretchedness. The weather added to the gloom, likewise the radio, mixing traditional Lakota chants with country-and-western tunes—the empty bar at 2 a.m. variety, Waylon Jennings and Hank Williams lamenting cheatin' hearts and errant men seeking solace in a whiskey glass. Most bizarre: Williams's fifties-era rendition of "Kaw-Liga," about a cigar-store Indian who never gets a kiss from a wooden Indian maid. To hear that on a reservation radio station was like watching an *Amos 'n' Andy* rerun on the Black Entertainment Television Network. When Paul Revere and the Raiders began singing "Cherokee Nation," Leslie rolled her eyes.

Looking for an uplift, we stopped off at the chamber of commerce in Kyle. Inside, the varnished floor gleamed like a yacht's deck, the mounted heads of bison, elk, and antelope protruded from pine-paneled walls above paintings by Native American artists, and leather easy chairs only needed to be occupied by well-heeled sportsmen to complete the picture of a high-end hunting lodge.

Twenty-year-old Cole Hunter, seated behind a computer screen, manned the office with his younger sister, Kylie.

Cole, slim and tall, was the talkative one, good-humored and smart. He had to be. His task was to plant seeds of commerce in uncongenial soil. He told me that 80 percent of what money came into the reservation left it within twenty-four hours, because there was almost nowhere to spend it. A handful of groceries and shops and little else.

"We've got a shop local campaign, to promote local businesses," he said in the musical accents of the Upper Midwest. "We partner with the Badlands National Park and Mount Rushmore to get people to visit the reservation. It's not scary, it's a third world country, yes, it is, but there's good people and bad people, and the majority of us aren't bad, if you just approach us nicely."

"Some people don't?"

"Some people come here and ask: 'Where are your teepees at? Where are your villages?'"

"They're being smart alecks?"

"No. They seriously want to know where are our teepees and our horses so we can chase buffalo. And we tell them, you know, we're a developed nation."

"Are these Americans?"

Cole nodded. "Most of the educated people come from overseas, and they're more interested in how we live today. Like the other day, I had a guy come in here from London. He was making a film about modern Native American life."

It will be a pretty bleak film, I thought after a few more minutes of conversation. Cole told us that the unemployment rate on Pine Ridge was 80 percent.

"That's stunning," I said. "The rate in the Great Depression was only twenty-five percent, and that was considered a catastrophe."

"Yeah, and that's just one of the factors. Teen suicide is a crisis . . ."

"And the drop-out rate," Kylie interjected in a shy undertone.

"Heart disease, diabetes, cancer," her brother went on. "Our life expectancy is, for men, fifty-five, and I think it's sixty, sixty-four for women."

Kylie, again in her quiet voice, said that only some of her friends—those who hadn't dropped out—went on to college, and hardly any of them made new lives for themselves off the reservation.

"Most of them come back."

"It's the reason I didn't go away to college," said Cole. "Because I didn't want to be away from my family. We live just down the hill from our grandmother, and our aunt is just down the road. On the reservation, we're so close together, in this one little area. Here, the family unit is so important."

Was it fair to say that family bonds tied young Lakotas to the reservation, but at the same time it did not offer them any opportunities?

"Yeah. It's a love-hate thing."

We'd seen cattle on the drive through the reservation. Was there any agricultural work to do?

Cole shook his head. Most of the big ranches were owned by whites. "Some of them married into the tribe," he said. "Or they found some other way to get in, but they found a way."

Whites, however, offered one vital service to the Lakota.

"Before diabetes, heart disease, cancer, alcoholism is the big killer on the reservation. Anything that can go wrong with alcohol is on this reservation."

"Even though it's dry," said Kylie.

"Like I said," Cole added, "eighty percent of the money that comes in goes out."

And much of it flows into Whiteclay, Nebraska, only a mile from the Pine Ridge border. The town exists solely to peddle alcohol to Indians. Stateline Liquors and three other establishments sell four million cans of beer a year. Their customers aren't from town; twenty people live in White Clay, twenty-eight thousand "on the rez."

"White businessmen saw an opportunity, and they took it," Cole said. "That's corporate America, that's capitalism. I mean, what're you gonna do?"

There probably were a host of reasons why Cole had not succumbed to drink, or to more direct forms of self-destruction. His wry sense of humor had to be one of them. One anecdote he recounted was of the time, in high school, when he went to Washington, D.C., with a program to acquaint minority students with the workings of government.

"It was a big culture shock for me. I'd seen only people like us, and there were Mexicans, blacks, all kinds of people. I thought, *We're all from the same country?* It was so funny, because we were all in this big room and they still singled us out." He imitated the high-pitched voice of the host. "'We have some special guests with us today, from South Dakota! From a *Native American* charter school in South Dakota!' We had to stand up, and I said [to myself], *Oh, dear Lord, in a room of minorities, we're a minority.*"

On the Big Foot Highway, newly paved with federal stimulus dollars, we rolled south toward Wounded Knee. Ahead, a cavalcade of cars and tribal police cars, lights flashing, cruised slowly in the right-hand lane. SACRED HOOP RUNNERS: SLOW DOWN! read a message painted across the cargo door window of an SUV bringing up the rear. Leslie let up on the gas, and we passed a line of teenage Lakota jogging at the roadside, chests thrust out, determined looks on their faces, batons flying eagle feathers in their hands. Spectators cheered the runners on. I signaled Leslie to stop, lowered the window, and asked an older man wearing sunglasses and a cowboy hat if this was a reservation marathon. No, he said. It was a relay race to instill spiritual power in Lakota youth, so they would live sober lives according to the Lakota Way. Each band of runners covered two or three miles, then passed its batons to another band.

The course started in the Black Hills, as holy to the tribe as the temple wall is to Jews, passed through parts of Wyoming and Montana, and ended where it began, completing a five-hundred-mile circle around what had been, long ago, the heart of Lakota lands. The sacred hoop envisioned by Black Elk, the great shaman.

We heard more about the dysfunctions of reservation life, and lost traditions, at the Wounded Knee cemetery, where a stone obelisk marked the mass grave in which Chief Big Foot and 152 other victims of the massacre were tossed on December 29, 1890. Individual graves surrounded the monument, including those of Lost Bird Woman, a survivor who died in 1919, and Lawrence LaMont, a Vietnam veteran killed by a federal marshal's bullet during the standoff in 1973.* Over some graves, strips of red, white, yellow, and black cloth tied to stakes snapped in the wind.

"Those represent the four sacred directions, a color for each," said a man wearing a windbreaker and a Los Angeles Angels baseball cap. His face looked as hard, pockmarked, and brown as a walnut; black, mournful eyes flanked a large, blunt nose. "Red is East, stands for dawn, new beginnings. South is yellow—that's youth and strength. Black is West, for inner reflection. White is North, that's where we turn for wisdom from the grandfathers."

His sepulchral voice fit the setting.

"And you are . . . ?"

"Carl Broken Leg." A rough hand shot out of his jacket pocket, then he jerked his head toward a cluster of frame houses and trailers—the village of Wounded Knee. "I'm from right over there."

While Leslie read the grave markers, Carl attached himself to me and expounded on the massacre. I was familiar with its history, but it seemed the polite thing to listen, and so I did. We were standing, said Carl, on one of the hills from which the Seventh Cavalry had fired on Big Foot's band of Minneconjou Lakota, camped down there—he pointed toward Wounded Knee Creek, and I realized that was where Leslie and I were stranded the day before. With clouds scudding in the wind and sunlight and shadow dancing over a landscape much the same as it had been on

---

* Oglala Lakota protesting misrule on the reservation, joined by other Native Americans and American Indian Movement militants, seized Wounded Knee and held out against a seventy-one-day siege by federal law enforcement authorities. A Cherokee, Frank Clearwater, was also killed. Although the protest did not improve conditions on Pine Ridge, it sparked a revival of Native American customs, ceremonies, and languages throughout the country.

that bitterly cold day in 1890, I could almost see the bodies ripped by the troopers' carbines and Hotchkiss guns.*

But more than lives were lost. Black Elk: "When I look back from this high hill of my old age . . . I can see that something else died there in the bloody mud and was buried in the blizzard. A people's dream died there. It was a beautiful dream . . . the nation's hoop is broken and scattered. There is no center any longer, and the sacred tree is dead."

All of that seemed as distant as the Middle Ages in the wired America of the twenty-first century, but it wasn't. It had happened a mere fifty years before I was born; I was in fourth grade when Black Elk died, at eighty-seven.

Carl's account of the "battle" consumed twenty minutes, but it was only a prelude to a homily on today's ills (like Cole Hunter's, with some additional refinements: when liquor can't be had, hair spray is boiled down to its alcohol base and drunk) and then a soliloquy on the Lakota's illustrious yesterday.

"Everyone was strong and healthy," he said in that somber voice. "We could walk or run or ride for miles because our bodies weren't weakened by booze and drugs and diabetes and heart disease because of a bad diet. We could see for miles and miles. We didn't need glasses . . ."

The oration went on for a while longer. I doubted the Lakota had been quite the supermen he described. Their past, compared with their dismal present, shone with a brilliance it may not have possessed.

"I don't drink or smoke or do drugs myself," Carl said by way of conclusion. "I'm a sun dancer. I follow the Lakota Way."

He probably needed someone to talk to, get a few things off his chest, yet I couldn't shake the impression that he expected something from me. Not payment for his tour-guide services, which I hadn't asked for. What, then? Pity? Acknowledgment that the wrongs whites inflicted on his people were responsible for the wrongs they were inflicting on themselves? I wanted to say, "Okay, I get it. But the massacre was a hundred and twenty-one years ago. Your people have to get their act together. No one is forcing them to buy four million cans of beer a year."

Whatever he wanted from me, if anything, that kind of speech wasn't it, and I kept my mouth shut. Besides, what did I expect? Branded as

---

* At the time, state of the art in weaponry. The Hotchkiss fired a 42 mm exploding shell at the rate of forty-three rounds per minute.

intractable savages, subjected to wars of extermination, their languages and cultures suppressed, the original Americans had been made homeless in their own land, and in some sense still were. *The nation's hoop is broken . . . There is no center any longer.* When a nation loses its center, each citizen in it loses his or hers, the moral compass is demagnetized.

At the Shell station in Pine Ridge, seat of tribal government, I was feeding Fred his twice-daily ration of gas while Leslie took the dogs for a walk. She came back, trailed by a middle-aged man.

"Phil, he wants . . . ," she started to say.

"I need a little cash for gas money, so my kids don't have to walk home from school in the rain," he said, slurring his words a little.

"Nope," I said. "No way."

Then, after I swung the truck into the parking lot, two women roared up an alley in a banged-up Chevy. The driver saw me and hit the brakes. "Hey, you. Wanna DVD player?" She reached into the backseat and shoved the player out the window, wires dangling from the jacks. "Twenty bucks." I shook my head, fairly sure it was as hot as her eyes were bloodshot. "I'll take ten," she said, and when I refused again, she peeled off in search of another prospective customer.

The Red Cloud Indian School, beyond town off Route 18, is a Jesuit institution, kindergarten through high school. Having been trained by the Jesuits, I was drawn to it. And a donation card I'd picked up indicated that it offered hope in a place that, so far, struck me as hopeless. "More than 93% of graduates pursue higher education following graduation," read one side of the card. "Five Red Cloud Upper Elementary students received awards at the 2005 South Dakota Media Fair . . . Red Cloud Lower Elementary students read over 2,500 books." As if to guard against unwarranted optimism, the flip side delivered more bad news: "On the Pine Indian Reservation Today . . . Per Capita Income: $6,143 . . . Infant Mortality Rate: 2.6 times the national average . . . Suicide Rate: 72% higher than national average . . .

Why does anyone live here? I wondered.

In the Lakota Heritage Center, inside the original mission school building, I put that question to Tamarie Red Cloud, a tall, slender, striking young woman with glossy black hair, her sleeveless blouse baring arms liberally tattooed. She was ringing up sales in the gift shop with a coworker, Angel White Eyes. If anyone had roots in Pine Ridge, Tamarie did: she was a direct descendant of Chief Red Cloud, buried in a cemetery behind the school that bears his name. She'd lived all over the country, an army brat, but when her career-soldier father was killed in Iraq she moved back to the reservation with her mother and her young son.

"What I like most is being close to family," she said, then thought for a moment and added with a grin, "It's also what I dislike the most."

"It's a big, supportive, loving family," she elaborated, "but I have an uncle who gets up at six in the morning, walks two miles into White Clay, and sits there and drinks all day, comes home in the evening and goes to sleep. Just like a job . . . I used to drink myself, but when I got pregnant, I sobered up on my own. A lot of people have kids and keep doing what they're doing. I had to break that cycle. My son is my life. I want him to grow up in a loving environment so he'll know, be nice to your girl-friend, be nice to your wife. He's a powwow dancer."

She thought that the revival of ancient customs, like powwows, helps guide young Lakota onto a new path. "It's not the Lakota Way to drink. There are a lot of people who have gotten sober, a lot of people who sit up and say, 'I'm really proud to be an Indian, so why am I doing this?' A lot of people are on the straight road."

Leslie had a question: did Tamarie resent white people who copy Native American practices, like playing pipe music in fancy massage spas, con-ducting sweat-lodge ceremonies at fat farms?

Tamarie laughed. "A lot of Indians get upset about that, and the Chiefs and the Redskins and the Braves. It doesn't bother me if you guys want to name teams after us. We're still here, and we're not going anywhere."

The skies were stupendous as we drove back to Interior. The plural *skies* was appropriate because they were so vast and varied, tattered clouds racing from horizon to horizon, like ragged airships. The land beneath was a bright, eye-hurting green where the sun broke through, dark and muted elsewhere, and it looked as if it had been recently shorn and its hair had just started to grow back; the grass, topped with tawny tufts, appeared to be the same length all across the hills rolling on toward the Badlands. Beneath the fantastic rock formations, the flats and valleys, catching the late sun's slanting rays, shone like lakes of light, and the pathologies afflicting Pine Ridge, awful as they were, seemed worse for the beauty of the setting, like a terrible crime committed in a splendid mansion.

22.

INDIANS AND WHITES AGREE ABOUT ONE THING: THE DAKOTA BAD-lands are bad lands. That is the meaning of the Lakota word *mako sica*. French fur trappers called them *les mauvaises terres à traverser* (bad lands to cross). A fair day was in the forecast; we were going into Badlands National Park on a buffalo hunt—with cameras rather than guns.

Wild bison roam the park's prairies, sharing them with blackfooted ferrets and prairie dogs. Bighorn sheep range through the mountains. Our first stop was the Cowboy Corner gas station in Interior. There was no twelve-step program for Fred's drinking habit. To avoid facing the truth—I'd bought too much truck—I did not look at the numbers flashing on the pump. A man walked out of the convenience store, wearing a silvery beard forked like a fish's tail.

"Now that's an unusual beard you've got there," I called out.

He glanced my way. "Yup. It covers up a lot of ugly."

Equipped with backpacks, water bottles, binoculars, camera, compass, GPS, and Tanka Bars (a version of Indian pemmican made from dried berries and buffalo jerky), we drove to park headquarters and picked up a map, the back side of which issued warnings: "Weather can change rapidly . . . seek shelter from the thunder showers, hailstorms, and occasional tornadoes that descend on the Badlands with sudden fury . . . Observing a bison up close in the wild . . . is extremely danger-ous. This is not a zoo . . . they may attack. *Never* approach a bison closely.

They can run faster than 30 miles per hour . . . Rattlesnakes, spiders, and stinging insects are found within the park."

"Think we'll live through this experience?" Leslie said, half jokingly, which is another way of saying half seriously.

The Badlands Loop Road wriggled across a wide, green plateau through what must be one of the weirdest landscapes on Earth—like a city designed by a mad architect. Buttes that resembled Mayan temples; chimneys, spires, minarets, cones, pinnacles, pyramids—every shape we could imagine and quite a few we couldn't: gigantic rock mushrooms, enormous golf balls perched on stone tees tall as telephone poles. We stopped at the start of the Medicine Root Trail, shouldered our packs, and tramped off into a profound silence. (Prohibited from running in the park, Sage and Sky were confined to quarters in the truck.) After covering only half a mile, I discovered that my foot still had some healing to do and had to take a break. Sitting down, I munched a Tanka Bar for breakfast and glassed the prairie for bison, the mountains for bighorns, but saw none. The buff-colored mountains were banded in vivid reds— fossilized soils tracing the history of the Badlands from the present day (near the top) back to a layer of grayish black shale (at the bottom) that was a sea floor seventy-five million years ago.

If it weren't for the wind, the stillness would have been absolute. Looking at the bizarre formations in the eerie quiet, I felt as if we were astronauts on an alien planet. The earth shrugged its shoulders, and what had been sea bottom rose to become, many millennia later, a humid, subtropical forest; the climate grew cooler and drier, and the forest was transformed into an arid savanna; the earth shrugged its shoulders again, lifting mountains, and erosion patiently sculpted them over the ages. In the Badlands' crumbling rock the fossil shells of enormous sea turtles had been found, the remains of giant marine lizards, the bones of prehistoric sheep and saber-toothed cats. I pictured, eons into the future, a paleontologist from our successor species scratching his own brain-bulging head at the discovery of a human skull, a homesteader's plow-share, or maybe the preserved frame of a truck like Fred. *Incomplete fossil records and fragmentary artifacts suggest that our primitive ancestor Homo sapiens inhabited this area in the anthropocene epoch . . .*

We walked another mile, and the prediction of unpredictable weather proved accurate. A gray awning drew over the sky. It began to drizzle, then rain, then pour. The "waterproof" labels on our jackets were grounds for a false-claims lawsuit. Drenched, we slogged back to the trailhead and continued our hunt by road. We saw not one buffalo but did pass through prairie dog towns—cities, really—and watched the inhabitants pop out of their burrows, peer around, and scamper from hole to hole, emitting birdlike chirps. Leslie mused upon one of the great mysteries of nature: why are rats repulsive and prairie dogs cute? On the return leg, at a bend in the road hemmed on one side by sheer cliffs, we came upon a herd of bighorn sheep, all ewes and kids. A crowd of bipeds had gathered to observe and photograph them. They—the sheep, that is—were in the late stages of a wardrobe change from winter white to summer tan, shedding in huge patches that made them look disreputable. Camouflaged against the brownish heights, the animals perched atop rocky steeples or scampered down what appeared to be perfectly vertical bluffs. One kid, no bigger than a small dog, hadn't yet got the hang of disobeying the laws of gravity and stranded himself at the edge of a dropoff. His piteous bleats drew his mother's attention. She trotted to the base of the cliff and stood there, apparently to give him confidence. He found a way out of his predicament, and the two ambled across the road. They were quite tame, the kid coming right up to me, as if expecting to be fed, before he opted for the grass on a sloping meadow.

—

She would have stood out anywhere, twenty-one years old and not far under six feet, two thirds of it taken up by her bare legs, tapering down from the cuff of her shorts into a pair of iridescent purple Doc Martens. I was slouched beside a campfire, sipping an after-dinner scotch, when she sauntered over, draped in a mauve sweater over a pink tanktop, costume jewelry clattering from around her long neck.

"Hi! I'm Dani. That's us, over there." She pointed at a tent and a small red car, beside which stood a tall young man with long, sandy-brown hair. "My brother, Alex. Okay if I hug your dogs?"

Sage and Sky, leashed to a picnic table, were at their charming best, tails like furry metronomes. Dani missed her dog. She and her brother were driving from Baltimore to Portland, Oregon, and had decided to visit the Badlands. Dani was captivated by the geology—she'd graduated from Johns Hopkins a couple of weeks earlier with a degree in planetary science.

Alex joined us. Wearing wire-rim glasses, thin, and about six-four, he had the look of a slightly underfed scholar. He was in fact a graduate student in mechanical engineering at the University of Maryland and not sure he liked it.

"All I'm doing is crunching numbers. I'm taking a little time off to figure out what I really want to do." He waited a beat. "Actually, I'm on the run from the law—I got a parking ticket."

Leslie came out of the trailer, and Dylan's voice trailed her through the open door. He was singing an anthem to the rambling life, "Let Me Die in My Footsteps."

"We made Chicago in one day from Baltimore," Alex was saying. "Got into South Bend and checked in at a motel, but the rooms were full of bedbugs and we checked out and drove on to Chicago. Got in at three a.m. but couldn't check in till eleven, so we popped some uppers and walked around the city for eight hours."

Glancing at their tent, I noticed several purple hula hoops, two plugged into a power outlet. Electrified hoops?

"I'm a hoop dancer," Dani said. "Those two are lighted. I'm recharging the batteries."

She promised to stage a performance after dark.

They were a delightful pair, students on a cross-country adventure, separated from me by a gap of nearly fifty years, but we had the road in common. The road collapses differences in age and any other difference you can think of.

Then Ansel Woodenknife showed up to tell me how he'd gone from the reservation to the Food Channel.

———

The skies had cleared, stars came out, undimmed by smog or city lights, and we sat at the picnic table and talked till midnight. Woodenknife has an agile mind that's likely to go off in unexpected directions; the conversation hopped and skipped and made sudden turns, but it began with fry bread.

Thirty-four years ago, his mother-in-law wanted to start a restaurant, but, she told Woodenknife, she needed something different to attract customers.

"At the time, my mother was making Indian tacos on the Rosebud Reservation and selling them out of a cooler. So she came down and said

I'll teach you how to make Indian tacos. That was the draw on the café and what a draw it was."

The secret ingredient that made her fry bread so tasty was ground-up timpula—wild prairie turnip. Word spread. Customers flocked in from all over South Dakota and Nebraska. The Wooden Knife café became a must-stop for tourists visiting the Badlands.

Then, six years ago, the café was discovered by the Food Channel, and after Woodenknife appeared on national TV the business fell victim to its own success.

"We got so busy we couldn't keep up. We closed. We'd expected to reopen when things slowed down, but they never did."

But that didn't mean retirement. The restaurant's demise gave birth to the Wooden Knife Company, which sells fry bread mix and native foods online, and to nationwide chains like Walmart, Safeway, Stop & Shop. Woodenknife has picked up badges of recognition—voted Minority Small Businessman of the Year in 1989, inducted into the South Dakota Small Business Hall of Fame in 2003, appointed by the governor to the state tourist board. The fry bread taco has carried him a long way from the Rosebud Reservation, where he was born, yes, in a log cabin in 1954, and made it only through the ninth grade.

"So did your mother create the Indian taco?" I asked.

"No. Just about every tribe west of the Mississippi would like to claim to have started the Indian taco. What I think happened . . ."

He then presented his theory, and it taught me two things: if you ask Ansel Woodenknife a question, you will not go begging for an answer; and fry bread was as crucial to the survival of the plains Indians as the introduction of the horse. The theory went like this. After they were confined to reservations, the tribes could no longer migrate; the men were not allowed to hunt. They nearly starved on meager government rations until the women figured out that by mixing a little of this with a little of that and cooking it in lard, a substance they'd never heard of before, they could provide a meal.

"The mother could feed her family," he said. "What a relief! Her kids weren't starving anymore. And that's why fry bread is such a pivotal food in American culture. It was a monumental step."

"I'd never thought of fry bread as the salvation of the Indian people," I said.

"In a lot of ways it is. People talk about obesity on the reservations, that fry bread is this terrible thing that's causing death. Those same people were never subject to a hundred-and-fifty-year change in everything . . . Most species never survive that, having to completely readapt in a hundred and fifty years."

From there, the conversation branched off like a vascular system into Lakota beliefs, and Woodenknife's traditional upbringing, and his hopes to preserve those traditions for his children's sake.

"I embrace other cultures. Because I was given so much of my culture as a youth, I'm not threatened by other people's. It's sad to me that other people don't have as much of their culture as they should. It's sad that that's disappearing . . . Just a few weeks ago, a friend of mine that's a photographer came out here. He leads retreats. There was a lady there from Italy, and we were talking about my culture. I asked: 'What do you know about yours and your gods? Not the crusade God but your beautiful gods. You had river deities, forest deities . . . power points where you could reach out and be beyond who you are. Know your gods. Know what made you Italian . . . What a thing you can offer the world—a slight bit of color in a gray, gray world.'"

He'd quickened a memory in me. In 1973, I'd visited an ancestral village in southern Italy. A distant cousin took me to a mossy, vine-choked stone bridge built in the sixth century. "We've been here at least since then and maybe from before that," she'd said, and I'd felt, well, *something*. A connection, and a sense that I could be a perfectly modern American and yet remain bound to an ancient past.

"What a beautiful thing to hand the world," Woodenknife said. "One time I was giving a talk at a small college, and the young kids, all white, were asking me about my heritage. And I said"—his voice fell to a half whisper—"'I'd like you guys to close your eyes for a minute. Imagine yourself waking up on a foggy, chilly morning, and you roll out from underneath your furs, and you hear a drumbeat, ba-boom, ba-boom, ba-boom . . . And you start walking up this grassy hill, and as the fog starts to lift you see four men on a hill holding up a skull, and they're chanting. As you get closer, you see other men pounding on a hollow log, and you look around, and there are women and children, and you get there and they turn around and look at you, and you realize they have red hair. Those were Celts, singing in the morning sun, as they had for a thousand years . . . You guys had a rich, rich, beautiful culture.'"

In one sense, Woodenknife's story is like Filemon Sanchez's—a Horatio Alger saga; but in another, it's the story of a man who walks in two worlds. He's an all-American entrepreneur and a Lakota shaman, or, as the Lakota put it, "a teacher of the way." A teacher of the way, he said, "is a book, an encyclopedia of a whole way of life," and it takes years to become one.

Under the wing of a mentor (Woodenknife's was named Runs Close), a promising candidate is guided through levels of knowledge and understanding. Knowledge and understanding of exactly what he would not reveal; the deepest mysteries of Lakota religion aren't shared with outsiders. At some point in his instruction, the apprentice takes part in the sun dance, the most sacred ritual of the plains tribes. He fasts and takes sweat baths for four days; then his mentor pierces his chest in two places with a knife and inserts into the incisions pegs attached by ropes to a forked pole. The sun dancer dances to the pole and back three times and, on the fourth, leans back with all his strength, ripping the pegs from under his skin. This is not a test of manhood but a rite of self-sacrifice. He has offered his flesh to Wakan Tanka (the Great Spirit) for the good of all the tribe.

There in the darkness, I pictured the man sitting across from me stripped to the waist, blood trickling down his chest. I couldn't reconcile that with the image of the fry bread wholesaler, shipping orders to Walmart. How did he do it?

"It's a very delicate walk to walk in both worlds," he answered.

He's had a lot of practice walking that walk. He was one of twelve children, crammed into a cabin without electricity or running water, near the town of Corn Creek.

He remembered the itinerant Indians who stopped in to help cut wood or work cattle and at night told stories by the light of lard-oil lamps, men with names like Quick Bear and Six Toes. He learned tribal lore and history from his father's first cousin John Lame Deer, a famed Lakota holy man. He was fond of Six Toes, who'd lost his family in a fire and wandered about with a tin cup, an army blanket, and a double-bit ax.

That was one world. Then something happened that changed Woodenknife's life forever. At age nine, he was kidnapped by the U.S. government and thrown into the white world.

"March of 1963, two guys from the Indian agency showed up at the Indian school with Dad. I thought I was in trouble. They put me in a station wagon, Dad tried to fight them, and the cops arrested him. They took me to Pierre, South Dakota, and gave me to a family in Philadelphia. Parents had no recourse. The government sent you to wherever it thought you needed to go—"

"Ansel," I interrupted, saying that I'd heard about Indian children plucked off reservations without their parents' consent and sent to boarding schools or white foster homes, but I thought that had ended a hundred years ago.

"No, it was practiced till 1977. It was part of the assimilation process. Send an Indian over here, over there, and he'd become white . . . And so they shipped us all over, and I'm one of them. They put me on a plane, and when we got to Philadelphia I ran away from the guy who was supposed to escort me. They caught me and gave me to this family. They were an Italian family, and they were nice to me, but it wasn't my family, and so I kept running away. I didn't know where I was going. I didn't know where Corn Creek, South Dakota, was. I could've been running toward the ocean for all I knew, but I just kept running away till they couldn't deal with it anymore. I got sent back to the reservation as an incorrigible."

That was in 1966. After three years away, Woodenknife discovered, as did thousands of other Indian children torn from their roots, that he'd become a stranger to his family.

"I never really came home," he said. "I lived at the house, but everything was different after that . . . My brothers and sisters didn't know what to do with me. They were glad to see me, but it was like I came back from the dead."

He related all this with neither bitterness nor sadness. I think he was one of the most serene men I've ever met.

"When you got home, were you an angry kid?"

"Oh, sure. I fought a lot. Boxed for fourteen years. Carried a chip on my shoulder. Went through the gamut and . . . One of the tests. I passed."

"You said you boxed?"

I'd had twenty-three amateur fights when I was young. Looking at Woodenknife in the hazy light falling through the trailer's curtained windows—the thick neck, the muscle-bunched shoulders—I knew I would not have wanted to face him in the ring.

"I probably did it because I had a lot of anger, although anger does you no good in boxing. It taught me how to handle my anger. Then I started fighting in tough-man contests. I rodeoed, rode bareback and bulls . . ."

I caught a flickering out of the corner of my eye. It was Dani, walking back and forth while she twirled her lighted hoops. Because she was almost invisible in the moonless night, they appeared to be spinning on their own power, like miniature Ferris wheels. *I'm talking to a Lakota shaman who's also a successful entrepreneur*, I thought, *and over there a Johns Hopkins graduate is dancing in the dark with electric hula hoops. How weird, how wonderful.*

The constellations rode the ecliptic westward, and the conversation turned with them, back to the purpose of my journey. What bound the atoms of America to one another? Or was it becoming ever more atomized?

"I don't think so," Woodenknife answered. "Getting to meet you and your culture solidifies mine. I embrace that. If you don't embrace it, you fear it. If you fear it, you lock it out. I'm not like that, and I don't think most Americans are like that. We have to learn from each other . . . To me, one of the most valuable things about this country is learning different cultures . . . That's the most colorful fabric I've encountered in life. I don't go up to people in fear."

"Well," I said, "what about people who aren't like you?" Who are angry and afraid of the Other, of the immigrant, of the homosexual, of the secularist or of the evangelical, of the black or brown face or, for that matter, the white face?

"*No*," he answered in a kind of growl. "Your grandparents who came over had to study everybody that was here intently, not only to get along with them or to work with them, but to be an American. We as Native Americans had to study you very intently to be able to live amongst you in a hundred and fifty years. Your grandparents didn't have that much longer, either. And so they made the investment of self into another culture. Because we all believe in this country that we're people who are free to be people. You get that, and you don't have to fear anybody anymore. You know, I've never lost the fact that I'm a free person. The government may hate me because I'm an Indian, but my ancestors walked freely, and by God, if it kills me, I'll walk freely too."

He was a Lakota Whitman.

> *Afoot and light-hearted I take to the open road*
> *Healthy, free, the world before me*
> *The long brown path before me leading wherever I choose.*

"I really believe that when we start taking ourselves back, we'll have more to offer the world," he said. "I don't want a gray world."

"You mean taking back our cultures and where we come from."

"Absolutely! You want to talk about the fabric of this country, that's it."

"So rather than a melting pot, it would be a . . ."

"A blanket of color, all sewn in the shape of the U.S."

"A beautiful image," I said, and looking at him across the table I felt that I was in the presence of a great soul. Earlier, he'd said something that now came back to me: "If I have too much, someone else has too little." It was the Lakota way to share, and he didn't want more than his share. He didn't want to become the fry bread king of America, with a chain of coast-to-coast Indian Taco Bells. He'd earned enough to educate his children and ensure a decent retirement. Reflecting on that and on his thoughts about freedom, I grew confessional. You're never free till you're liberated from your own passions, admittedly a secondhand idea. But that didn't make it any less true that we are manacled by the voice that cries, *I want, I want.* Once upon a time, I was eaten alive by ambition—for more recognition, more praise, more money, a bigger house, and then a still bigger house. No matter how much I had, I was like the Johnny Rocco character in the movie *Key Largo*, who, when asked what he wants, answers, "More! That's right! I want more!" I was always unhappy. It had taken me years to work my way out of that. Years of thinking and study, mostly in the ancient Stoics: Marcus Aurelius, Seneca, Epictetus.

Woodenknife motioned in recognition—he'd been there. "Well, I pulled up tonight and see a man visiting with two people he'd never met before. I see two dogs laying contentedly that didn't bark at me, and I see a small, self-contained trailer, and *that's enough.* Here you have more than any king could want. You're free to move about, free to engage."

I threw out the idea that America's binding force was its unboundedness. You could travel across every state line on the map and never have to show a passport, and knowing you had the freedom to go, just go where you pleased, even if you never went anywhere, liberated your mind to think as it pleased.

"Well, when you can live as you are, and I can live as I live, and we don't ask people to make reservations for us, then we free them up as well as ourselves. Anytime somebody has to shift position just because of you, you've come into more than that person's face, 'cause you've taken their freedom and exchanged it for something you probably don't even value . . . There's a lot more to this country than the next toy."

"Oh, God, yeah!"

"You know, we're fast becoming this nation that's forgotten to give our kids that freedom of movement. If you give your kids nothing, give 'em the land."

"Do I love that one," I said, and I surely did. "Those two, Dani and Alex, they're brother and sister," I said. "I'm seventy, she's twenty-one, he's twenty-seven, and yet there's this commonality."

"Reaches across generations. And it reaches across all the segregations that the world demands we put up. Those segregations weren't meant for you and me. They're meant for those who want to be in control."

23.

ALEX INVITED US OVER FOR COFFEE—FRENCH-PRESS COFFEE with cardamom, no less—and Dani performed with impressive dexterity, twirling a hoop around each shoulder, another around her waist, and a fourth around her knees, all at the same time. We felt a bit of a letdown when she and her brother left, bound for Oregon.

I was still set on photographing wild bison. Long ago, Lakota shamans went on vision quests, imploring Wakan Tanka to show them where the herds were. Having bonded with a shaman the night before, I hoped that some of his magic would rub off on me. My vision—a guess, really—was that we'd better our chances of spotting buffalo in the Badlands Wilderness Area, a more primitive part of the national park offering escape from crowds and signed trails.

We banged along the gravel Sage Creek rim road, parked, then hiked a sloping ridge down into a basin riven by wooded creeks, overlooked by far-off buttes and mesas, and webbed with buffalo trails as easy to follow as the man-made kind. Cholla sprouted yellow summer blossoms, mallow scattered orange across the sweep of bluestem and cordgrass. I loved it, two people alone in a vast and beautiful desolation, walking in the tracks of wild buffalo.

But after tramping more than an hour, we hadn't seen a single animal. My foot was throbbing again, even though we'd covered less than three miles. We sat down by a pond, in a tallgrass meadow half hidden by cottonwood and more willow. Only us and swallows and ducks and jack-in-the-box prairie dogs and trees, sibilant in the warm wind. All quite magical. I took off my shirt, Leslie removed hers; I shed my jeans, she wriggled out of hers, and . . . Rocks began poking in uncomfortable places, the bugs found us while fleeing predatory swallows, and the luxuriant grass looked like ideal tick habitat. Realizing that this was not a Cialis commercial, we looked at each other, started laughing, got dressed, and headed back.

There were three of them about 250 yards away, two grazing, one lying in the shade of a solitary tree. I pulled the camera out of my backpack and began a stalk, crouching at first, then crawling on hands and knees. When I'd closed to within fifty yards, I raised my binoculars and was awed by their size. Each bull, weighing close to a ton, looked like he could take on Fred and win, humped shoulders mantled in a knotty brown cape, hindquarters the color of burned wood, horns burnished by sunlight hooking out from a shaggy head as big as a Volkswagen's front end, dripping a beard and perforated by tiny black eyes.

I was too close for safety and too far for a good shot—I didn't have a long lens. I dropped into a shallow ravine, slithered up the side to the lip, and realized that the ravine would bring me to within thirty yards. Thirty miles an hour, the warnings on the back of the map said. How long would it take to cover thirty yards at thirty miles an hour? Not long enough to keep me from looking like roadkill. The light was right now, and the bull was beautiful in it, hide shining as if it had been shellacked. I framed him and took two or three shots. Possibly he'd heard the shutter snap; he raised his head and looked at me with a kind of baleful stupidity. Enough. This was really, really stupid on my part. I slipped back into the ravine.

"It's Buffalo Phil," Leslie said when I returned. "I was having flashbacks to tenth grade."

"What happened in tenth grade?"

"We read 'The Short, Happy Life of Francis Macomber.' He was killed by a buffalo. A Cape Buffalo, but that's close enough."

"Actually, it was his wife. She shot him in the head."

"Oh."

North by northwest toward Rapid City on South Dakota 44. The Buffalo Gap National Grassland, sparkling in the clear morning, stretched for forty or fifty miles. Far off to our right, the Badlands formed a jumbled skyline, the cliffs and buttes dusty and wrinkled, like elephant hide. Fred's tank was half full when we gassed up in Caputa, but I had to stop and find out if the town had been founded by a lost relative who couldn't spell his own name. A Caputo in these parts might explain why the pizza we'd eaten the previous night had been more than edible. The man behind the counter in the general store had no idea of the name's origin. He summoned Ryan Olson, a tall cowboy sporting a black goatee and Wyatt Earp mustache.

"My great-granddad built this store in 1908," he said. "It was a mercantile for when they built the railroad. Our ranch is right across the highway. Been in the family more'n a hundred years."

The ranch also had a place in the history of American cinema: it had been the location for the movie *Dances with Wolves*. Ryan was proud of that and showed us a wall full of photographs taken during filming. "Interesting," I said, "but what about this name, Caputa?" I pronounced it as I do my family name, with a short *u*. He corrected me: it was *Ca-pew-ta*. He'd heard it meant "railroad stop" in a foreign language but wasn't sure which one. Could be Swedish or Norwegian.

Outside, Leslie asked Magic Droid to translate *Caputa* from Swedish, then from Norwegian. For a change, MD was at a loss.

The road began a sinuous climb into the Black Hills, which aren't hills but mountains, isolated out on the Great Plains, as if a chunk of the Rockies had broken off and floated out onto that ocean of grass. It was a pleasure to look up instead of out for a change, a pleasure to see trees again, and there was an abundance of them. The dark green of the spruce and ponderosa bristling up the mountainsides, interrupted by bright alpine meadows, gave rise to the Lakota name Pahá Sapá (Black Mountains). To the Lakota, as to the Cheyenne, they were the center of the world, for practical as well as mystical reasons. Trout abounded in the streams; bison grazed in the open mountain parks; sheep inhabited the high, granitic peaks; elk and deer ranged through the forests, which also supplied wood for fuel and poles for lodges. In *The Oregon Trail*, Francis Parkman describes riding into the hills with a Lakota band whose sole purpose was to cut trees for lodge poles. But for some, the journey was also a kind of religious pilgrimage. One day, while hunting deer, Parkman came upon an old man, "seated alone, immovable as a statue among the rocks and trees."

"His face was turned upward, and his eyes seemed riveted on a pine tree springing from a cleft in the precipice above . . . Looking at the old man for a while, I was satisfied that he was engaged in an act of worship, or prayer, or communion of some kind with a supernatural being."

Because we were near Mount Rushmore (and as a fan of the movie *North by Northwest*), Leslie insisted that we visit. I expected to hate it, and I did. Keystone, near the entrance to the monument, looked as if it had been designed by a Disneyland imagineer, and the highway was a gallery of trashy billboards. PAN FOR BLACK HILLS GOLD! SEE THE CONATA MYSTERY! REPTILE JUNGLE! OLD MACDONALD'S FARM—SEE THE PIG RACES! If the Black Hills had been sacred to the Lakota, that part of them had been thoroughly desanctified. Inside the gate, tourists swarmed, gawking at the massive faces carved out of a mountain.

For the sake of balance, we then went to the Crazy Horse Memorial, begun in 1948 by the sculptor Korczak Ziolkowksi and still a work in progress. For twenty dollars, we got to see, from a distance, the colossal torso of the Sioux chief astride a colossal horse, its head more than twenty stories high, its eye as wide as a passenger car is long. Another eleven dollars would have bought us a ticket on a tour bus to the construction site. Instead we headed out past the gift shop and snack shop and the Laughing Water Restaurant onto U.S. 385. Beyond the claptrap, the scenery was grand and unspoiled, but I couldn't take my eyes off the road for long. The two-lane teemed with bikers roaring up to Sturgis. They weren't the badasses of old, but middle-age dentists and accountants riding with their middle-age mamas, all garbed to look like Marlon Brando in *The Wild One*.

Deadwood was an Old West theme park, retailing its fame on the HBO series, its violent, gold-rush past, and its two most celebrated residents, Wild Bill Hickok and Calamity Jane. What it is to Old West mythology, Sturgis is to the motorcycle subculture. Seven hundred thousand bikers rumble in from all over the world to the annual Sturgis Motorcycle Rally to party, race, and show off their machines for a week. The old post office has been converted into the Sturgis Motorcycle Museum & Hall of Fame. Every store peddles leather biker wear and accessories; the bars have names evoking the thunder of 1,000-cc engines: the Full Throttle Saloon, the Loud American Roadhouse.

Bike Week was a month away when we passed through, and the town was quiet enough to hold church services on the main street.

I don't need a big vocabulary to tell you where you we camped that night, twenty miles up the road from Sturgis: it was in Spearfish, in Spearfish Canyon, through which flows Spearfish Creek, so-called because the Indians found it ideal for, well, you can guess. A local diner, however, appealed to the meat eater, serving up buffalo burgers and Leslie's new favorite beer, Buffalo Sweat stout.

Spearfish was where I met Whitey Wenzel, a biker's biker, in his man cave, a garage with enough tools to equip a dozen mechanics, an air bench—a pneumatic lift used to work on motorcycles—and two customized Hondas, both under canvas shrouds. His hand clamped down on mine, a row of teeth precisely aligned showed beneath his mustache, light blue eyes sparked like an electric bug killer in August as he sat down and gave me an oral history of the Sturgis Rally.

"Go back to 1938, Pappy Hoel, he had the Indian motorcycle franchise in downtown Sturgis. Him and his buddies racin' around down there, the old racetrack, maybe an eighth-mile circle, and that's how it got started. It got to be a club thing. They were called the Jackpine Gypsies."

"And somehow the word spread?"

"I don't know when stuff got sanctioned, the sixties probably, when it got more organized. But it was always their little deal. People would come and stay in Pappy Hoel's backyard, tentin' and campin', y'know, and then baboom, baboom, baboom. Seventy years, dude!"

"You raced . . ."

"Top-fuel Harleys."

"What?"

He let out a laugh that was a little bit cackle, a little bit whoop. "Don't know what that means, do yuh? Nitro bikes. Drag racers . . ."

And Whitey was off. I'd run into a few talkers on the trip, I was to run into more, but he was world-class, sentences colliding, careening off on tangents, every one an exclamation delivered at maximum volume, as if I were deaf, though it could have been that he'd had to shout so much over the explosions of those nitromethane-fueled dragsters that yelling had become his natural mode of speech.

"My first year was 1976. That's what we come out to do was to race bikes on the drag strip. There were seventeen thousand people, ten thousand in city park, and it just exploded! We were some of the instigators . . . Fire burnouts! Dump a little gas on the road, light it on your tire, get your back wheel on it, smoke it, and then spin it all the way out. Fire burnouts!

We were doin' them middle of the week, hootin' it up, and well, it got outta hand, everybody racin' and ba-ba-ba. And there's a little knoll up above city park, and all these outlaw bikers up on the knoll. Well, the city brought out the water truck and watered down the road to slow the whole thing down, and the outlaws shot the water truck full of holes! Boom! It was over, the last time everybody stayed in city park. I was layin' under a trailer with three, four buddies while the gunshots went overhead. The next morning they brought in all the cops, the National Guard, dogs, and more firehoses, and cleared the whole park out, and that was the last time . . . This is all common knowledge. Now last couple summers here—"

"Let me interrupt a—"

"Hey! Lemme finish this story! Last couple summers I ran into a guy out here, and we got to talkin' about Sturgis and ya ya ya, I said it's my thirty-second year blah blah blah, and is this your first year, and he told me, no, he was here in '76 . . . He starts talkin' about these guys doin' fire burnouts and the water truck comin' and shootin' it full of holes and the . . . ba-ba-badaboom . . . and it all blew up kaboom! Worst time he ever had, and he ain't been back since. And all I could think of was, it was the best time I ever had! And I been goin' back ever since, haven't missed one! I called buddies and told 'em about this guy had a bad time, and everybody, 'What, is he fuckin' crazy? The best time.' Y'know, how many? Girlfriends? How many these years I've been comin' to Sturgis? I come home after bein' away ten days, two weeks, house is empty, furniture's gone, the whole works . . ."

I managed to squeeze in a question: "How many girlfriends?"

"Half a dozen that period of years. Been single my whole life. I been blessed never bein' married. And jobs! Oh, you ain't goin' to Sturgis, you're workin' for me now, oh, yeah, we'll see how all that pans out!"

For the next hour, I spoke perhaps a dozen words while Whitey barreled along, telling me about growing up in St. Paul, Minnesota, cutting school to build motorcycles with his two brothers, and working in his father's concrete business, and how he was the alcoholic son of an alcoholic son of an alcoholic, and had learned how to fight by pulling his mean-drunk father off his mother. "'C'mon, old man, you wanna beat up on somebody, let's see what you've got.' I was probably fifteen, sixteen years old."

Whitey had been sober since 1993, but before that, he bellowed, "I drank professionally . . . Now listen to this! Our drink of choice was Cuervo. Night I quit drinkin', we were dumpin' the tequila shots on the bar and then snortin' 'em through a cocaine straw! That's how they do it in Mexico."

He'd learned how in Mexico, on a wild ride with his racing buddies in 1986. "Took ten days to get down, eleven to get back. We ended up twelve hundred miles into Mexico on fuckin' motorcycles. Had to put 'em on flat cars crossin' Copper Canyon, sittin' in the club car drinkin' with the fuckin' Mexicans."

Biff. Bang. Boom. His voice pummeled me. I felt like Joe Frazier's sparring partner.

"Gotta show you somethin'. One of my original motorcycles. Built it in the eighties." He took the cover off one of the bikes, a long gray-and-black machine that looked, standing still, like it was doing a hundred. "Seventy-nine CBX Honda engine. Chassis, I built, and the body, the exhaust, the rear wheel, all that's custom work. Motor is six cylinder, twenty-four valves, four cam shafts, four drive chains, six carburetors. Got a lock-up clutch, and you gotta follow to the back of it now."

He brought me around to the rear fender. On it was a sticker: WFO— WIDE FUCKIN' OPEN.

"That's my philosophy on this bike." He whooped. "Let's see whatchya got. Wide fuckin' open separates people real quick! Now this one is all hot rod, too." He unveiled the other motorcycle, a gorgeous assembly of ebony black metal and chrome polished to a blinding finish. "Ninety-six ST-Eleven Hundred. A rocketship! This is a hundred-and-fifty-mile-an-hour bike, and I can prove it. A lotta these guys talk big speed about their motorcycles, especially the Harley guys. This'll smoke a Harley. Read on the back."

Two words printed in big letters on a plate: SEE YA.

Then he got onto the changes in Sturgis since the WFO days of fire burnouts and gunshots on Main Street.

"In them days the cops come through city park and they'd see half a dozen bikers sittin' around, they'd say, 'Go on home, rally's over.' Cops don't do that anymore. Hang around, spend some more money! Stay till October! Seven hundred and forty thousand bikes last year. Look at this number." He pulled out a newspaper clipping from a drawer. "Last year, eight hundred and seventeen million economic impact on the state! This is all common knowledge. Eight hundred and seventeen million fuckin' dollars into the state! Of course that's why they want us to stay."

But not all the changes were to his liking. He stood and swung over to his "Wall of Fame"—photographs of him on the bikes he'd built over the years—and whipped out one more bumper sticker. It read: IT USED TO BE ABOUT MOTORCYCLES. NOW IT'S A FUCKIN' FASHION SHOW.

"The nineties, Harley-Davidson," he said, for the first time at a normal decibel level. "Every fifty-five-year-old man had to have a brand-new Harley with the shiny pants and the belt buckle and the hat and the kerchief and the new new new, the new pickup and the new trailer, everything new. Well, they're just wannabes."

A wannabe is something Whitey is not; nor is he a usetabe. He still rides, at sixty-three. He'd taken over his father's concrete business in Minnesota but cashed out eighteen years ago, knocked around, and settled in Spearfish with his bikes and trailer and tools.

"I love my lifestyle . . . This is the dream! Livin' the fuckin' dream! Look at this . . ."

From his workbench he picked up a yard sign reading WHITEYVILLE.

"So we're in the town of Whiteyville."

"The planet, dude!" he said, hooting. "Whiteyworld. It's all good in Whiteyworld."

———

We took a hike into the wilds, six miles round-trip, to work off breakfast and give Sage and Sky some liberty.

The trailhead was an eleven-mile drive down Spearfish Canyon Scenic Byway, which I added to my list of favorite roads. It paralleled Spearfish Creek, tumbling through the canyon, a narrow, twisty corridor walled by palisades of yellowed rock streaked with black. The creek's runs and riffles threw off crystalline glints in the sunlight, and the pools below the fast water, shouldering up to the steep banks, were the color of burned butter.

The trail, an old miner's route, followed Iron Creek, a tributary of the Spearfish scarcely wider than a ditch. Granite cliffs shot up a hundred feet or more, pine and spruce clutching the crags above. I'd read that the Black Hills were formed by volcanic uplift at the end of the Cretaceous Period 125 million years ago. Erosion eventually exposed much older formations, dating back two billion years. On that timescale, the Ice Age was last Saturday. As I gripped a rock to pull myself up a rise in the trail, it occurred to me that I may have touched a remnant of the earth's adolescence, when the only living things were single-celled organisms. Thoughts like that help me to not take myself too seriously.

About a mile in, we saw a plastic-covered sign tacked to a tree beside the creek. It was a placer-mining claim, filed by a Wyoming couple.

Gold!

The discovery of it in 1874, by an expedition under the command of George Armstrong Custer, brought on the Black Hills gold rush. Thousands of white prospectors poured in, in violation of the 1868 Fort Laramie Treaty that promised the Black Hills would belong to the Lakota for as long as the grass grew and the rivers flowed. The invasion led to the Battle of the Little Bighorn in 1876 and to the defeat of the Lakota a year later, after which the U.S. government decided that the grass would grow and the rivers flow no longer and seized the Black Hills. There was just too much money there to leave them to savages. By 1880, the gold mines were yielding four million dollars a year. This is not all ancient history. The Homestake Mine, founded in 1876 by George Hearst, father of William Randolph, remained in operation until 2002 and took out forty million ounces of gold worth half a billion dollars. Nor is it ancient history to the Lakota. In a 1980 case, *United States v. the Sioux Nation of Indians*, the Supreme Court ruled that the taking of the Black Hills had been illegal and offered the Lakota compensation of $106 million. The tribe refused the settlement, and although the fund, invested in an interest-bearing account, is now worth more than $700 million, they still refuse. They want the Black Hills back.

Which isn't likely to happen soon. When gold topped eight hundred dollars an ounce in the eighties, a new rush came to the Black Hills, then faded when the price fell. But now, I thought, looking at the placer claims, maybe a third rush was in the offing. Gold had hit a new high: fifteen hundred an ounce.

We hiked on. Blue flax and violet Venus's looking glass decorated the stream side. Cow's parsnip made white bouquets—the Indians used the mashed flowers as insect repellent. The dogs were in their glory. Dashing unfettered through rough country is in a setter's blood. Sage seemed to recapture some of her youth, sprinting off into the woods not to be seen for five or ten minutes, and when she returned to check in, she would look back at us and—we swear—smile.

Near Ethel was a trailer named Cyclone—so I should have known what was coming. First rain, then hail. Stones as big as ball bearings pelted me as I came out of the campground shower. I felt like an adulterer caught by the Taliban. In an earlier storm, we'd discovered that Fred's hardtop had sprung leaks; the sealant in the roof rack bolts had cracked. The problem was worse now. The dogs and their bed and everything else inside was soaked. Once again, Ethel became a dog house. Leslie and I played Scrabble, shouting "twenty points!" above crashes of thunder, the hammering of hailstones and rain against Ethel's metal hide.

WELCOME TO BELLE FOURCHE
THE GEO. CENTER OF THE U.S.

The historical marker paid its respects to Lebanon, Kansas, but noted that with the admission of Hawaii and Alaska to the union in 1959, the navel of America had moved to South Dakota. Latitude, 44 degrees, 58 minutes north; longitude, 103 degrees, 46 minutes west.

Belle Fourche means "beautiful fork." It was so christened by French fur traders (they did get around), who maintained a post at the confluence of the Belle Fourche and Redwater Rivers. The locals pronounce it *Bell-Foosh*, which would have revolted those Frenchmen. The town is much larger than Lebanon, with more than five thousand people, and a lot more vibrant. The streets were jammed with cowboys when we got there, the day after the storm; the state high school rodeo championships were being held at the county fairgrounds.

Leslie decided she needed a new pair of boots and popped into Pete's Clothing & Western Wear. I picked out a shirt, my old one having succumbed to travel fatigue. Noticing that Pete's didn't have a dressing room, I asked the saleswoman if it would be all right if I took off my T-shirt to try the new shirt on.

"Did you take a bath this Christmas?"

I said I took one every Christmas and Easter.

"Then you pass the test."

Like Lebanon's claim as the center of the contiguous United States, Belle Fourche's title as the other center is somewhat fictitious. The actual spot, said a marker, was twenty miles away. We went into Belle Fourche's Museum and Visitor Center to ask directions and fell into a conversation with a volunteer, Mary Jane Steinbrecker, and the director, Rochelle Silva.

I remarked that their town looked a good deal more prosperous than Lebanon, and Steinbrecker confirmed the impression. It thrived on ranching; cattle drives still took place when herds were moved off the plains to summer pastures in the Black Hills. Some citizens were employed in the coal mines across the state line in Gillette, Wyoming, others in the bentonite plant nearby. She gave me a pamphlet: *Bentonite—the Clay of 1000 Uses*. A bit of an exaggeration. The pamphlet listed 126 products that used the mineral, from "abrasive wheels" to "Zelite water softeners." Then Silva produced a map, showing the route to the "real" middle of the United States. She lamented that people thought of the Midwest as fly-over country. If I wanted to know what held the nation together, I was in it; the Midwest and its rock-ribbed values were the glue.

Fourteen miles north on U.S. 85, then west on old 85, a dirt road. Black specks in the distance marked a herd of Angus; the white specks were antelope. Otherwise, we saw grasslands rolling on and on and on without a tree in sight.

"What is it with no trees anywhere?" Leslie said, as if their absence offended her. "We live in Arizona, a desert, and there are trees there."

MD answered: rainfall on the Great Plains insufficient to sustain trees; frequent fires seared the soil, preventing seeds from sprouting, but grasses survived because of their hardier root system.

Mile upon mile of . . . space. And after eight of those dusty, jaw-rattling miles, we arrived at the actual, the genuine, accept-no-substitutes center of the United States. A crude, hand-painted sign, riddled with bullet holes, dangled from a barbed-wire fence: THE TRUE CENTER OF THE NATION. Fifty or so yards away, an American flag fluttered on a lean-ing pole. A plaque at its base noted the latitude and longitude. And that's all there was to it, the second heart of the big two-hearted heartland.

THE CINNAMON BUN

I am very discriminating about this pastry. Those sold in Hum-phreys Bakery, on Massachusetts' Martha's Vineyard (now, sadly, out of business), were my gold standard. A Humphreys cinnamon bun first graced my mouth about fifteen years ago, after a morning of striped bass fishing, and I'd never found its equal anywhere. Throughout the journey, I sampled the offerings in diners and cafés every chance I got. Highlights of my survey: the buns served at the KOA Spearfish Diner in Spearfish, South Dakota, scored a six on a one-to-ten scale. Those baked at the Chicken Creek Café, in Chicken, Alaska, rang up an eight.

And then there was the Tetsa River Campground, milepost 357.5 on the Alaska Highway in British Columbia. A sign at the roadside made an outrageous claim: WELCOME TO THE CINNAMON BUN CENTER OF THE GALACTIC CLUSTER.

I entered, tingling with mixed doubt and anticipation. The buns, hot out of the oven, were lined up in a display case, the white glaze dripping down their sides like sugary icicles. I asked the young waitress if the galactic cluster referred to the Virgo Cluster, in which the Milky Way was but one of a thousand galaxies. She wasn't sure; the come-on was her dad's idea. I bought one and held it to my nose to savor its bouquet before biting into it. It was dense yet as soft as room-temperature butter. An explosion of complex flavors. The icing with its suggestion of vanilla. Cinnamon, of course. Accents of brown sugar, and did I detect a suggestion of pecan? Humphreys had had all the advantages, access to the best ingredients ferried over daily from the mainland. Here was a backwoods cabin in the middle of the middle of nowhere. I took a second bite to be sure, and, oh, it slid down my throat like a slim Elizabeth Taylor in a velvet dress.

Score: Off the charts.

I cannot verify that the Tetsa River Campground is the cinnamon bun center of the Virgo Cluster, whose galaxies contain somewhere around 260 trillion stars. If only one out of every hundred billion has a planet capable of supporting life intelligent enough to create a cinnamon bun . . . well, you see why the claim may be over the top.

PART THREE

Ocian in View

Fred and Ethel.

24.

A SAILOR WOULD HAVE SAID WE MADE 198 MILES OF NORTHING that day, so I'll say it because I felt, on U.S. 85—as I had on all the other roads since we'd crossed into Kansas—that we were voyaging on a dryland sea. The prairie's undulations were swells, the buttes and hills far off were islands, and I could think of the drill rigs in the North Dakota oil fields as offshore platforms.

We docked at a campground on the Heart River near Dickinson. We'd been on the Great Plains for two weeks and, except for the Black Hills, had seen no end to them. My eyes tired, as if overstretched from staring at the stretched land, I walked the dogs along the river, then through the campground. This one was different. In place of half-million-dollar rigs towing boats and ATVs and other vacationer playthings were abused pickup trucks with company logos on their doors and commercial plates on their bumpers; trailers that had a decidedly lived-in look, with weathered awnings sheltering rickety lawn chairs, corroded barbecue grills, and tools and equipment.

Next to one, three brawny young guys in work boots were wrestling acetylene tanks and what appeared to be a generator into the bed of a Ford F-350. Any one of them could have carried the generator on his back if the truck broke down. They told me that they would be heading out to the rigs in the morning. The campground was their home for the time being, as it was for most of the others living there: welders, electricians, construction workers, roughnecks. North Dakota was undergoing an oil boom. Beneath the western third of the state and extending into Montana and Saskatchewan, embedded in shale rock, lay the largest oil deposits discovered in North America in forty years. The Bakken Field—spoken in tones of awe—was going to be pumping a million barrels a day, nearly as much as Texas. Bad news for the Sierra Club, I supposed, but good news for North Dakota. It had the lowest unemployment rate in the country—a little over 4 percent—and with workers and their families migrating from as far away as Alaska and Georgia, a reverse housing crisis: contractors couldn't build houses fast enough.

The reason for our next move, a one-hundred-mile detour eastward, actually began with my mother's death ten years earlier. Afterward, my gregarious, joke-telling father had plunged into a cycle of depression and fits of self-pitying rage. He would sit silent and inert for long spells, then grow snappy and demanding, then curse God for taking his wife of sixty-two years, leaving him to face his final years alone. Moving to Scottsdale with my sister and brother-in-law didn't help. In time, he began to drive everyone in the family nuts, even my sister, who is almost saintly in her patience. Although he was as mentally and physically fit as you could expect a ninety-year-old to be, she hired a home health-care worker to keep him company and to take him off her hands for a few hours each day.

A retired emergency-room nurse who'd grown up on a North Dakota cattle ranch, Allie Addington was then in her seventies, an indestructibly cheerful widow with a zest for life. He started to spend more time at Allie's apartment in Mesa than he did at my sister and brother-in-law's house. They took trips together, went to concerts and out to dinner. They began to call each other "dear" or "darling" or "honey." Allie liberated him from the prison of his grief and restored him to at least a semblance of the man we once knew.

He died in her arms two years later. He'd woken up, startled, at four in the morning, complaining that the room was spinning. "I knew something was wrong," Allie told me later. "I said, 'Joe, talk to me,' but he just looked at me with those soft brown eyes of his, he took two or three breaths, and then he was gone."

When my sister called from Arizona and mentioned that Allie would be thrilled if we visited her younger brother, John Ellison, in Mandan, North Dakota, I couldn't gripe that it was out of our way. But I had another motive. A couple of years earlier, Allie had revealed that she and John were the great-grandchildren of a cavalry trooper killed with Custer at the Battle of the Little Bighorn, Private Archibald McIlhargey. Her brother had photocopies of his army records. I wanted to look at them and to talk to John about his ancestor. His story would be a link to the places we'd already been. The Black Hills gold rush had been the first act in a three-act western tragedy, Wounded Knee the third, and in between was the Little Bighorn. Custer's Last Stand! Like the siege of Troy, an actual event so fogged in legend that it occupied some twilight realm between the factual and the fabulous.

A really big pool player with a really big stick could have shot a cue ball down I-94 from Dickinson and broken a rack at Mandan. The only vertical objects out there were the oil field pumpjacks, nodding up and down like grazing dinosaurs.

John, a retired optician, met us at a diner on Main Street for a heart-healthy brunch of fried eggs, bacon, and biscuits in gravy. A stocky, wide-faced man of seventy-one, he was, like his sister, talkative and outgoing. He was also a bit sentimental, tearing up easily when he spoke of his boyhood or his maternal grandmother, Rosalie, daughter of the ill-fated McIlhargey.

"I was born with a clubfoot, and the doctors said there was nothing they could do for it. My grandmother would massage it when I was little, every day, she would gently bend my left ankle into place. It worked so well that by age five or six I was ridin' bareback over these Dakota hills. When I was older, I'd say to her, 'Grandma, I don't want you ever to die,' and she'd say to me, 'Don't you worry, I'll come back to see you.' And you know, sometimes when I'm shaving, I'll feel a warm hand on my shoulder. I don't know if it's her. I try to keep an open mind about things like that. Or maybe I'm just getting old and nuttier'n a fruitcake."

He remembered listening to his grandmother's tales of her early childhood at Fort Abraham Lincoln, headquarters for Custer's Seventh Cavalry. She had no memories of her father; she was two years old when he was killed and could recall only the stories she'd heard from her mother, Josie, about the undersize but handsome Irish immigrant.

"My great-grandfather was with [Marcus] Reno's battalion. He carried a message from Reno to Custer that the hostiles' village was a lot bigger than Custer thought. But Custer never listened to anybody, the son of a bitch."

He showed us photocopies of McIlhargey's enlistment papers and other records. Chilling for its understatement was this paragraph in his great-grandmother's application for a widow's pension, dated July 27, 1878: "She further declares that said Archibald McIlhargey, her husband, died in the service of the United States . . . at the battle of the Little Big Horn, Territory of Montana, on or about the 25th day of June, 1876 . . . that the exact cause or manner of his death has never been known to her knowledge, he being mutilated by the Indians in what is known as the Custer Massacre."

Josie was awarded the pension: ten dollars a month.

For a while John talked about the here and now: the Missouri River flooding that caused evacuations in Minot and brought volunteers to sandbag the levees in Bismarck; the oil fields drawing people from all across America. "I see license plates from places I've never seen before. Thank the good Lord for those oil wells out there—North Dakota may be pumping more oil than Texas." Then he suggested we go to Fort Lincoln, now a state historical park a few miles south of Mandan. We could see Archibald McIlhargey's company barracks, a replica of his bunk and footlocker, and a note with a biographical sketch and a brief account of his role in the battle. In his old white Cadillac, John led us to the park. Before saying good-bye, he urged us to visit the Little Bighorn battlefield.

"Y'know, when you're out there, you can still hear 'em fightin'."

Fort Lincoln, nestled above the Missouri, embraced by green hills mottled with yellow sweet clover, didn't look like the cavalry posts in the movies: no stockade walls and blockhouses. The two-story house Custer shared with his wife, Libbie—the last house he'd ever live in—stood solitary, facing a grassy parade ground bigger than two football fields.

That parade ground had been awash in mud on the drizzly, foggy morning of May 17, 1876, as the Seventh Cavalry passed in review before setting out for the Montana Territory, guidons fluttering, horse tack and sabers jiggling and clattering while the band played the regiment's marching tune, "Garryowen."

Bright and airy, the barracks for Company I, McIlhargey's outfit, looked more comfortable than the cramped, stifling quonset huts I'd lived in when I trained at Quantico, Virginia. Commanded by a brooding Irishman, Captain Myles Keogh, the company was one of five that made up Custer's battalion. It was haunting to walk between the two ranks of bunks and read the thumbnail sketches of the men on the note cards pasted to footlockers painted pale cavalry blue. And there, as John had told us, was "Archibald McIlhargey. Born 1845, Antrim, Ireland. Died: June 25, 1876 . . . He carried the first message from Major Marcus Reno to George Custer, reporting that Indians were in front of his command in strong force."

Detached from I Company to serve as Major Reno's striker, probably because he was an experienced soldier, he crossed the Little Bighorn with Reno's small battalion of 131 troopers on that hot June morning in 1876. Its mission was to attack the Indians from the south, while Custer charged from the other direction—a pincer movement.

As the battalion approached the huge Indian village, Reno ordered his men to dismount and form a skirmish line. The warriors counterattacked in such numbers that, as Reno later reported, "the very ground seemed to grow Indians." At that point, he scribbled his hasty message and told McIlhargey to deliver it to Custer, who was on the opposite side of the river, looking down on Reno's fight from a high bluff.

Carrying the message—a message he couldn't even read because he was illiterate—was what doomed McIlhargey. He galloped up the bluff and handed it to Custer, who read it without expression.

So I'd read in various accounts of the battle. But there in the sunlit barracks, I wasn't thinking about the golden hero. Either John and Allie's great-grandfather remained at Custer's side, waiting to hear if he was to deliver a reply to Reno, or he was told to rejoin I Company. Two possibilities with the same end. Custer's force was annihilated; the sole survivor of I Company was Captain Keogh's horse, Comanche. Private Archibald McIlhargey lay dead at age thirty-one.

25.

BEFORE MOVING ON TO THE CUSTER BATTLEFIELD, WE OVER-nighted in Theodore Roosevelt National Park, a swath of wilderness that hugs about sixty miles of the North Dakota–Montana state line. Ethel was nudged into a primitive campsite, meaning that we had to rely on her water tank and stored battery power. She wasn't all that reliable. Scummy dishwater continued to bubble up through the shower drain when her gray tank filled; so under cover of darkness, I committed an environmental misdemeanor by draining the contents into the ground. It would have been a felony to empty the black (sewage) tank in the same way, but I managed to scavenge a bucket and drained the mess into it. I hadn't thought things through; now I had to empty the bucket. To mitigate my crime, I crept off into the woods with a camp shovel, dug a hole, dumped the contents, and quickly covered them up.

Dissatisfied with my South Dakota bison photographs, I wanted to see if I could do better in North Dakota. A sizable herd roamed the park. The morning expedition was to follow the Jones Creek trail, where, a ranger informed us, buffalo had been sighted recently.

I have a good sense of direction, I'm good at reading maps; however, reminders come now and then that I'm not as good as I think I am. I couldn't find the trailhead. Which led to our first road quarrel.

"We must've gone by it," Leslie said. "Let's go back and start over."

"Think we made a wrong turn somewhere," I said, pulled over, got out of the truck, walked in circles, studied the map and the terrain, then rummaged for my GPS.

"What are you doing?" she asked, irritably.

"Trying to figure out where the hell we are," I answered, irritated by her irritation. Another of our differences was coming out, namely, I am deliberate and she's not. What I take for deliberateness she takes for slow-mindedness.

I found the GPS and turned it on and waited.

"Now what?"

"It takes a couple of minutes for the GPS to acquire satellites."

"*Let'sgobackandstartover.*"

Five weeks on the road, living in a closet with wheels. I blew up, reaching through the door to smack the dashboard. "Goddamnit! You're like some goddamned impatient sixteen-year-old!"

Leslie shouted back, "That's better than being a geezer who takes all day to find out where the hell he's at! Doy-de-doy-de-doy." She did her best imitation of Mr. Magoo checking maps and coordinates at glacial speed.

Our first quarrel. My mind flew back to Key West and Harry Wade, the retired Alabama cop who doubted our marriage would survive the trip. Fortunately, all our fights, like bottle rockets, sizzle and fizzle. I fulminated; Leslie jiggled her foot. Then we collected ourselves, Leslie mollified by my realization that, yes, she was right. We had to go back and start over.

The Jones Creek trail wound through country as wild as when Teddy Roosevelt came out to the Badlands from New York to hunt, ranch, and recover from a near-paralyzing grief: his wife and mother had died in the same house on the same day. The rugged desolation woke the conservationist in him, and in the three years he'd spent running Elkhorn Ranch, he established his reputation as a rough-and-ready frontiersman, decking a cowboy in a saloon brawl, capturing outlaws. Roosevelt had flaws to match his virtues—he liked war a little too much—but wouldn't it be *bully*, as TR liked to say, to have another president who can win a barroom fight and run down outlaws, especially the kind who wear suits and ties and have degrees in finance?

Okay, back to the buffalo hunt. Two miles in, we were graced by the appearance of a lone bull. He stood about two hundred yards off, swatting flies with his tail, its tuft brushing dust from off his massive hindquarters.

I dropped my pack and fumbled for the camera. Just then, the bull trotted up a slope, his movements at once ponderous and graceful, then folded his legs and lay down on a narrow bench shaded by an overhanging cliff. I could not stalk up to his secure perch without startling him into a charge. We watched him for a while through binoculars, and it was enough just to see him, at rest in his solitude.

A high priest and priestess of the Airstream faith, Larry and Lou Woodruff, greeted us when we returned to the campsite. They were towing a new Excella, which was to Ethel as a Lexus is to a Volkswagen Beetle, circa 1968. Having spotted the little Globetrotter, they'd felt compelled to meet her owners, whom they assumed to be coreligionists. I was sorry to admit that we didn't own Ethel, and that we were neophytes. But I knew Rich Luhr, the guru of Airstreaming. They did, too; they'd written for his magazine. I asked their advice about Ethel's quirks, particularly her gray tank's tendency to fill up in no time and flood the shower stall. Larry advised that I buy a portable holding tank. It is equipped with wheels, so it can be rolled to a dump station. I was very excited, which shows how far removed from indoor plumbing we'd become. Then, turning from sewage to wildlife, he suggested we drive the park's loop road at dusk, when elk came out of hiding.

The loop road was thirty-two miles long. We felt as if we were on safari, there was so much game. Buffalo bulls crossed the road in front of us; the fluid late afternoon light was perfect, and I got my photographs. Farther on, as we slowed for a sharp turn, a bison of awesome bulk lunged out of the brush and plodded down the road straight toward Fred. I stopped. A steel "moose bar" protected the grille and headlights, but I wasn't sure it would hold if the bull mistook Fred for a rival and butted him. A few yards short of the truck, when we could hear his plate-size hooves striking the pavement, he angled off slightly and kept on coming, right on the centerline, and passed the driver's side close enough to brush the side-view mirror. I could have poked him with my finger, which I most certainly did not. I sat motionless, holding my breath. Fred is six feet, four inches top to bottom, and that bull's hump rose to the roof. Leslie snapped a picture, and all you can see is my nose and a mass of dust-streaked brown filling the window.

Through the side-view, I watched his slow procession. He veered into the right-hand lane, as if he knew the rules of the road. I grinned at Leslie, she grinned back, and we drove on.

I have a pedantic streak, a habit of lecturing, and I was going on and on, explaining the habits of elk, how they lay up in high timber during the day to conceal themselves in the shadows until twilight, when they move down to feed in the valleys. Leslie threw out her arms and bowed up and down. "O great Chingachgook, O learned one, tell me the ways of your elk brothers." Her way of asking me to please shut up.

But I must have instructed her well, because she spotted them first, way off on a meadow under a fissured limestone cliff. A bull with a rack like a tree, a spikehorn, and four cows. On the other side of the road, in the very last light of day, two hundred bison were bedding down for the night, as many as Roosevelt might have seen in the 1880s.

Thoreau: "The West of which I speak is but another name for the Wild; and what I have been preparing to say is, that in Wildness is the preservation of the world." That's an often misquoted quote, *salvation* being substituted for *preservation*. But I preferred the error; I felt as saved as any Christian born again in a megachurch.

Montana's official nickname is the "Treasure State," but most people know it by its unofficial moniker, "Big Sky Country." I don't know about the sky, but the state sure is big. It's as far from the North Dakota to the Idaho state line as Boston is from Detroit. The eastern third of the state, which we entered on a ninety-nine-degree scorcher, is often called "the Big Empty"—with justification.

The familiar signposts of the Lewis and Clark Trail reappeared. We hadn't seen them since leaving Missouri. The interstate girded the Yellowstone River, so we were following the Corps of Discovery's return route from the Pacific. It had split up in July 1806, with Lewis and several men making a reconnaissance of the Marias River, while Clark and several more proceeded down the Yellowstone in dugout canoes. On August 3, 1806, they reached the Yellowstone's confluence with the Missouri, having covered more than six hundred miles from its source in about two weeks.

If the river had been anything like it was on June 29, 2011, Clark's party would have done it in, oh, a day and a half. The mountain snows, deep enough in places to bury a semitrailer, continued to melt in the summer sun, and the Yellowstone looked like a torrent of froth-flecked chocolate milk. It had breached its banks and in a few spots threatened to drown the Northern Pacific tracks running alongside. I'd fished it the previous September and hoped to again on this trip. Rods, waders, flies were stowed in the rubberized carrier lashed to Fred's leaky roofrack. They were going to stay there.

We left I-94, went south on I-90 into the Crow Indian Reservation, and rolled into the 7th Ranch, a few miles from the Little Bighorn Battle-field National Monument. The owners, Chip and Sandy Watts, shaved the peaks and raised the valleys of the cattle market by operating a camp-ground on their property. An American flag snapped on a clover-spangled hill above the parked trailers and RVs, one of which was the biggest we'd seen to date, a jet-black beast towed by a Mack or Kenworth diesel.

The Wattses had named their ranch in honor of the Seventh Cavalry. Virtually everything in the neighborhood had a Last Stand theme. A settlement nearby was called Garryowen, a short stretch from the town of Benteen (for Captain Frederick Benteen, one of the regiment's battalion commanders). Custer, of course, got the lion's share. Streets, roads, even convenience stores paid some sort of homage to the "boy general"* from Monroe, Michigan. It's long mystified me why so much adulation has been heaped on a rash officer who, intoxicated by his own mystique and ambitious for promotion, led more than a third of his regiment to their graves. Had he lived, he probably would have been court-martialed.

Our tour of the battlefield was delayed after Leslie, alarmed by my road diet (lots of summer sausage, Fritos, beef stew, and, yes, Spam), insisted that I consume more fruits and vegetables. My counterargument—that my father made it to ninety-four despite eating fried eggs and toast swabbed in bacon grease almost every morning—availed me nothing. So I dined that morning on a tub of mixed melon, grapes, and pineapple. Then, to avoid shaving and brushing my teeth in the same sink where we washed dishes, I trooped off to the campground bathroom. I was a few yards from the door when an invisible hand gripped my gut, and I hurled the melon, grapes, and pineapple. Sweat erupted on my forehead. I ran inside to a stall and vomited again; then diarrhea struck.

---

* During the Civil War, Custer was promoted to the temporary rank of brigadier general at age twenty-three. After the war, he reverted to his previous rank of captain. He was a lieutenant colonel at the Battle of the Little Bighorn.

I stumbled back to the trailer and flopped on the bunk, with stomach cramps and dry heaves. Leslie took my temperature—a hundred and one.

"So much for fruits and vegetables," I croaked, and spent the day in bed, where Leslie fed me boiled white rice and ginger ale. I vowed to increase my intake of meat and fat as soon as possible.

———

Sometimes I enjoy having my mind changed. On the patio at the Custer battlefield visitor's center, we sat in on a "battle talk" delivered by a National Park Service ranger, a man with a wiry build, hair like strands of iron, and a martial bearing. He did not demolish my opinions of Custer, but by the time he was through, I saw the flamboyant Yellow Hair in a somewhat more favorable light. Because our mental states are often determined by the condition of our bowels, it may have been that I felt better about him because I felt better all around; no foreign objects had gone down my throat that morning, only the familiar slide of fried eggs, fried potatoes, and corned beef hash.

The gist of the lecture was that Custer wasn't the author of the catastrophe. He was both its flawed protagonist and a mere supporting actor in a much larger national drama. It went like this.

The country was in bad shape. The financial panic of 1873 had brought on an economic crisis: banks and businesses went broke, unemployment soared (that sounded familiar). Some way had to be found to improve the chances of the disgruntled masses and of Civil War veterans, who were clamoring for the land promised them for their service. Out in the West lay millions of unclaimed acres occupied by "savages." The solution?

"By clearing the West of Indians," the ranger said, "the nation would be developed and good times restored."

Resolved to do just that, Washington gave the Lakota and Cheyenne an ultimatum: move onto reservations or you'll be considered hostile. The Indians refused. Custer's regiment was part of three army columns ordered to find them and force them to obey the summons. That brought our lecturer to Custer's tactical mistakes: failing to heed his scouts' reports that one hell of a lot of Indians were camped on the Little Bighorn; dividing his command in the face of a superior enemy force. Eight thousand Indians in a single encampment was unheard of, and as we could see—the ranger motioned with an arm—the thick tree cover along the river and the labyrinth of hills and coulees made it almost impossible to determine the actual size of the hostiles' village.

The decisive moment came when it appeared that Lakota scouts had discovered the presence of the Seventh Cavalry.

"Custer's fear was that he'd lost the element of surprise. He was afraid that the Indians would break up into small bands and scatter over the plains, and the army would waste months tracking them down."

And so he attacked, galloping off to an early death and the reward of having stuff named after him.

The Seventh Cavalry monument, three granite blocks inscribed with the names of the 263 soldiers who died in the battle, rises atop Last Stand Hill.* Names and names, each one representing a life, somebody's father, husband, brother, son. And there, on one of the panels, we saw ARCH'D MCILHARGEY. All around, enclosed by an iron-picket fence, marble headstones marked the places where the men had fallen. RHIP (Rank Hath Its Privileges) applied even in death: the officers' markers bore their names, but the enlisted men's all had the same inscription: U.S. SOLDIER, 7TH CAV. KILLED JUNE 25, 1876.

Was one of them McIlhargey? Although there was no record of what he did after conveying Reno's message, I doubted he'd remained with Custer, waiting for a reply. Custer had committed his battalion to an attack; he or an aide probably ordered McIlhargey to rejoin his unit.

On nearby hillsides, down in ravines, more headstones poked up through the grass in clumps. Now and then we came across a red granite marker for an Indian warrior. LAME WHITE MAN, A CHEYENNE WARRIOR. DIED HERE JUNE 25, 1876 WHILE DEFENDING HIS HOMELAND AND THE CHEYENNE WAY OF LIFE. Or: UNKNOWN SIOUX WARRIOR, DIED HERE JUNE 25, 1876 WHILE DEFENDING THE SIOUX WAY OF LIFE.

A hot wind blew as we headed to where I Company, cut off from Custer, had made its own last stand. Broken clouds lunged from the horizon to reach across the immense sky. Hills bright with clover tumbled down to the Little Bighorn Valley, the silver river snaking through stands of high timber. Except for the segments of the interstate occasionally

---

* Fifty-five more were wounded. They and other survivors were from Reno's and Benteen's commands, which regrouped on a hilltop and held off an Indian siege for two days before help arrived.

visible, the scene looked much as it had 135 years and one week ago. Even the heat was the same.

The commander's marker was in the middle of a cluster of head-stones: M.W. KEOGH, CAPTAIN, CO. I, 7TH CAVALRY. FELL HERE JUNE 25, 1876. His troopers' embraced his, as if protecting it. U.S. SOLDIER, 7TH CAVALRY . . .

I recalled John Ellison's comment: "You can still hear 'em fightin'." And I almost could—rifle fire and arrow hiss, the deafening pound of horse hooves, thousands of them, shouts, screams, the terrible bray of wounded animals, warriors' cries, "Hi-Yi-Yi, Hoke-Hey!" (Come on!), and the shrill of their eagle-bone whistles. A prickling went up the back of my neck. Somehow, I knew that one of those stones, eloquent in its ano-nymity, marked the ground where Private McIlhargey had stood before a bullet or arrow found him.

We'd gone out of our way to see this battlefield, and I was glad of it. I stood there for a moment, as much to pay homage to the dead, trooper and warrior alike, as to thank the great-granddaughter who had given my father so much of herself.

26.

FORT SMITH, ON THE BIGHORN RIVER, IS SO SMALL YOU COULD walk across the whole town during a Super Bowl commercial and be back in time to watch the next play. After filling a shopping bag or two with oatmeal and canned goods at the local market, we ran into a friend of Chip and Sandy Watts, Don Kray, a cowboy who'd grown up on the Crow reservation. Old enough, at seventy-five, to remember when some of his Indian classmates in grammar school still lived in tepees, Kray had a face like a fissured hillside, a ready laugh, and a hand missing two fingers. He'd lost them years ago in a well-drilling accident. We drank strong coffee in his barn-red house, its front adorned with cow and buffalo skulls, its tidy interior with black-and-white photographs of brandings and cattle drives that looked as if they'd been taken in 1870.

Despite his age and mangled hand, he still worked cattle, when there was work to do. Not much was left.

"It's changed. Usta be just two, three big ranches around here, and all the farmers had cattle. There was one year I got five, six thousand calves branded. Almost all gone now."

The big outfits got sold off into ten- and twenty-acre parcels—ranchettes occupied by spacious log homes—and the fly-fishing guide replaced the cowhand as folk hero. Kray became an anachronism, and he didn't know the names of half the people in town, small as it was.

"Ever feel like a bastard at a family reunion?" he asked, chuckling.

He guided us through his photo gallery: cowboys lined up on

horseback, their hats raised after the last branding on a ranch in 1996; his father, his two wives, both dead now. Lucille, his second, a heavy smoker, succumbed to cancer, and after her death his first wife returned.

"She was gonna stay a few days. Stayed eight years. She had a pot-bellied pig, ole Nellie. The pig got mad at me, and she left. I should say the pig left and took her with."

"Do you have any kids?" Leslie asked.

"None that I know of. Haven't seen any with three fingers on their right hand. Two, three stepkids . . ."

Which brought him to a picture of a mare that a stepson had given him. She threw him about ten years ago. "Bucked me right off, ironed me out good, goddamned right she did, and it feels different at sixty-five than it does at sixteen."

Among the images of family members and horses and cowhands pushing cattle, one stood out for its incongruity: a helicopter.

"The vice president stopped by here. That was one of the helicopters he was in." Kray paused, frowning as he searched for a name. "*Cheney.* He came here for fishing. There was *four* helicopters and more goldanged people around here."

Leslie asked, "Do you get along with the fishermen, or do you fight with them?"

"Oh, I don't fight. I just like to antagonize 'em. I start a little story and wait four, five days and then really build somethin' in their minds. Most of 'em that know me don't listen to me anymore. They've heard it all."

He thanked us for stopping by. Not many people in town talked to him, possibly because of those false fish stories he cooked up.

Crossing the road to Polly's Café for lunch, I was tempted to think of Don Kray as one of a vanishing breed; but then, cowboys have been vanishing for at least a century and somehow never quite disappear.

No one was fishing the raging Bighorn, and business was slow at Polly's. We were it. The waiter, who doubled as cook, was thrilled to have something to do. While he flipped burgers on the stove and we examined the hefty trout and walleye on the walls, three women in identical Red Cross vests came in. One, a brunette with a southern accent, asked in a tone of suppressed desperation, "Where can we get some gas?"

"We're not in a crisis situation yet," said the blonde, "but we've come a long way, we've got a long way to go, and there's a lot of distance here between gas stations."

Relieved to hear from the waiter/cook that gas could be had nearby, the trio sat down to lunch. They were volunteers, summoned from their homes—the brunette was from Kentucky, the blonde from California, and the third, a lean woman with cropped gray hair, hailed from Colorado—by the ongoing floods. Their field of expertise was mold control, but they were now bringing food, clothing, and bedding to flood victims in Montana. The California woman told us about one man on the Crow reservation. Floodwaters had washed out the road to his house, gouging a sinkhole thirty feet deep and a hundred feet across. There was no way he could get to his place to salvage his belongings, and the reservation didn't have the money to rebuild the road.

"The poor guy tried driving his truck overland, but he bogged down in a ravine and then had to call for a wrecker to pull him out," the blonde said, distressed. "The place is a total loss, and he's got six kids."

I felt sorry for that man and at the same time heartened by those women who'd left their distant homes to come to the aid of strangers. They reminded me of the volunteers who'd flocked to Tuscaloosa. I'd read or heard somewhere that the individualism in which Americans pride themselves had curdled into a pathological selfishness. Yet there were still some who believed that we're all in this together.

The morning was one of those that make you wish you'll never die. We set off at exactly 9:10 a.m., a record time for us, and rolled toward Livingston and a visit with our old friends Jim and Linda Harrison. Way off west of Billings, a ruffled white line shone on the horizon, like a shoal of low clouds, and the clouds rose with each mile till they revealed themselves to be the snowy rims of the Absarokas and the Beartooths. The Rocky Mountains, the backbone of the continent. The Great Plains were behind us.

We pulled into a campsite on the Yellowstone, in the Paradise Valley. For me, it was a kind of homecoming. There, thirty-six years earlier, I'd rented a cabin on a tributary called Pine Creek and finished my first book, *A Rumor of War*. The valley had been all rangeland then; now some of the ranches had been chopped up into vacation properties but the Paradise was still heartbreakingly beautiful, the shoulders of the Absarokas on the east side and the Gallatins on the west mantled in firs, the peaks in ermine white, and the swollen Yellowstone below, surging through the flatlands as through a mountain gorge.

After settling in, we detached Fred and headed for the Harrisons' restored ranch house and a dinner of pork ribs, white beans, salad, fruit pie, and three—or was it four?—bottles of Bordeaux and Côtes du Rhône. Linda said that we were guinea pigs for a new recipe. After weeks of eating out of tin cans, we would have been happy if they served breaded boot leather. As it was, Jim being the great gourmand of American letters, a former food columnist for *Esquire* magazine, the meal would have been praised by his friends Mario Batali and Anthony Bourdain.

Afterward, while Sage and Sky frolicked in the yard with their old friends Zilpha and Mary, we talked. I should say, Jim did. Like Whitey Wenzel, the South Dakota biker, he's a champion conversationalist. No one has ever accused me of being taciturn—long ago, Leslie nicknamed me "Talkie-the-Dwarf" because I'm a five-foot-six-inch blabbermouth— but in Jim's presence, I grew as word-bound as Gary Cooper (though not as tall). Linda and Leslie, both as economical in speech as Jim is extravagant, were reduced to near-total silence. I don't recall what we talked about, mostly because Jim speaks in a low rumble and switches subjects so quickly that following his trains of thought is like trying to follow electrons bouncing off one another in the Large Hadron Collider. But I'm sure we were entertained—he has one of the most original minds I've ever encountered.

Before we left, he gave us a signed copy of his twenty-ninth book. Better than twice my production, and I wondered aloud not only how but why he kept at it.

Jim, an Olympic-class smoker, sucked on an American Spirit and growled, "I don't have enough hobbies."

We were going to spend the July Fourth weekend at the 63, a dude ranch. I didn't see myself as the dude-ranch type, but I'd promised Leslie. Despite the lecture delivered by Carol Springer at Meramec Farm, she wanted to ride, and had chosen the 63 because she'd stayed there on a family holiday when she was thirteen, as her mother had in her childhood.

Four thousand miles and forty-five days of hitching and unhitching, hooking and unhooking had tired me, and we still had around four thousand more to go before we reached Deadhorse. Dude ranch or no, I looked forward to getting off the road and into a cabin for a few days.

Sage and Sky would have to make an exchange, too: the truck bed for a kennel. Dogs weren't allowed on the ranch. To give them some liberty before their imprisonment, as well as to work off the Harrisons' pork ribs, we took a hike into the Absaroka Wilderness, climbing in an early morning chill to Pine Creek Falls, where water blasting down for a couple of hundred feet made such a noise that we had to shout to make ourselves heard. Mists rose dense as steam and sparkled in the broken light. The whole scene had the sublimity of a Hudson River landscape.

We'd seen no one on the way up but ran into a constant stream of hikers on the way down. As usual, the presence of other people brought out the crab in me; and, as usual, Leslie tried to curb my grumbling.

"Phil, are you the only one who's allowed to hike here? You're part of the human race, too. You're just like them, you're a tourist."

"I'm not a tourist. I'm a traveler. There's a difference."

"Like you're better than everyone else? Who do you think you are? God?"

"Nope. But I'm god*like*."

I grinned; she groaned and said, "That's going to get you a smiting from a higher power."

For the umpteenth time, we joined Ethel to Fred, then headed to the kennels outside of Livingston. It was hard, leaving our two buddies. Sage, who loathes kennels, looked at us with melancholy setter eyes that asked, "Will we ever see you again?" We felt better, and so did she, when she and Sky were led to their cage—the kennel owner called it a "suite"—and saw two blankets with dog bones on top. Sage scarfed hers down and then ate Sky's.

The 63, so named because it was started in 1863, had been a dude ranch for more than eighty years, owned by the same family, the Cahills. It was now run by the third generation, Jeff and Deanna Cahill. Jeff, a fortyish man wearing a cowboy hat and glasses that lent him a professorial air, escorted us to our cabin. It perched on the lip of hill and had a deck looking down on the meadow where we'd parked truck and trailer. We flung ourselves on the double bed. Oh the joy.

Two dozen guests jammed into the lodge for dinner. The atmosphere was congenial, the staff solicitous. What fun not to have to cook and clean up, to be *served*. I was getting used to being a dude. We sat at a table with Jeff and Deanna. Earlier, Leslie had told them of her previous visit in 1967 and of her mother's thirty-two years before that. Deanna must have conflated the two, because she asked, "So Leslie, you were here when . . . the nineteen fifties . . . the forties . . . or thirties?" Leslie winced, and whispered, "I'd better get a facelift or at least buy some wrinkle cream."

At first light on July Fourth, we stood on the deck and watched the wranglers, Bob, Bill, Carol Ann, and Analiese, drive our horses from the pastures into the corrals. I was assigned to a paint, McCrae, which pleased me because he'd been named for one of my favorite characters: Gus McCrae, the jokey, good-hearted cowboy in the novel *Lonesome Dove*. Leslie drew Buck, a lively gelding. She asked Jeff if "Buck" was for what he did to riders or for his buckskin color. Jeff assured her it was the latter.

In groups of four to six, we mounted up and rode off. I could think of no better way to spend Independence Day than riding through those mountains, a symphony of light and space. The Rockies, like the Black Hills, rose from the bed of a shallow inland sea and were built by the same geologic event: the Laramid orogeny. It was a long construction project. Eighty million years ago, tectonic plates began to grind and crunch against each other. Fifty million years later, the work was done: a mountain chain three thousand miles long and nearly three miles high. Fast forward a few more epochs, and Ice Age glaciers plow canyons and gorges and bring forth lakes and rivers as they melt, the rivers carrying boulders and silt and the fossilized remains of marine creatures that lived two hundred million years ago. We could find them now, Jeff said, embedded in the shale slides coming off the mountains. Fantastic. Crustaceans and fish that once dwelled in a primeval sea, entombed today at altitudes of eight and ten thousand feet.

McCrae, unfortunately, sounded as if he were soon to be entombed. Climbing a hill, he huffed and wheezed like a two-pack-a-day smoker. But I was delighted with him, and that was unusual. I have never been able to warm up to a horse the way I do to a hunting dog. I don't trust horses. They're prey animals, likely to see almost anything as a threat. A piece of windblown newspaper, or a damned leaf or two flutters by, and you with your fine education and your portfolio of midcap stocks fly over the beast's head and wind up badly bruised if you're lucky, hospitalized if you're not. But McCrae was reliable, responsive, composed, with an alert intelligence in his eye. He seemed to like me. For the first time ever, I'd established a relationship with a horse.

For the next two days we loped and trotted across alpine meadows quilted with lupine and larkspur and Indian paintbrush. We climbed a trail along Mission Creek, white water so solid that it looked like a snowbank in motion.

A square dance was held in the bandstand one evening after dinner. The caller was the 63's manager, Karl, a German immigrant who'd immersed himself in the folkways of the western United States. He knew all the moves and steps. With Teutonic thoroughness, he made us rehearse before playing each tune on his sound system. Fiddles screeched and banjos twanged, and we clomped around while Karl barked in a slight German accent, "Gents to the center, form a Texas Star . . . Promenade your partner . . . Swing your corner . . . Allemande left with the old left hand." I was reluctant to participate in this summer-camp activity, certain I would make a fool of myself. And I did. Most of the other guests seemed to know what they were doing. Even eight-year-old kids were reasonably competent, while Leslie and I, well, struggled.

We retired to the pool room and library, tried our hand at a game of eight ball, then we sat down and talked to the wranglers Analiese Apel and Carol Ann Liesen. We would have confused their names if not for their contrasting appearances: blonde Carol Ann stood six feet; dark-haired Analiese might have made five-one with a strong wind under her. There were other differences. Carol Ann was demure, the daughter of a cowboy and a cowgirl; she'd been home-schooled because the Idaho ranch where she'd grown up was seventy miles from the nearest school. Analiese was a city girl from the east side of St. Paul, Minnesota, a girl with attitude and an ironic wit.

"I had a gangster phase," she said. "I wish to delete that phase of my life . . . You know, tight jeans, sloppy shoes, oversize shirts I stole from my brothers, blingy earrings. I listened to rap music, smoked cigarettes, and thought I was pretty cool. I'm glad that's over."

"So was your gangster phase stylistic, or were you really a gangster?"

"People don't take eighty-pound mall rats into gangs. My oldest brother, Tony, he's twenty-five, and he still thinks he's a gangster. The night that everything changed was the night we found him with his eye socket crushed in because somebody had jumped him. And after that night, everything kind of fused into perspective. This isn't the life I want, this isn't the kind of person I want to be, this isn't the kind of place I want to be in. I want to be gone."

That summer six years ago—Analiese was fifteen—she landed a job at a Girl Scout camp in Wisconsin, where she learned to ride and then to teach riding.

"It was a shocker, going from urban to country. We had no TV, no papers, no contact with the outer world. I mean the music we sang was about frogs and bubble gum and worms. It wasn't, you know, 'I'm going to smoke some crack and find me a prostitute.' Very different from what I'd grown up with. But I got a new appreciation of the things that mattered. My saving grace is actually horses."

She'd lived in sixteen different places since then and attended three colleges, going, she said, "wherever the wind takes me. I don't get too involved in places, so I can easily uproot and go somewhere else."

"So I take it there's no guy in this picture," I said.

"Far too much work. I have a horse named Peppa. She's all that I need in my life at this point in time."

Carol Ann's path to the 63 had been more traditional. "I grew up riding. My parents cowboyed most of their lives. I grew up in that lifestyle. It's just something you learn automatically," she said in a self-effacing way.

She was twenty years old, and this was her third year at the 63. She'd worked guest ranches every summer but one since she was thirteen, and she'd learned a few things, like the difference between dealing with the public and caring for large animals.

"The public you can leave at the end of the day, but the animals you have to see every day. You know, people give their kids, like, goldfish for a pet, and if the goldfish dies it's no big deal. But if your horse dies, it is. To have something that big relying on you to keep its life intact, it's definitely a big deal."

Carol Ann and Analiese's day began before dawn and ended after sundown. They rode out in semidarkness to round up the ranch's herd and drive it to the corral. They curried and brushed and picked hooves and with the two male wranglers saddled and bridled two dozen horses, and at the close of the day they took off the saddles and bridles and turned the horses loose. It was a life that put them out of synch with 99 percent of Americans their age.

"We don't blend in very well with our generation," Carol Ann commented, without regret. "They get so far away from nature, they get so far away from, you know, what built them," Analiese added. "There's a disconnect, it's more about things than about places and people. It's 'Ooo, I lost my iPod, my life is over.'"

"I have a laptop, mainly for school, and a cell phone because I have to," Carol Ann interjected. "But I do love my iPod."

There was no TV on the ranch, and Leslie thought that its absence was a blessing. "I work on the East Coast," she said. "I drive to work every day, and I listen to the radio, I watch TV, although I hardly listen to it anymore because all I want to do is throw things at it. These people are screaming at those people, and you really do get a sense that things are just flying apart. But I have to say that on this trip we've hardly run into any angry people."

"It has to do with media," Analiese said. "What makes the ratings is pissed-off people, the weirdos. I mean you hear more about Lindsay Lohan than you do about crop prices. There's such a disconnect—this is a whole new spiel—of people from their food source. Children think milk appears in a jug or it just falls from the heavens.

"I think the country definitely is in disarray. At the same time, to grow as a country, we need to have conflict, and conflict is healthy, conflict is good. But the media has this awesome way of blowing it out of proportion. It would be nice not to have this skewed perspective on the television. Yes, there are extremely left wing and extremely right wing, but the middle ground very rarely gets reported on. And you know, there's a huge disconnect between urban life and rural life. There's *nooo* sense of community in that respect."

I reckoned that the young woman who'd morphed from city-street hip-hopper to Montana wrangler knew both sides of that rupture. But I wondered where she was going with this.

"The first step would be to educate kids on the country they live in," she said. "Emphasize history, emphasize geography, emphasize lifestyles outside of your own. There are kids out there that haven't even seen what a cow looks like except *c* is for *cow*."

"They can go down to the grocery store and buy themselves a hamburger patty," said Carol Ann. "They don't know beyond that point what goes into that animal to get him to that stage. Growing up like I did—I won't lie, the first calf we butchered was little Pee-Wee, and I cried. Yes, you're sad when your favorite calf has to go to the market, but you learn to deal with it. You learn to appreciate what you eat and where it comes from and the work that goes into it."

So I guessed where we'd gone was back to the same idea Carol Springer had tossed out: "It's not a great evolutionary thing to be so distant from where your food comes from." True connectedness doesn't come from electronic gadgets; it comes from a connection to the land and the origins of what you put into your stomach.

We took a last ride the next morning and, during a final lunch with the other dudes, listened to a guest crying over spilled milk. Namely, that the Environmental Protection Agency planned to compel dairy farmers to clean up milk spills as if they were oil spills, but had to back off when outraged citizens rose up in protest. By this time, we recognized the signs of modern mythmaking: the guest had cherry-picked putative facts from the Internet to confirm his preconceptions that the government is out to get us all. If he'd made the effort, he would have learned that the EPA was seeking not to pass a new law but to *repeal* an old one, on the books for years, that put milk spills on the same footing as oil spills. The problem was too much information. A twenty-first-century American can access more of it in ten minutes than an eighteenth-century American could in a year, yet the dominion of falsehood remains. It can be stated as a kind of mathematical principle: the degree of ignorance on any given subject is directly proportional to the amount of information available about it.

27.

AFTER REUNITING WITH SAGE AND SKY, WE TOOK I-90 TO Three Forks, Montana, where the Jefferson, Madison, and Gallatin Rivers, tumbling from their origins in the Rockies, join to form the headwaters of the Missouri, at 2,341 miles the longest river in North America.* Lewis and Clark arrived there on a Thursday morning, July 25, 1805.

Reading from Clark's journals with his capricious punctuation and spelling, we stood about where Clark had, looking at the Jefferson's confluence with the Madison, both running high and fast. Climbing up Fort Rock, we could see the Gallatin surging around a rocky, shrub-covered bluff to give itself to the Missouri, two parts water and one part mud.

To stand at the source of a great river is to be present at a perpetual beginning. I felt a mixture of wonder and humility, and could only imagine Lewis and Clark's emotions, knowing that theirs were the first European eyes to see the headwaters. The French explorer Jacques Marquette had named the Missouri in 1673 (corrupting an Algonquin word for the tribes that lived at its mouth, Oumessourit [people with canoes]), but Lewis and Clark had the privilege of naming its three major tributaries.† They had put them on the map.

---

* The Mississippi is 2,320 miles long.
† For President Thomas Jefferson, Secretary of State James Madison, and Treasury Secretary Albert Gallatin.

From atop Fort Rock, I-90 showed in the distance; otherwise, the explorers would have found much that was familiar.

July 7, 2011, was very hot, and July 25, 1805, was *verry hot*. And one other thing they would recognize. Leslie slapped her arm and said, "Mosquitoes most troublesome." Clark wrote, "Musquetors verry troublesom."

In the journals there is no mention of Lewis's dog, Seaman, attempting to escape the heat and bugs by hurling himself into the river. Sage and Sky tried it and almost took me with them. If I hadn't dug in my heels and practically strangled them with the leashes, the three of us would have been on our way to St. Louis.

The whole trip, Leslie had been anticipating a big test for Fred and Ethel. The very words *crossing the Continental Divide* conjured in her mind a road winding up and up for hours, sheer drop-offs, the truck struggling, possibly overheating, the trailer scraping guardrails, sending pebbles hurtling down into crevasses. The highway did wind upward, though not for hours, and Fred's big V8 hauled Ethel as if the grade were a bowling lane. Near Butte, hemmed in by slablike rock formations, we passed under a bridge. A green-and-white sign hanging from it said: CONTINENTAL DIVIDE. ELEVATION 6393.

"Wait, what! Is that it?" Leslie asked. She sounded crushed.

"Yes. From here on, all the rivers flow west."

"No, I mean, is that *it*? Where's the struggle?"

"Well, we could always drive back down and try walking up, if it's a struggle you want."

Butte, Montana, born as a gold camp in the 1870s, grew into a boomtown, burned down in 1879, was rebuilt and boomed again with the discovery of copper, much in demand as electricity was developed, went broke in the Great Depression, revived during World War II, then became a kind of company town for Anaconda Copper, which dug the Berkeley Pit in 1955—at the time the largest strip mine on Earth—and operated it till 1982, when it shut down and Butte entered another decline, its population falling from a high of sixty thousand to its present thirty-four thousand.

Pollutants from more than a century of mining are still being cleaned up. Butte is a paradigm of the western mining town's natural history: from tent camp to boomtown to Superfund site—the largest such site in the United States. The downtown business district, called Upper Butte, has architecturally distinguished buildings, some empty or half empty, their sides painted with "ghost signs" of long-vanished enterprises. With the headframes of old shaft mines poking up here and there, it has the look and feel of a city in the midwestern rust belt.

The Berkeley Pit is its most dramatic attraction. A mile long, half a mile wide, seventeen hundred feet deep, and partially flooded with ground-water chock full of arsenic, sulfur, and heavy metals, it's the only toxic waste dump in America open to tourists.

We could see no sense in paying money to look at a contaminated hole in the ground and pulled into a campground outside the city, on Blacktail Creek. Two Canadians touring the United States were parked next to us. I had a postprandial drink with them, Reggie and Mark, father and son. They were electrical contractors involved in another extraction industry—the tar sands oil fields in northern Alberta. After delivering a seminar on how oil is produced from tar sands, Reggie volunteered that he'd made $320,000 the previous year, and his wife $100,000. I hoped he and his son would live long enough to enjoy their riches. Both were, to be polite, on the stout side, guzzled beers like soda, and smoked as I've never seen anyone smoke before or since. Each had four packs of Marlboros stacked in front of him, and it appeared that wouldn't be enough to last the night. The Berkeley Pit was less toxic than the air around our picnic table.

"We're your biggest suppliers of oil, you know," Reggie declared.

Yes, I knew that. With Saudi Arabia in second place.

"And that's as it should be. We're not unstable, like over there in the Middle East. We're not likely to have a revolution or a war. Hell"—he blew out a cumulus of smoke as he laughed—"we haven't got enough people. Thank God you're here to protect us. Otherwise, somebody would've invaded us by now."

I replied that we Yanks were only too pleased to guard our friendly neighbor to the north, then leashed up Sage and Sky and walked them along Blacktail Creek, making sure they didn't drink.

For the 120 miles from Butte to Missoula, U.S. 12 was the paved twin of the Clark Fork River, following it bend for bend. Beyond Missoula, the highway turned away from the Clark Fork and crawled westward through the Bitterroot Mountains to Lolo Hot Springs Resort, a short hop from the Idaho state line. Expecting a magical town with natural grottoed baths, Leslie was a little let down to find a bar and grill, a couple of outbuildings, and two swimming pools that charged seven dollars for a dip, a thin towel, and a wire basket for your clothes. But the campground on the other side of the road was lovely, set beside clear, swift Lolo Creek and backed by a cliff of smooth, rounded rock that resembled papier-mâché, its top plumed with spruce and fir.

Across the road, at the side of the bar and grill's parking lot, was a . . . well . . . a *thing*. A thing that looked as out of place among the mountains and the forests as a Ferris wheel in St. Peter's Basilica. An enormous blue steel box sitting on wooden blocks the size of compact cars. Two huge cylinders were attached to the front by pipes a foot in diameter. A chain-link fence, hung with NO TRESPASSING signs, enclosed the monster, and outside the fence, a pair of security guards wearing hard hats and safety vests sat under an awning, looking bored to distraction.

"What do you suppose that is?" Leslie asked.

I couldn't suppose. "We'll find out in the morning. Don't think it's going anywhere."

I walked over to the Thing the next day. Two new security guards were on duty, a bald, hulking man, Glenn, and a sparky Korean woman, Tangerine.

"I was born in Seoul. My mother left me in the hospital," she offered by way of explaining how she'd come to be named for a citrus fruit. "Spent my first year and a half in a foster home, then an American couple adopted me and brought me to Missoula. They named me. Back then, in the seventies, I was the only Asian, and on top of that I was named Tangerine, and it really sucked. It's better now. There are a lot more Asians in Missoula, and more blacks, and I don't get fucked with anymore."

Having presented that capsule biography and commentary on a changing America, she informed me that the Thing she and Glenn were guarding was owned by the Imperial Oil Company, a subsidiary of Exxon-Mobil, and had been on its way to the tar sands fields in Canada. Tangerine said it was a "test module," although she didn't know what it tested.

Two hundred feet long, thirty-six feet high, twenty-eight feet wide, it weighed half a million pounds.

"What's it doing here? How the hell did it get here?"

Glenn took over. Its saga began in South Korea, where it had been built. It was shipped across the Pacific to the West Coast, then floated on a barge up the Columbia and Snake Rivers to Lewiston, Idaho, where it was loaded onto a flatbed carrier with twenty-four axles and ninety-six wheels. Goliath trucks pushed and pulled the megaload through the mountains, up U.S. 12. Traffic stalled, trees were cut down to make room for its passage, and as word leaked out that the oil companies planned to turn the highway—a scenic byway—into an industrial truck route, local residents objected. Ad hoc citizens groups joined with environmental organizations like the Sierra Club and filed suit to put U.S. 12 off limits for giant rigs. A federal judge ruled in their favor, temporarily enjoining the oil companies and the transportation firm from using the road. And so the Thing's long journey ended, for the present, right here at Lolo Hot Springs.

Now, Glenn continued, a band of protesters were planning a demonstration, which was why his and Tangerine's employer, Knighthawke Security Services, guarded the rig round-the-clock.

I didn't see any protesters. Where were they?

"They're camped out somewhere up Fish Creek Road. Don't know where exactly—that road's thirty-one miles long. Some of 'em are from as far away as Florida, and I'd like to know how much gas they used to get here and protest extracting oil that gas is made from. Everybody has the right, but if you're going to be honest about it, you should bike up here, or walk, not burn gallons and gallons of gas."

I would have been hypocritical to argue. We'd covered 4,250 miles from Key West and had consumed roughly 350 gallons, give or take.

We determined to find the protesters later.

Meanwhile, a campground neighbor told us that we had to see a field of blooming camas flowers just across the line in Idaho. We found the field, watered by a meandering stream, blanketed with purple blossoms.

The camas is an edible tuber and is thought to have given the Bitterroots their name. It was introduced to Lewis and Clark by the Shoshone, the tribe to which Sacagawea, the fifteen-year-old girl who guided them through the mountains, belonged. Camas helped sustain them in their severest test: the crossing of the Bitterroot Range in the fall of 1805. Thinly clad in buckskins and moccasins, they climbed steep, snow-drifted trails for ten days, ran low on food, and at one point were reduced to eating one of their pack horses. A ranger at a Forest Service station told us that the Lee Creek trail approximated a segment of their trek. We decided to hike it, to get some idea of what the explorers went through. Of course, it was summer, and we had plenty of food, and a way out, so it would be a pretty faint idea.

The first half mile was easy. Sage and Sky ran back and forth, jumping into ponds and streams, happy as two bird dogs could be, especially when Sky flushed a big ruffed grouse. Then the trail grew as steep as a staircase—without the stairs. Up and up into the twilight cast by spruce and lodgepole pine, and so many hairpin switchbacks that it took fifteen minutes to gain a hundred feet of altitude. Sage's limberness astonished us, although I had to carry her over deadfalls obstructing the trail. At six thousand feet we rested, acknowledged that we were no Lewis and Clark and Sage was no Seaman, and headed back down.

After soothing sore muscles in the hot springs, we cooked up mac and cheese for dinner, built a smoky campfire, and hung out with our neighbor Steve and his ten-year-old daughter, Emily, a tall, bright girl. Steve, a well-built man with bristly gray hair, was divorced. He'd picked up a wreck of a small, boxy aluminum trailer for nothing, got it ready for the road, and was taking a trip with Emily "to get to know her better."

He worked for a truck dealership in Missoula and knew all about the Thing. It had been in the news for weeks. It was a kind of local celebrity, and its arrested progress inspired Steve to utter a few remarks about liberals and environmentalists in a tone that declared he wasn't either.

Emily stopped him in midsentence and asked, "Wait a minute, Dad. What do you mean when you say *liberal*?"

Taken aback, he hesitated for a beat. "A conservative thinks that people should be responsible for themselves and can handle their problems without help from the government. A liberal is someone who believes that people should help other people and is all for the environment and nature."

Emily piped up. "Then I guess I'm a liberal."

She grinned, and so did her father. He was getting to know her better.

We batted politics around and talked about the economy, Steve saying that he'd worked for another truck dealership until 2010, when, after years of downsizing, pay cuts, and cuts in benefits, he got laid off.

"I was out of work for nine and half months. Then I got a job in the same business. I hate it. The guy I work for"—grimacing—"yells all the time. But the pay's good. Y'know one thing I did learn was that I could live on a lot less than I thought when I was drawing unemployment."

I resisted reminding him that unemployment compensation was a liberal invention. But I did not resist a gentle dig when, after I complained that the campground's uncured pine firewood produced too much smoke, he gave us an armload from his stack of seasoned hardwood.

I thanked him. "That's neighborly of you, Steve. Keep that up, and next thing you know you'll be a liberal."

He laughed. "I'll consider myself an open-minded conservative."

We woke up to an unusual sensation: cold. Burrowed into our sleeping bags, we watched our breath plume. I jumped out, dressed in about two seconds, put coffee on, then went outside to check on the dogs. They lay huddled together for warmth, and I had to crack the ice crusting their water dishes. After weeks of broil and bake, I fairly wallowed in the frigid air.

Today was our day to find Protesters of the Thing. They turned out to be camped miles down a rugged dirt road, prompting Leslie to ask, "If you hold a protest in a forest and no one sees it, is it still a protest?"

At last we came upon a line of dust-filmed cars and pickups, heeling over on the right side of the road, a few so plastered with stickers and decals advertising almost every environmental issue that you could hardly tell what color they were. A hand-lettered sign over a latrine read SHITTER, and a bedsheet hung from poles declared NO TAR SANDS. We were there! A wan young woman and a young man whose beard and hair were innocent of a barber's touch directed us to the Welcome Tent, a lean-to beneath which sat two more beards, one black, one gray. Glued sticks hung from a tree branch overhead to form the letters *RRR*. The graybeard told me that it stood for Round River Rendezvous, an annual gathering of mountain-man trappers in the 1840s. That puzzled me a little.

This was an Earth First! protest, right? Not an encampment of mountain-man reenactors?

"Nick will explain. He's our media relations guy."

Graybeard picked up a radio and summoned Nick Stocks, a twenty-seven-year-old whose facial hair was confined to sandy stubble. I asked Leslie's question: if this was a protest, what was the point of holding it in the middle of nowhere? Or was I under a misimpression?

I was, Nick answered. This was the annual rendezvous of Northern Rockies Rising Tide, an affiliate of Earth First!

"Every year there's a rendezvous in a different part of the country. Different local communities spend some time bidding where the next year's rendezvous is going to be, and then the community decides where. We bid to come here to draw attention to the shipments, the big rigs, the Alberta tar sands, issues that pertain to Montana."

That seemed to evade the question, so I rephrased it: "How are you going to call attention to these issues way out in these woods?"

"Well, the rendezvous is not a protest in itself. It's a gathering of the Earth First! community. There are a lot of traditional features to a rendezvous . . . There's generally an act of civil disobedience of some kind where we call attention to a local issue."

That was to happen on July 12, but he didn't know what form the civil disobedience would take. Earth First! being an ultrademocratic organization—some would say anarchistic—every action is debated, decisions arrived at by consensus of everyone involved. In this case, that would be about 150 people.

"But we can safely say that there will be a protest at the end of the rendezvous."

I saw, or rather heard, why Nick had been chosen as a media spokesman. He was a fast, forceful talker, firing words on semiautomatic with hardly a breath or pause between them. He claimed—and news reports appeared to bear him out—that Northern Rockies Rising Tide's opposition to the shipments had grassroots support from groups as diverse as the Nez Perce and Salish Indian tribes, the Missoula City Council, and people who didn't share its lefty politics, like biker clubs and Tea Party partisans, even, he said, "gun-totin' rural folks."

"Because they don't want to see mining equipment that's built out of country going to another country," he explained. "People who live up and down U.S. 12 need to use the road for access to hospitals, ambulance service. That's been a big issue for these folks because these loads are so big and no one can get by them unless they pull over. They do a rolling blockade."

Some of the loads, he went on, had violated an Idaho law prohibiting blocking a highway for more than fifteen minutes at a time. The oil and transportation companies had chosen the highway for a reason: the mega-loads cannot pass under the bridges and overpasses on interstates. There are none on U.S. 12.

When I brought up security guard Glenn's objection—burning gallons and gallons of gas to protest extracting the oil that produced the gas—Nick sighed. He'd heard it before.

"The people we're up against—ExxonMobil makes more money than most small countries—wield huge, huge influence. To oppose them, we need to transport people, but we don't have the resources to transport everybody. We have to use the tools of this world to move toward the world we want to see. To me, that argument is one of saying, Well, if you're true to your own beliefs, you'd isolate yourselves from everybody and not have anything to say to anybody and just stay in your own woods."

We went off on a tour of the encampment, and it had all the organizational elements that Earth First!'s antipathy to organization—the top-down kind, anyway—seemed to deny: a sanitary kitchen and a staff capable of feeding everyone; a medical staff trained as wilderness first responders (an herbalist included); roped-off areas for "morning circle," as the daily assembly was called, and for workshops on subjects from knot-tying to legal issues to, Nick said, "metaconversations about the future of the kind of world we want to live in." Backpackers' tents and lean-tos made of tarps were pitched on hillsides; banners splashed with slogans and artwork were draped from the trees. One young woman was washing her feet in Fish Creek; full bathing was forbidden because it would pollute the stream. All in all, the rendezvous had the combined flavors of a scout jamboree and a kind of Woodstock without the music; and though most of the campers were under thirty, a handful looked like they'd been at Woodstock.

"It begs the question if it was glued together in the first place," Nick remarked when I asked if he thought the country was becoming unglued. He then went into a long commentary on the alliance of big government and multinational corporations that ignored the needs and wishes of local communities. If the nation's seams were becoming frayed, that was why.

"We look toward more community-based decision making, we look toward consensus, we look toward local engagement as the map to the future we'd like to follow. In a lot of ways, we reflect what the conservative right says: Y'know what? Maybe we need less federal government. Maybe we need more decision-making power on the local level as opposed to on a federal level."

A Jeffersonian vision, if you will—yeoman citizens in voluntary association, each with a voice as strong as a CEO or a U.S. senator or a corporate lobbyist. Easier said than done.

28.

IMAGINE SKI-CHALET ROOFS SEVEN THOUSAND FEET HIGH—THAT'S what it looked like on both sides of the highway that ran through the Selway-Bitterroot Wilderness. Alongside, the Lochsa River was a constant boil of rapids and standing waves, never a yard of calm, just white water churning like surf in a hurricane. Looking at it, Leslie said, had the same hypnotic effect as watching the Yule Log endlessly burning on TV. We pulled over and walked out onto a footbridge to take pictures of the torrent. Another traveler was there, and when I said I wouldn't go down that river unless a doctor told me I had only two weeks to live, he said that he'd just rafted it with a guide. "That took guts," I said, thinking, *You and your guide are out of your minds.*

The Selway joined the Lochsa, and together they tumbled into the Clearwater, and the highway turned sharply to follow that river northwestward. We stopped for the night in Orofino, an old gold-mining town. The campground was sandwiched between the river and a railroad siding crammed with idle logging cars. A sign on each read: WARNING— CAR MAY TIP OVER. We kept our distance. Orofino stood at a ford frequented by the Nez Perce hundreds of years ago, the spot marked by rust-colored sculptures of an Indian woman on foot and a warrior on horseback. Lewis and Clark had stopped there to scout for timber suitable to make dugout canoes. They certainly would not have recognized the place today. Porsche owners were holding a rally, and new Boxsters and restored 911s filled the parking lot of a riverside Best Western.

In the track of the Corps of Discovery, we passed through Lewiston and into Washington the next day and made a discovery of our own. Eastern Washington looks like western Nebraska—plateaus as treeless as the moon out to the horizon, with only patches of camas to relieve the monotony. A hundred and fifty miles of this brought us to the Columbia, nearly a mile wide, bounded by high, stark cliffs that could make you think you were in the Middle East. We dipped into Oregon, crossed a bridge back into Washington, and headed west, the tan-and-brown cliffs tiered like layer cakes assembled by a novice baker.

Suddenly, they appeared atop the ridgelines on both sides of the river: white steel poles taller than twenty-five-story buildings, turbine nacelles the size of school buses, blades from tip to tip as long as a 747's wingspan, some still, some twirling slowly. The wind towers went on for five miles, fifteen, twenty, fracturing the skyline, and transmission towers marched into the distance like giant robots. I'd seen wind farms in New Mexico and Texas, but these were wind ranches, wind *countries*.

"Jesus H. Christ!" I snarled. "Does it ever stop?"

"What's the matter?" Leslie said. She recognized the reemergence of Phil-the-Crank. But I couldn't, or wouldn't, keep him in the box.

"I hate wind farms. I loathe them. They totally fuck up a landscape. They make me love oil and coal companies."

"Phil, we use energy at home, and we're using a lot in this truck," she said reasonably. "Wind doesn't pollute like other energies do. And sorry, but this landscape isn't all that attractive anyway."

"I beg to differ."

"Would you rather see some coal-fired plant blowing crap into the air?"

"A generating plant takes up a few acres, not a zillion square miles."

"So you'd rather see that?"

I felt liberated from the bonds of environmental correctness as I answered, "Yes. Damn right I would."

She replied that a desk was waiting for me in a coal company's PR agency. A really nasty coal company that blasts the tops off mountains and poisons streams and runs up safety violations.

Leslie phoned her mother, Molly Ware, from our campsite in a state park on the Columbia, and mentioned that I was in high agita about the wind towers. Molly suggested that I talk to locals to find out what they thought, and so I did. While Leslie stayed behind to wrangle dogs and edit a story on wrinkle creams, I drove a few miles north into Goldendale, the Klickitat County seat. Ever since we'd arrived in the county, Leslie had said "Klickitat" at every opportunity; it rattled off the tongue, though the consonants sometimes collided and it came out "klickityclack."

Like a lot of the counties on the Great Plains, Klickitat was in a state of chronic recession, which gave its twenty thousand inhabitants this one consolation: they'd barely noticed the nationwide recession. Goldendale occupies a few square miles on a rolling plateau of cattle pastures and wheat and alfalfa fields. To the southwest, Mount Hood, symmetrical as a pyramid, rises in Oregon; northwest, Mount Adams lords it over the Cascade Range. It was mid-July, and both were white two-thirds of the way down.

I drove around town for a while. Although fine Victorian houses graced the streets and the absence of farm-size shopping malls had saved the downtown from becoming "historic," signs of dilapidation appeared almost everywhere: double-wide trailers on cement blocks, houses that hadn't felt a paint brush for a long time, junk-cluttered yards, potholed pavement. The town, and Klickitat County, had been doing fairly well up into the nineties. Agriculture was a mainstay of the economy, as it still is. Logging and a lumber mill provided jobs, and the Columbia Gorge Aluminum smelter, a few miles upriver, employed twelve hundred people. Then the county got whacked by a three-punch combination. A left hook from the environmental movement restricted logging to save the northern spotted owl, and the timber industry, already in decline, tanked. Reaganite Republicans followed up with a right cross by deregulating electrical utilities; soaring, unpredictable energy costs rocked the Columbia Gorge plant. Low world prices for aluminum threw the knockout blow. The smelter shut down in 2003, almost overnight, and most of its workers packed up to find jobs elsewhere. Goldendale's population plummeted from five thousand to three thousand. The only new residents were welfare recipients. The state government encouraged people on public assistance and food stamps to move to Klickitat County because the low cost of living saved the state money. I presumed that the down-and-outers shambling down Goldendale's sidewalks or idling on front stoops were among the refugees.

But the county had one thing that no one could take away: it had literally inherited the wind.

Mike Canon retired in Goldendale after a career with the United Nations, working on redevelopment projects in eastern Europe following the collapse of the Soviet empire. After he and his wife renovated a Victorian house, he needed something to keep himself busy and he landed a position as the county's director of economic development. It was keeping him busier than perhaps a sixty-eight-year-old man would want to be.

I dropped in at his office, in a nondescript building across the street from the handsome, art deco county courthouse. Canon had the look of an eminence, dark brows peppered with gray, a swirl of foam-white hair. A few years ago, he said in a scratchy voice, Klickitat County reminded him of eastern Europe in the early nineties.

"Working for the aluminum company had been like working for General Motors or Ford. It was going to be there forever, and suddenly it wasn't there. You had people who lost their whole careers. You don't restart, you're done. That's what hit 'em. When I first moved here, I loved to go to antiques shops. Well, the antiques stores in Goldendale were selling used plates, used glasses, not necessarily that old, not anything like fine, collectible antiques. These were people selling their furniture just to get through the next year."

"More like pawn shops?"

"That would be it. People were downhearted. And that's what's turning around. Now there's a whole sense of hope."

Hope generated by the wind, blowing from the west down the Columbia River corridor, from the north, south, and east across the unbroken plateaus. In 2009, a San Diego company, the Canon Power Group (no connection to Mike Canon), broke ground for a wind farm that will be the largest in Washington when it's finished. One hundred and seventy-six towers, representing a billion-dollar investment, will cover ninety square miles and generate enough power to light up a million homes.

Nature's endowment of wind might have been returned to sender if not for a man-made gift: transmission lines. Installing transmission lines is astronomically expensive, but here they were already in place, built years ago by the Bonneville Power Administration, which operates hydroelectric dams on the river. Put simply, all that Canon Power had to do was tap into the grid and export electricity to its customers in southern California.

The project, called Windy Point/Windy Flats, was about two-thirds completed and already paying the county two million dollars a year in property taxes. The money was going to repaving roads and streets, improving schools and hospitals and firefighting districts. An isolated hamlet of one hundred souls, Bickleton, had bought an ambulance with the revenues, its first. The farmers and ranchers who leased their land to the power company felt like they'd found oil. In addition to lease fees, they shared in the profits. "Turn and earn" was how they put it, and what they earned was up to eighteen thousand dollars per year per tower.

"That's very good for a dryland wheat farmer," Canon said. "That's big time."

I thought that would be big time for just about anybody—a dryland writer, for example.

There had been objections about the aesthetics, the ruination of the skyline, but most people welcomed the wind farm. "They're happy to see it," said Canon. "It makes money for them."

Brandy Meyers was happy. I met her at a restaurant, Marie's Sod Busters, where she dined on coffee and a protein drink. "Lost thirty pounds, so far," she said.

Meyers was a Goldendale native who'd left and returned. She graduated from college in 2000 with an accounting degree and worked for an engineering firm in Kennewick that sent her all over the country. Yet she always felt a tug, pulling her back to the land her great-great-grandparents homesteaded in the nineteenth century.

"No place like Goldendale, where the mountains meet the river," she said. "But there were no opportunities, no reason to come home."

Until the Windy Flats project gave her a reason.

"I said, all right, I'm ready to go back."

She was hired as the wind farm's administrative manager, her husband worked on the construction of the towers, and some of them rose on the leased pastures of her parents' wheat and cattle ranch. The whole family reaped the harvest of wind.

"We round up cattle right under the towers," she said, laughing at the picture. "The key is, there's hope."

I strolled around the business district for a while. It wasn't bustling, but it was a lot more alive than the haunted downtowns on the Great Plains. A few coffee shops, four bar and grills, and the offices of the *Goldendale Sentinel*, a weekly. A newspaper! I had a soft spot in my ink-stained heart for print journalism, so I popped into the *Sentinel*, which had a staff of four: Lou Marzeles, the editor and publisher; a general manager, Karen Henslee, and two reporters. The most recent edition was in a hallway rack—fourteen pages brimming with local news, ads, and classifieds. STATE, CITY TAKE ON MORE STREET PROJECTS . . . HONOR ROLL OUT FOR GOLDENDALE HIGH SCHOOL . . . BASKETBALL YOUTH LEAGUE STARTS MONDAY . . . But it wasn't quaint. A line above the masthead read: THE SENTINEL IS ON FACEBOOK AND TWITTER.

Marzeles made some time for me. My memories of newspaper executives were of the *Chicago Tribune*'s editor Clayton Kirkpatrick and its publisher Stanton Cook, WASPs supreme in sober suits and ties. Marzeles, with his shock of rebellious gray hair and open-neck shirt, looked like a Beat poet. He had, however, played in journalism's big leagues in New York and as a reporter and assistant features editor at the *Washington Times* in Washington, D.C. Two years ago, he moved to Goldendale, a long way, in more than mileage, from where he'd been. Was it a culture shock?

"It's the smallest town I've lived in in a long, long time. I grew up in New Hampshire. It's definitely a unique place. I'll tell you the impact it had on me. Shortly after moving here, April of 2009, within six weeks my wife passed away. We'd come here because her family was from Yakima, she was born and grew up in this area, so we came here because she had this strong sense that she had to get back to her family. We had no idea anything was seriously wrong with her till we got here, and she was found to have very advanced liver cancer. She was gone very quickly."

Marzeles found himself alone in a strange place. No family, no friends, no one he knew. He chose to stay, captivated by the beauty of the mountains and the Columbia, and by the warmth of the townspeople. They made him feel at home.

"Living in big cities, you think that a sense of community is a kind of fable," he said. "You see the old *Andy Griffith Show*, and you think, yeah, that's a fantasy. But it does exist."

In 2010, the *Sentinel*, published every week since its founding in 1879, went up for sale, and Marzeles bought it with a partner. Given the state of print journalism, you could say that was foolish, rather like the famed tale told in business schools about the man who starts a buggy-whip factory the year that the first Model T's rolled off the line. On the other hand, small, local papers were flourishing, while the grand flagships (like the *Chicago Tribune*) were foundering. And Marzeles's instincts told him Goldendale was where he should be. He'd caught the contagion of optimism, of expectation spread by those white blades, turning in the wind.

"I always get the feeling that something is about to break through in a significant way around here. I can't put my finger on it, but I want to be a part of it."

———

On July 11, a day late, we celebrated Sage's thirteenth birthday, something of a bittersweet occasion. We knew she wouldn't be with us much longer; she'd already outlasted the average setter by a year. We gave her an extra helping of canned food and two extra milkbones. Then I took her for a walk.

"That little pest isn't coming with us?" she asked.

"Nope. Just you and me."

"Like the old days."

"Right."

We trooped across the park to the banks of the Columbia, where I sat her down for a lecture.

"Now listen. I'm taking you off lead. Do not jump into that river. That's the Columbia. It will take you right down to the Pacific Ocean. I repeat, *do not* jump in."

"Okay."

"Promise?"

"Promise."

She ran off, with a semblance of her old, graceful lope. True to her vow, she stayed ashore, ranging through corridors of cottonwoods and birch, sniffing the rushes along a tranquil backwater. A great blue heron lofted from the branch of a dead tree leaning over the pond. Sage stood momentarily still, content to watch it fly.

———

The man and his girlfriend stood outside the Simcoe Café & Desert Room, smoking cigarettes. Like all smokers in these times, they had a furtive air, as if they were junkies shooting up in a back alley. As we approached the door, the man looked at me in surprise.

"Hey! You've got a brother in town!"

"I don't have a brother anywhere."

"Yeah. Dave Johnson at the coffee shop. Your brother. You look just like him!"

"Sorry. A sister is all I've got."

We went inside and sat at a table in the crowded little bar and ordered dinner. Leslie confined herself to a club sandwich. Sticking to my no-fruits-and-vegetables vow, I selected hot turkey with gravy on white bread and mashed potatoes.

The nicotine addicts returned and sat down with their friends. The man pointed at me.

"He's got to be Dave's brother. Doesn't he look just like Dave at the coffee shop?"

The drink in front of him wasn't his first of the night. A dozen or more pairs of eyes fixed on me, and everyone agreed that yes, I bore a striking resemblance to coffee-shop Dave. A fantasy flitted through my brain. My father had spent much of his working life on the road, so maybe . . . But no . . . Feeling uncomfortable as the object of the patrons' stares, I motioned at a row of Plexiglas cylinders suspended over the bar that could be spun like lottery bins. They were filled with dollar bills, enough to tempt a virtuous soul to robbery.

"What are those?"

"Those bills used to paper the walls before the smoking ban," answered a customer at the bar, a tall man with a bandito mustache. "Three layers thick, grimy with smoke. So the owner washed them in a washing machine and then iron dried 'em, each and every one, and put 'em in there."

"Guilty of money laundering," Leslie said.

Mustache laughed. "Yeah. One guy had accidentally pinned a hundred-dollar bill to the wall. Too drunk to see the difference. So after the washing, he came in to reclaim it, and he got it back."

On the way out after dinner, we passed the establishment's Desert Room, where tournament poker games were held every Wednesday and Sunday nights. A sign listed the prices for chips, ranging from ten to a thousand dollars.

A hundred pinned to a wall, by mistake. Thousand-dollar chips. Maybe things in Goldendale weren't so bad, after all.

"All right," I said to Leslie, "I'm trying to learn to love wind farms."

"How's that coming along?"

"I might be able to tolerate them, but I'll never love them."

We were in the *Sentinel*'s office the next day. In a role-reversal, Marzeles had asked to interview us about our trip for a story in the next week's edition. While we waited for him, we chatted with Karen Henslee, a crisp, businesslike strawberry blonde. Among other things, she handled the classifieds, and she'd observed that there were considerably more help-wanted ads since the wind farm began to revive the county's fortunes.

But her optimism was more tempered than others'. She wasn't sure how many permanent jobs would be created; the wind farm's scale troubled her, the towers' lights going on forever at night; and, she said, she and a lot of people were "holding their breath" waiting to see if the power company was going "to come in and utilize our wind and make our skyline less attractive and then run on down the road without leaving something here for us."

"They've talked about removing the [hydroelectric] dams from the river. We've got to figure out some way to get our power, unless we're going to go back to dirt floors and candles and lamps."

"Or whale oil," I said.

"Right. It's really difficult to run your computer on that."

She felt protective of her little town, liked "the wilderness look to it," and didn't want to see that spoiled.

"My husband was born and raised here; his grandfather was the livery stable blacksmith. So his family has been here forever. And my great-grandfather built the Loops Road in 1913. We have generations and generations, and I like that. I love driving through the gorge. It's the most amazing view. Every time I drive down it, I'm overwhelmed by it. I like that I know a lot of people in town . . . You stop and talk . . . One thing that happens in small towns that you probably wouldn't get in a big town is that when personal disaster happens, you're going to have so much more community that gathers around. It's an incredible thing. I know personally because I lost my youngest daughter five years ago, and it was different here than I can imagine it would be in a big city where you've got people who'll come around and talk to you for a couple of weeks and then everybody's life goes back to normal, and there you are. Here you've got people who will invest time, a community who knows who you are."

And, she said, echoing many others we'd spoken to, those bonds of family and community and neighbors helping neighbors were the bonds that held the country together. The laws and regulations passed in Congress or by the state legislature affected the citizens of Klickitat County, of course they did, but to them Washington, D.C., and Olympia, Washington, seemed to be in foreign countries.

"How about Seattle?"

"*Especially* Seattle."

She said that somebody had mentioned that eastern Washington and Oregon should be one state and the western halves another because the politics were so different.

"It was kind of a joke at first, but I've heard more and more people talking about it. I don't think you could do it, but it would be interesting."

Marzeles stepped in to tell us that he was ready. "The Cascade Curtain. Washington keeps its liberals west of the Cascades," he said. "Kind of a liberal reservation. A few renegades escape now and then. They're usually caught and sent back."

29.

IN SPITE OF MY NEWFOUND TOLERATION OF WIND FARMS, I WAS delighted to see the towers in the rearview mirror as we proceeded west on State Route 14 into the Columbia River Gorge. Our destination, two hundred miles away, was Fort Clatsop, Oregon. There, on the Pacific coast, the Lewis and Clark expedition spent the winter of 1805–6 before setting off on its return to civilization.

As everyone knows, it rains almost constantly in the Pacific Northwest, so the previous day I'd scaled Fred's roof and caulked the leaky roof-rack bolts with silicone. I was confident my repairs wouldn't do the trick, but it seemed the attempt should be made. Later, we restocked Ethel's pantry with ... fruits and vegetables! As the memory of seeing me feverish and nauseous faded, Leslie's zeal to reform my diet had reestablished itself. Orchards and farms lay in green bands between the river and the bare, brown ridges near the campground. Wandering past these pesticide-free, organic Edens, we saw women garbed like eastern European peasants in long dresses, kerchiefs, and head scarves perched on ladders, picking ripe peaches. I reckoned they belonged to some sort of religious sect. Or maybe they really were eastern European peasants who favored traditional costumes. Stopping off at roadside stands, we bought peach and apricot preserves, strawberries, onions, zucchini, and various other artery-friendly foods

It's a safe bet that there aren't any romantics among the civil engineers and heavy equipment operators at the Washington Department of Transportation. The song of the open road is not their song. This is as it should be. You wouldn't want an inspector to overlook a critical crack in a bridge because he's writing lyrics in his head or daydreaming about stardom on *American Idol*. We cannot, and should not, look to them to create a name for State Route 14, an exhilarating name to give it the distinction it deserves. Sometimes a highway's numerical designation communicates the allure of the vagabond life, lends itself to rhapsody—Highway 101 or Route 66, for example. But there is no magic whatsoever in the anemic "14"; it does not beckon, it says nothing, promises nothing of the grandeur the traveler will see driving the road in its eighty-five-mile passage through the Cascades and the Columbia River Gorge. The river was below us and on our left, of such breadth that it looked like an elongated lake, frilled with white caps in a brisk west wind. Fishing boats and sailboats drew greenish wakes across the blue water, and a few windsurfers cracked over the waves. Across the river, wooded ridges climbed toward Mount Hood, as white and sharp as a shark's tooth.

Two lanes defined the road; there were many bends and small towns. Towing the trailer, Fred had a top speed of forty miles an hour. Even so, we would be out of the gorge by midday. We did not want to be out of it, not yet, so a mere hour or so after leaving Maryhill State Park, we pitched into an isolated campground three miles up a side road in the heart of the Cascade Range.

There, my skills in backing up Ethel, considerably improved, were put to a severe test. After hauling her up a gravel road not much wider than she was, I had to back her uphill into a tight little space. Leslie got out and directed me . . . *A little left . . . okay . . . no, more left . . . right now . . . too much . . . You're jackknifing!* I broke out in sweats of frustration. *Straight now . . . Straighten out!* It was looking pretty grim till I was rescued by another Airstreamer, a Californian named Hal, who stood beside the driver's side window, instructing me on each nuanced turn of the wheel. In no time at all, the trailer slipped into her slot as neatly as my laptop's power cable into its port. Months later, my sister-in-law gave me a book for a Christmas present. It was titled *How to Back Up a Trailer . . . And 101 Other Things Every REAL GUY Should Know*. Hal was a real guy. Me? Not so much.

Drinks with Real Guy Hal and his wife, Joey, brought on another bout of Airstream envy. Their model was bigger than Ethel and had a full-size refrigerator, a full-size shower, and a full-size bed. Leslie looked with longing at the shower. She hadn't used Ethel's, not once. It bothered her to bathe in a broom-closet enclosure containing a toilet, not to mention that Ethel's small water tank compelled thirty-second shipboard showers in no-hookup campsites, and that the drain clogged often. She chose campground bathrooms, and those had their drawbacks.

Excerpts from her blog, July 12:

> This morning I attempt to shower at the Maryhill state park campground, which actually charges for the privilege . . . 50 cents for 3 whole minutes . . . I trek to one bathhouse where there's ONE shower whose occupant has clearly put in five dollars' worth of quarters . . . Then trek to another bathhouse, where the regular shower stall has nowhere at all to put clothes . . . The handicapped stall has a little spot for clothes, and I take it . . . But wait. The coin machine is jammed. So I leave clothes and stuff, hop over to the other stall and occupy both for 3 minutes.

We saw Beacon Rock the next morning. Clark sighted it on October 31, 1805: "A remarkable high detached rock Stands in a bottom on the Stard. Side near the lower point of this Island on the Stard. Side about 800 feet high and 400 paces around."* ("Stard" was Lewis's abbreviation for "starboard.")

Seagulls began to appear, heralds of land to sailors and, to overland travelers, of the sea. It was near Beacon Rock that Clark observed rises and falls in the Columbia, which he correctly ascribed to tides. It was the expedition's first encounter with tidewater. He recorded it matter-of factly. There was more emotion eight days later, when the Corps of Discovery camped at Pillar Rock. He wrote in the notebook he kept to record courses and bearings, "*Ocian in view*! O! the joy," and then in his journal, "Great joy in camp we are in *view* of the *Ocian*, this great Pacific Ocian which we have been so anxious to See."

Actually, Clark and the men had mistaken the lower Columbia estuary

---

* The explorers first called it Beaten Rock and later changed it to Beacon Rock. Its exact altitude is 848 feet.

for the "ocian"; they had another twenty miles to go before reaching their goal. It took them a lot longer than it did us. Half an hour past Pillar Rock, we entered Astoria, a working seaport and the oldest continuously inhabited city west of the Mississippi, founded in 1811 as a trading post by John Jacob Astor's American Fur Company. (Santa Fe is older [1609], but its habitation was interrupted for about twenty years, its Spanish settlers driven out by a revolt of the Pueblo Indians.)

Astoria's maritime atmosphere was welcome, all the more so because it was authentic, as opposed to the contrived nautical ambience of tourist towns, where there is always at least one tavern called the Ye Olde Something-or-Other and *shop* is spelled *shoppe*. We crossed a bridge and hooked southward on U.S. 101, found that a state park campground was full, and fetched up back in "K" land—a Kampground of America trailer park. Predictably, it rained, off and on, for the whole two days and nights we were there. Just as predictably, my repairs to the roof rack proved only partially effective, so whenever there was a letup, I dragged the dog bed outside in attempts to dry it off, and toweled Sage and Sky, their matted fur a reproach.

On a wet, chilly, windy morning, we paid a visit to Lewis and Clark National Historic Park, where a replica of Fort Clatsop stood under sitkas more than two hundred feet high. An announcement came over the PA system that two spaces were open on a kayak tour that was leaving immediately. We answered the call, piled into a van with other adventurers, and drove to the launch point, a mile away on the Lewis and Clark River. A bald eagle perched in a tree. Two rangers led us in a few loosening-up exercises, then we eased ourselves into two-man kayaks and proceeded downstream, stopping frequently to listen to ranger Shawna's lectures on the Lewis and Clark expedition and local ecology. We learned how to tell the difference between sedges, reeds, and grasses. "Sedges have edges," she instructed. "Reeds are round, and grasses are hollow." Also how to distinguish a fir tree from a spruce: the tips of spruce branches point upward. I tried to think of ways to put this knowledge to use in my future life. Shawna was fascinated by Lewis and Clark's encounters with grizzly bears and told a few hair-raising tales, like the one about Lewis being charged by a bear after he shot a buffalo. With no time to reload his flintlock, Lewis ran into a stream, turned to face the charge, and braced his pike in the stream bottom, hoping the grizzly would impale itself before it swatted his head off his shoulders. Apparently impressed by this demonstration of resolve, the bear spun on its heels and fled.

At the end of our voyage, two hours later, it began to rain in earnest, and we retreated into Fort Clatsop, which Leslie insisted on calling Fort Ketchup. There, by candlelight in long cabins, the two captains caught up on their journals and classified their discoveries, more than three hundred species of plants and animals previously unknown to science. The Lewis's woodpecker, the Clark's nutcracker.

We put up our hoods and sloshed our way to a musket demonstration put on by a six-foot-five-inch guy wearing a ponytail and buckskins. In the twenty-first century, he was an eighth-grade teacher. He pointed out that this was a very Lewis and Clark kind of day. It rained all but twelve of the 106 days the expedition was camped at Fort Clatsop. The sun shone for only six.

A few years ago, a friend of mine taught me how to load and fire a flintlock rifle, a complicated business requiring a good deal of practice and, if you're being charged by a grizzly, an impervious nervous system. That the giant teacher kept his powder dry in such weather was itself a marvel. He shoved a ramrod down the barrel to make sure it was empty, poured in a dram of powder from his flask, rammed in a paper wad in place of bullet, cocked the hammer with its piece of flint, put a few more grains of powder into the pan, and pulled the trigger. The spark from the flint ignited the powder in the pan (whence "flash in the pan"), the flame shot through the touchhole in the barrel, and the gun went off with a most satisfying bang and puff of smoke.

I then learned that my own eighth-grade teacher (Sister Joan Clare, the reader may recall) had taught me an incorrect pronunciation of Sacagawea. It wasn't *Sacka-jah-WEE-ya* but *Sah-KA-ga-waya*. This was more knowledge I hoped to put to future use, perhaps at a cocktail party when conversation flagged.

Next morning, we crossed the Columbia's mouth back into Washington and stopped off at Cape Disappointment, the westernmost point reached by the Corps of Discovery. Clark marked his arrival by carving the inscription WM. CLARK. BY LAND. NOV. 19, 1805 into a pine tree. It had taken him and Lewis eighteen months and five days to get to the western ocean.

It took us fifty-six days. After I retrieved the plastic bottle I'd filled in Key West, we hiked a mile through forests swathed in fog and mist, and at last the ocean was in view. Across a hundred yards of sand, iron-gray breakers curled and crashed, making one incessant roar. As we picked our way through jumbles of driftwood, a beachcomber pointed out a baby seal, its white fur barely visible in the rocks of a jetty. To make sure Sage and Sky did not molest it, Leslie led them well away, then released them to gambol in the surf. I waded into the sheet of a receding wave, dipped the bottle, and shook it, mingling the Pacific waters with the waters of the Atlantic and the Gulf of Mexico.

I'd finished reading Bernard DeVoto's edited version of the explorers' *Journals*. From Lewis's grave on the Natchez Trace to the continent's western shores, I'd traveled with him and Clark, sharing vicariously in their hardships, their disappointments, their triumphs, their astonishment at a West whose breadth and beauty exceeded anything they could have imagined. In the places that had changed little since their day—the Missouri headwaters, the Bitterroots—they'd seemed almost living presences. I felt that I'd come to know them. I was going to miss them.

It was time to head north for the Canadian border.

SIGNS AND WONDERS

Some signs . . .

Outside Tok, Alaska: IGNORE THIS SIGN.

A bumper sticker in Maryhill, Washington: I'M OUT OF ESTROGEN AND I HAVE A GUN.

Another sign in Tok: WELCOME TO ALASKA. THE LAST FOREIGN COUNTRY FRIENDLY TO AMERICA.

Seen in Cannonville, Utah, printed on the back of an Italian tourist's T-shirt: IL MONDO È UN LIBRO, E CHE NO VIAGGIA NE LEGGE SOLO UNA PAGINA. (The world is a book. And who does not travel reads not even one page.)

A bumper sticker in Friday Harbor, Washington: DON'T BELIEVE WHAT YOU THINK.

Two billboards somewhere on U.S. Route 2: ADULT SUPERSTORE. DVDS. TOYS. LINGERIE. Ten yards from the entrance: JESUS IS WATCHING.

A bumper sticker in Tuscaloosa, Alabama: CAUTION. DRIVER UNDER THE INFLUENCE OF THE HOLY SPIRIT.

And a couple of wonders . . .

Salem Sue, the World's Largest Holstein Cow, stands on something even more unusual in North Dakota: a hill. Sue, made of reinforced fiberglass, was born in 1974 at a cost of forty thousand dollars. She is thirty-eight feet high, fifty feet long, and weighs six tons. The legend: In 1883, an early settler of New Salem, North Dakota, was plowing his field when two Sioux stopped by to see what he was up to. The older Sioux looked at a chunk of broken sod, dirt side on top, and turned it over so the grass side was on top. "Wrong side up," the younger Indian explained to the bewildered farmer. After thinking about it, the farmer realized that the prairie was better for grazing than plowing, and that was the beginning of New Salem's dairy industry.

The World's Largest Ball of Twine, Cawker City, Kansas. You have to make your own fun out on the central Great Plains. Back in 1953, Frank Stoeber, like many farmers, was a string saver— literally. He rolled spare pieces of sisal twine into a ball in his barn. But as time passed, instead of reusing the twine, Frank kept on rolling until, in 1961, he had wrapped 1.6 million feet into a sphere eleven feet in diameter. He turned it over to the town. Cawker City, to retain its title as holder of the World's Largest Ball of Twine (there are rivals), has continued the tradition with an annual Twine-A-Thon, in which anyone can wrap more scrap twine onto the ball. Spools and wrapping apparatus are provided. String and yarn are prohibited. Today, the ball occupies an honored place under a brick and steel gazebo. Forty feet in circumference, with a recorded length of 7.8 million feet of sisal twine, it weighs nine tons.

PART FOUR

Northern Lights

At the Arctic Ocean.

30.

THE PACIFIC NORTHWEST IS TO COFFEE WHAT KENTUCKY AND Tennessee are to bourbon. Every town and hamlet has at least one espresso shack; some have two or three on a block, serving up lattes, macchiato, or straight stuff brewed from every bean grown on Earth. Why? Did people need stimulants to stay awake, or just to cheer up under the perpetual gunmetal skies?

"Let's ask," Leslie said when, near Cape Disappointment, we stopped for lunch at a concession stand advertising wood-fired pizza and a brand of coffee called Stumptown.

It was run by a fiftyish white guy, Jim, and his much younger Vietnamese wife, Chee. Jim, who'd been a financial adviser in a previous incarnation, had met Chee, slender as a wand, her straight black hair falling to her waist, in Saigon a few years earlier, when he was vacationing in Vietnam. (Though I'd made two trips to Vietnam since the end of the war, it was still hard for me to imagine an American going there for fun.) She was preparing to enter a convent when Jim convinced her that marrying him was her true vocation.

They were proud of their pizza, made from a fine-grained imported flour, Ultimo Caputo (he asked if I was related; I wasn't), and with fresh tomatoes, herbs, and spices. They baked their own bread, a kind of focaccia, for their sandwiches. Leslie ordered a Mediterranean, with chicken, sun-dried tomatoes, olives, and other delicacies that were way too healthful. I opted for the meatball sub and asked for a cup of the Stumptown coffee. Way better than Starbucks, Jim boasted, and I took a sip and gave him an A for truth in advertising.

"A couple of young guys started it in Portland. Bought beans from all over, and don't overroast them like Starbucks. It's shipped to me overnight every day, and then we run it through a French press."

But why was coffee such a big deal in the Northwest?

Jim shrugged. "Starbucks got started in Seattle, that's all I know," he said. "There's been a backlash against the chains, back to small-scale coffee shops."

And because there are just so many things you can do with a cup of coffee, some espresso stands had resorted to gimmicks to get a leg up on the competition. "They got pretty edgy, bikini espresso, the baristas wear skimpy bikinis. A few of 'em got so edgy they were shut down." He didn't elaborate, leaving me to picture topless baristas, nude baristas, pole-dancing baristas in spike heels.

———

By late afternoon we were in Tacoma and looking for a campground with a vacancy, which was proving difficult. An all-day, all-night indie rock concert was being held in a Tacoma suburb and had drawn thousands. Finally, the map revealed a state park called Dash Point. It looked promising because it was hard to get to.

So hard that it confused the usually infallible Magic Droid. Her directions gave me whiplash. "In one hundred yards, turn right," she said in her Sister Joan Clare voice. "In half a mile, turn left on . . ." And more turns; Christ, she sounded like a drill sergeant with all her left-right-lefts. Then, in the heart of the Tacoma port district, I missed one, which required me to make a U-turn. In the best of circumstances, that's a tricky maneuver when towing a trailer, and these were not the best of circumstances, the street walled on one side with warehouses and no intersections on the other. A tiny hot-pink shack appeared in the middle of a cramped parking lot, hemmed in by buildings and in back by a tall fence. A picture of a scantily clad woman with enhanced breasts beckoned from a sign. DRIVE-THRU ESPRESSO. BIKINI BARISTAS. One of those edgy places. It was closed, which proved fortunate. I pulled in, intending to drive around the shack until I saw that the space between it and the fence was barely wide enough to accommodate a Mini Cooper. A glance in the sideview mirror showed me that Ethel had already hit a hanging plant, which Leslie unhooked and set on the ground. If I went a foot farther, Ethel's skin would be pierced by a low-hanging eave, and then she would topple the bikini baristas' place of employment.

Leslie waded into traffic on the main road, put up her hands, and imitated a traffic cop. I began to sweat from terror that I'd botch it and create a traffic jam of irate motorists flipping middle fingers and threatening bodily harm. Desperation is the mother of competence; I backed the trailer into the street without a kink, Leslie replaced the hanging plant, and we headed for the missed intersection.

MD was more confused than ever, but despite our chorus of what-the-hells, we followed her instructions, lefting and righting into . . . a cul-de-sac in front of a suburban house. Resorting to traditional land navigation, I looked at a map and found a way to Dash Point State Park. CAMPGROUND FULL, read a sign pasted to the entrance booth.

And that was why, for the second time on the trip, we stayed at a motel.

———

In a steady drizzle, fog, and bumper-kissing traffic, we inched up I-5 through Seattle. If Seattleites were a little more like the folks in the South and built churches instead of coffee bars, they would have been worshipping, and the freeway would have looked as a freeway should on a Sunday morning.

On a trip like ours, the two of us crammed for weeks on end in the truck's cab, it becomes almost impossible to ignore annoying quirks that would be otherwise overlooked. One of mine that bugs Leslie is what she calls "the wiper thing." When driving in rainy weather, I leave the windshield wipers off until there's a monsoon, then keep them whapping long after the sun has emerged. Also, I tend not to signal when changing lanes, and when I do I forget to turn the blinkers off. Personally, I think these traits are signs of advancing age, but Leslie has a friend whose nongeezer husband's driving habits are identical, and she and her friend have concluded they are linked to gender. Usually, my wiper/blinker behavior elicits a mild reminder from her to turn them on or off, as circumstances require. Now, it drove her nuts. To stop herself from grabbing the wiper controls, she spelled me at Fred's helm.

Bored with our sluggish progress, I made the mistake of reading an article in the *Seattle Times* about the city's attempts to deal with its traffic problems—not as bad as L.A.'s but getting there—by extending a light rail line out to its suburbs. Voters had overwhelmingly approved the project in a referendum in 2008, but it couldn't proceed because a commercial real estate developer named Kemper Freeman opposed it. He'd filed a lawsuit and sunk $1.1 million of his personal fortune into a political campaign to stop its construction. It seemed that Freeman, a kind of minor-league Donald Trump, thought that cars made America free and prosperous and that building mass transit was a socialist plot.

It was a mistake to read this article because I had been feeling pretty good about the country, much better than before we'd begun our travels. We hadn't run into hysterics in colonial militia outfits, calling for secession or spouting nonsense like "Government keep your hands off my Medicare." We'd met the couple from West Virginia who'd given up all they owned to succor the lost and the addicted, and black and white volunteers working side by side in the rubble of Tuscaloosa, and Red Cross women who'd come hundreds of miles to aid flood victims in Montana. Almost everyone we'd encountered had been kind and generous to us, reasonable in voicing their opinions when we asked for them. We'd heard from ordinary people some perceptive ideas about what put the *unum* in the American *pluribus*. I was encouraged and felt like whistling Copland's "Fanfare for the Common Man." Now this newspaper story made me wonder if I was deluding myself. Did the thoughts and wishes and opinions of the common man and woman count any longer, assuming they ever had? Here was a project that had won broad public approval and could do nothing but benefit the public, and it had been stymied by one plutocrat flexing his financial biceps, as if to remind us all that Democracy in America has become a process not of one man, one vote but of one million dollars, one vote.

31.

W E LIKED ANACORTES, A LIVELY TOWN WITH ENCHANTING
views of the San Juan Islands and, in the opposite direction,
of the northern Cascades. We did not like it so much that we
wanted to spend an entire week there, but Fred and Ethel delayed us.

He needed servicing in preparation for the three-thousand-mile haul
to the Arctic Ocean, but every garage in the area was booked up for days,
so we had to wait our turn. She threw another of her tantrums. In the
middle of the night, water began leaking from the toilet, and when I
flushed it the leak exploded into a fountain that flooded the compartment. I determined that a valve had cracked and, after consulting the
manual, further determined that fixing it was beyond my pay grade. We
dragged the trailer to a Camping World RV center fifteen miles away. The
service manager confirmed my diagnosis but said he would have to order
a new valve. Another wait.

Ethel was hauled back to our campground, on an Indian reservation
outside Anacortes belonging to a small coastal tribe, the Samish. The
weather—low skies, rain, fog—was perfect for a Bergman film, but we
could have been stuck in a worse place. For 270 degrees on the compass,
the views were captivating. Seagulls wheeled over Fidalgo Bay with quar-
relsome cries, dropping crabs on the rocks to crack the shells and get at
the meat; great blue herons patiently stalked tidal flats; harbor seals poked
their whiskered, doglike faces out of the water. When the sun raised the
curtain of morning fog, the San Juans were unveiled little by little,

conveying an impression that they were being created as you beheld them. Inland, in the rare moments when the clouds parted and the rain stopped, Mount Baker, nearly eleven thousand feet high, revealed itself in all its whitened massiveness.

The other ninety degrees, to the southeast, illustrated the principle that no attractive scenery shall go unpunished by industry. The Shell and Tesoro oil refineries defaced a long peninsula with mazes of pipes, colonies of storage tanks, and forests of stacks pumping mephitic billows of smoke.

A Samish, Larry Thomas, told me that the land for the refineries had been leased from his tribe during World War II for one hundred years, on favorable terms—favorable, that is, to the oil companies, not the Indians.

"All the tribes around here had been pushed onto that land," he said. "We're all related." He was a well-built, handsome man with a nutmeg complexion and an easygoing manner. "Because the refineries are so close is the reason why gas around here is so expensive," he quipped. "I'll bet if you filled up right under one of those stacks, it would be five bucks a gallon."

Thomas wore a plastic tag on his T-shirt identifying him as a SHELL-FISH COMPLIANCE OFFICER. His job was to make sure that commercial and recreational fishermen did not harvest oysters, clams, and mussels from the bays. Dire warnings with skulls and crossbones were posted all over. DANGER. TOXIC SHELLFISH. SHELLFISH IN THIS AREA ARE UNSAFE TO EAT DUE TO BIOTOXINS PARALYTIC SHELLFISH POISONING (PSP) AND/OR AMNESIC SHELLFISH POISONING (ASP). DO NOT EAT CLAMS, OYSTERS, MUSSELS OR SCALLOPS.

Abnormally heavy rainfall, Thomas explained, had raised the levels of the rivers spilling into the bays, and when that happened, fecal contamination increased. In a phrase, too much shit in the water. Human shit (faulty septic systems), animal shit (livestock, pets), manufactured shit (farm fertilizers). The bays had been closed for six weeks this year, he said.

"Been clamming here ever since I can remember and since before I could remember," he said wistfully. "I'm sure I was propped up on a stump when I was one or two while my grandfather and father dug for clams."

For some reason the toxins had not affected the salmon that assembled in the bays for their epic voyages up the rivers to their spawning grounds.

"Caught so many last year that the meat was equal to what you'd get off an elk. My wife told me to stop. The freezer was full up, she said, so just stop."

He was an avid hunter as well and had bought some land in eastern Washington, near the Canadian border.

"There's elk and deer up there, and I'm going to take my dad. He's seventy-eight, and he can still shoot straight. But he can't hike the hills like he used to. So I'll just sit him on a stump and push the elk into him, like he did with me when I was a little kid. I'll be paying him back."

He asked how long we were staying. I told him I didn't know; I was waiting for a trailer part to arrive.

"Hope you can stick around for the great canoe journey," he said, and described an annual event in which coastal tribes from Oregon and Washington, British Columbia, and as far away as southern Alaska paddle hand-built cedar canoes to converge on the reservation of a host tribe for a week of dancing and feasting.

This year's host was the Swinomish, cousins to the Samish, and the canoes would be arriving in Fidalgo Bay by the weekend.

"There'll be sixty of them," Thomas said. "Some of them have been paddling thirty, forty miles a day, on the water for three weeks."

———

Keeping ourselves occupied became an occupation in itself. With Sage and Sky in tow, we rode a ferry to the San Juans one chilly morning, when a fog bank that looked as solid as the earth lay on the water and only the upper halves of the islands were visible, so that they appeared to be resting on a crust of vaporous gray. Salt air, the clanging of bell buoys—Leslie was in her element. It's said that the chemical composition of human blood is remarkably similar to seawater. Hers must be identical. She is a sailor descended from a long line of Yankee sailors.

Rafts of gulls floated in calm Friday Harbor, and the town with its ferry docks and seafood shacks and ice cream parlors reminded us of Martha's Vineyard. We were in the West, yet *the* West, as the term is commonly understood, seemed far away, and the steamy Everglades, two months and five thousand miles behind us, might as well have been in another hemisphere.

We hiked in Deception Pass State Park on Whidbey Island, the largest island in Washington and definitely the noisiest. A naval air station is located on its northern end, and the pilots practice touch-and-goes daily, shattering the stillness of the old-growth forests. The trees—Douglas fir, western hemlock, western red cedar—rose higher than radio towers. The

New England oaks and pines were mere shrubbery by comparison. We paced around one cedar and estimated its circumference to be greater than twenty feet. It had been a sapling when Columbus mistook a Caribbean Island for India; in its adolescence when Lincoln issued the Emancipation Proclamation. It will be standing five hundred years from now, when fragments of the naval air station's runways and hangars and radar dishes will be dug up by the archaeologists of the twenty-sixth century and placed in museums, as we today display medieval broadswords and armor.* I recalled an oft-quoted line from Whitman's "Song of the Open Road": "Why are there trees I never walk under but large and melodious thoughts descend upon me?" It is a good thing to walk under such giants, not only for the large and melodious thoughts that descend. It puts things in perspective for those who think the transient trends and events of the present really mean something, and I highly recommend it as an exercise in humility for the self-important and the self-involved.

We climbed to the summit of Goose Rock, from which we could see the Pacific and, directly below, Deception Pass, between Whidbey and Fidalgo Islands. An outgoing tide surged along. In places, slick water flowed seaward like sheets of jade-green ice; in others, white water sparkled, whirlpools spun. But it was hard to appreciate the beauty and hear melodious thoughts with the planes screaming overhead.

Wordsworth, I thought, *you had no idea how much the world would be too much with us.*

We were driving back to the campground when we saw them, clustered at each corner at the intersection of Commercial Avenue and Twelfth Street. On the northwest corner, about twenty people, mostly silver-haired, carrying signs that said things like THANK YOU U.S. MILITARY and LET FREEDOM RING while a Merle Haggard tune blared from speakers hung from a light post and a row of American flags snapped in the breeze alongside the Gadsden flag from the Revolutionary War, with its segmented rattlesnake and motto DON'T TREAD ON ME.

On the northeast corner: a dozen citizens flew the UN's flag, and

---

* The oldest verified western red cedar sprouted in approximately AD 550, about a century after the fall of the Roman Empire. There is another on the Olympic Peninsula believed to be two thousand years old.

their signs flashed, UNITE FOR PEACE and WAR IS NOT THE ANSWER. We couldn't tell if the smaller assemblies on the other corners were allied with the northwest corner or its opposition.

The scene looked out of place in relaxed Anacortes; it almost looked staged, as if it were background for a TV movie about polarized America. We pulled over at the patriotic corner and got out of the truck.

The demonstrations *were* staged, in a way: a ritual that had begun two weeks after 9/11 and had been going on for one hour every Sunday since, as regularly as church services. Patriots on one side, peaceniks on the other. We learned this from a stocky, seventyish fellow named Dan, a retired California cop who'd flown fighters for the U.S. Air Force between the Korean and Vietnam Wars. He and the others belonged to an organization that started in Anacortes and now had chapters all over the state of Washington.

"That's our major point right here," he said, pointing at the sign he held with another man. Emblazoned with the emblems of the four armed services and the U.S. Coast Guard, it said, WE SUPPORT OUR TROOPS.

"We've got a Web site," he added over the music and the honking of car horns signaling support of the troops supporters. "Go hyphen Patriots dot com. Look it up."

I did, though not right then. The Go hyphen Patriots was founded by a couple, Andy and Mary Stevens, its stated purpose to hold a vigil in recognition of the soldiers in Afghanistan and, later, Iraq. I quote from the Web site:

> We stand in direct opposition to the "peace at any cost, "no war for oil," "anti-Bush, anti-establishment" crowd who organize and gather at the other corners of the intersection where we stand each Sunday . . . The group we stand in direct opposition to is organized and consists mainly of members of The Left Wing Socialist Celebration church . . . temporarily augmented by other fragmented groups with their own political agenda.

The Left Wing Socialist Celebration Church? I'd never heard of it; nor could I find a Web site for it. Maybe, being socialist, its collection plate didn't gather sufficient funds to afford a Web designer. Safe to assume that it was the fringe of a fringe (though perhaps larger than the Right Wing Socialist Celebration Church). I'm fairly sure that its entire membership, nationwide, was standing on that one street corner.

Dan said that the Go hyphen Patriots were not concerned with the political reasons why the troops had been sent to Iraq and Afghanistan, only with the fact that their country had sent them.

"If you remember thirty years ago, it was nasty to be in the military."

"Yeah, I was in then myself," I said as another motorist honked his horn.

"Okay. Guys came back from Vietnam and were spit on, this and that. That's not going to happen this time, because there's groups all over the country just like we."

Dan continued, praising the clarity, the consistency, and the politically neutral message of the Go hyphen Patriots, scorning the opposition's muddled, incoherent slogans. Gesturing at the northeast corner, he heaped contempt on one woman, presumably a priestess in the Left Wing Socialist Celebration Church.

"She takes things out of context she hears on the news and then writes a sign—she's political," he scoffed. Then he motioned across Commercial, at the southwest corner. "Do you see that guy's sign? His signs make no sense whatever."

Peering through the crowd, I read the only sign visible: RUG SALE.

"So there's four different groups here?"

No, he answered. The others were considered one; they had split up merely to take possession of three-fourths of the intersection. They were antiwar, which was not to say that the Go hyphen Patriots were prowar.

"Do you want the troops to come back?" asked Leslie.

"When the job's done, yeah. We want them to come home with their heads held high. We don't want them to come back with their tails between their legs, like we did in Vietnam. That was a war that could've been won early on, but then the politicians got involved. We're back to it again now, with the change in administrations. The politicians are involved. Most everyone here is a veteran."

I noticed one, slouched against a light truck plastered with bumper and window stickers (VIETNAM VETERAN, SOCIALISM = CHAINS) and a sign on its rooftop (IMPEACH OBAMA). The man stared at me, arms crossed over his chest, a hip cocked, lips tight beneath a shaggy mustache, and even without the sticker on his truck I would have known he'd fought in Vietnam by his stance and the air of sullen truculence. I'd run into dozens like him over the years. I'd watched their hairlines retreat as their waistlines advanced (along with my own), but the attitude never changed. Call it the Lost War Warrior syndrome. I'd suffered from it myself and felt relapses whenever I remembered a certain summer day in 1967. I was home on leave and waiting to cross a street in Chicago, my marine buzz cut as obvious as a uniform. A carload of college kids veered toward me, one yelling, "Hey, burrhead!" as he flung a bag of fast food scraps in my face. I can even remember the name on the bag: Burger King.

So I was all for backing the troops and welcoming them home, though the thanks of a grateful nation might be scant comfort to those returning blind or disfigured for life, or with traumatic brain injuries, or missing an arm or a leg or both arms or both legs, not to mention that all expressions of support and gratitude would be lost on the families of the ones coming home in metal boxes.

Turning to Dan, I asked, If the Go hyphen Patriots message was apolitical, then what was with the socialism equals slavery, the impeach Obama slogans? As far as I knew, the president supported the troops and their mission.

Well, yeah, the politics slipped out now and then, replied Dan. Did I see that flag over there, the yellow one? I did—the Gadsden flag. It was his. He'd flown it ever since he'd retired, and now he saw it all over the country because the Tea Party had adopted it. And, he added, the Go hyphen Patriots supported the Tea Party.

He feared that the country could blow apart if the economy worsened, because "there's a lot of hatred of government right now. We've created a society of gimmes. Gimme. Gimme. Gimme a house. Gimme my health care. Gimme my social security. See what I'm saying? We've got so many gimmes, who's going to do the work?"

I had to wonder if Dan himself might be in the gimme class. As a retired law enforcement officer, he must be earning a generous public-employee pension; as a veteran, he was eligible for free medical care through the VA. I didn't get a chance to ask; Dan rolled on farther and farther from supporting the troops, hitting more Tea Party talking points. Illegal immigration, the housing bubble, bailouts . . . He was getting pretty worked up, and Leslie felt obliged to join the fray. Allow me to note here that she does not relish confrontation.

"You don't think that the big corporations might be a bit of a problem, maybe?" she asked. "The big banks, the mortgage companies, and . . ."

"No!" said Dan. "I blame the government. It's cut and dried. The banks said, These people can't afford a house. We're not going to lend money to people in this area. What did the government say? Oh, no. If you redline, you can't borrow overnight funds from the Fed. What is that? Extortion."

Well, I thought, *holding up powerhouses like JPMorgan Chase and Goldman Sachs as spotless lambs, docilely led by reckless politicians, requires a willing suspension of disbelief that some might be unwilling to make.* But I didn't argue. I wasn't there to argue.

The demonstrators on all four corners were folding their flags and taking down their signs. I would have liked a word with the Left Wing Socialist Celebration congregants, to find out what was the question to which war wasn't the answer. But the Sunday ritual had come to a close.

"Well, we finally found them," Leslie said as we drove on. "Angry Americans. And right here in little Anacortes. Who would've thought?"

Ethel finally underwent toilet valve replacement surgery. The procedure cost only eighty-three dollars. She recovered nicely, and we were getting ready to leave for Canada when Rose, a Samish woman, asked us to the canoe gathering and the salmon feast that would follow in the evening. Best smoked salmon anywhere, she promised, and then moved on to invite other campground visitors.

Almost all of our popular mythology about the West features the mounted tribes of the plains, deserts, and mountains. As far as I know, no one has ever written a Zane Grey novel or made a John Ford western about the Indians of the Pacific coasts. It may be that so many of their tribal names turn the tongue into rotini. Whole cities and counties have been named for the Sioux and Cheyenne; the U.S. Army named a fearsome attack helicopter for the Apache, but could there ever be a city called Nuxálk? How about Wuikinuxv County? Could the army dub an attack helicopter a Kwakwaka'wakw? The only pronounceable eponym I can think of is a species of salmon, the Chinook.

These Indians of the western shores were skilled mariners, traveling, trading, and going to war in canoes hewn from the red cedar, small ones that served the same purpose as a family car does today and seagoing freight canoes as long as seventy feet. There are legends that some voyaged as far as the Hawaiian Islands. Their way of life, their whole way of *being*, was lost to European conquest. In more recent times, the multiple contagions of heart disease, diabetes, alcoholism, and drug addiction have swept through their reservations.

The great canoe journey began when the Suquamish tribe of Washington organized a "paddle to Seattle" in 1989. Since then it's spread to other bands, as many as ninety, up and down the coast from Oregon to northern British Columbia. Like the Sacred Hoop Run we'd seen in South Dakota, it's an invented tradition, and its purpose is the same: to gain a better future by reconnecting to the past.

The first canoe crossed Fidalgo Bay at 3 p.m. Long, black, and high prowed, it was paddled by eight young men and women wearing shorts and tank tops and the straw hats traditional among the coastal tribes. An older steersman sat in the stern, using his paddle as a rudder. A Canadian ensign flew from a stern post. Larry Thomas, watching alongside me, said that the crew were Saanich, from Vancouver Island. Ashore, a Samish delegation waited to welcome them. The Samish wore identical headgear. Very practical, Thomas told me. It shielded its wearer from the sun; the cone-shaped peak allowed rain to run off, and if you doffed it and turned it upside down, you had a basket in which to carry whatever needed carrying. He offered further ethnological information when I observed that the vessel, with its upturned prow and carvings of fierce animals, resembled South Sea islander canoes.

"Yup. It's been shown that we're closer in our blood to Hawaiians and Polynesians than we are to inland tribes."

He didn't say how this genetic link had been made, or who'd made it, but it was intriguing to imagine Hawaiian pilgrims planting a colony on the western edge of America thousands of years before Jamestown.

At a command from the steersman, the canoeists circled offshore, banging the paddle handles on the gunwales to time their strokes, then made for the beach and stood their paddles on end while the steersman, holding a feathered staff called a talking stick, rose and made a speech, first in Salish—the principal language among the coastal Indians—and then in English. He announced where the vessel was from, and that it had come in peace, and requested permission to land.

A Samish woman ashore, garbed in a black cloth dress embroidered in red, raised her arms and welcomed the visitors in both languages. "My dear people, I'm so happy to see you here in our territory. Please come ashore. Eat. Drink. Dance with us. I baked brownies for you."

That drew a cheer, and drums beat and the crew thumped the thwarts with the ends of their paddles.

This ritual, Thomas explained, was known as "the protocol" and had its origins in the time before European contact. Arriving canoeists had to declare their peaceful intentions before they could be allowed to land. Not that there was any chance a war party would storm the beach; the ceremony was purely symbolic.

Far out on the bay, ten or twelve more canoes were making for Fidalgo Island, the paddle blades flashing silver as they were drawn out of the water. As they came closer, we heard the rhythmic *thump ... thump ... thump* of the handles beating against the gunwales in between the strokes. Minutes later, they were all lined up side by side and made quite a sight: the upturned paddles with their diamond-shaped blades, the stern flags, the feathered talking sticks held high, the bowsprits carved into the shapes of fish and wolves, the canoeists in bright, themed T-shirts.

Each one followed the protocol punctiliously, and their Samish hosts invited each to land, the woman in the black dress alternating with a man attired like a backyard suburbanite in sneakers and shorts with cargo pockets.

"We are glad you came through the islands," he called. "Too many of us were pushed off those islands, forced onto reservations inland, away from the things we knew and loved." *Thump, thump, thump* went the paddles. "We are here to show the government that we're still here, and we're here to stay!" Louder thumps, cheers. "They can't take our land from us anymore. They can't take our culture, our language ... The ancestors watching and listening are happy to hear the languages being spoken." More thumps. "It warms my spirits to see so many youths here. That's what this is all about, to bring back our culture to our youth. Welcome to our shores. We have food. We have clean toilets. We have showers."

And that drew the most vigorous thumps of all.

"Makes you think, doesn't it?" said a white guy next to me. "We took a lot from these people."

Yes, we had. Yet because the plagues of body and spirit continue unabated in Indian country, you have to question if the attempts at cultural revival, all these sun dances and Sacred Hoop Runs and canoe journeys and powwows, are an effective cure. Maybe, as natural immunities are built up to certain diseases, it's a process that will take not years but generations.

After the last canoes had landed, the feast began. We joined the crews and filed past steam tables laden with smoked salmon (it lived up to Rose's promises) and meat loaf and king crab, with rice, potatoes, green beans, and fry bread. Singing and dancing followed. To drumbeats, men droned the songs peculiar to their tribes, some dirgelike, some with a melodious lilt remarkably like sea chanteys. Women and girls, traditional robes thrown over their street clothes, danced barefoot. It was very moving, and a little odd, watching and listening to those ancient ceremonies while just a mile away tankers lay docked at the refinery, its tangled geometry of pipes and stacks and girders lit up like a city, and the smoke obscuring Mount Baker's moon-plated slopes.

———

Leslie was staging another work stoppage as dog wrangler. A couple of days earlier, Sage and Sky had chased a campground rabbit and, once again, nearly had her airborne. She tied them up, thereby forcing them to watch "bunny TV," slavering over rabbits they couldn't reach ten yards away.

About an hour after dawn, I walked them past the canoeists' encampment, where bell-tents made a nylon village and the canoes were drawn up on a pebbly beach. The crews were taking part in a ritual cleansing. They stood in a line, stepping up one by one to a woman who held a wooden bowl of smoldering sage in one hand, an eagle feather in the other. Each paddler would dip his or her hands in the smoke, then symbolically bathe hands, feet, and arms in it. That done, the woman would waft the smoke over the back and back legs with the feather, completing the rite by tapping the right shoulder to indicate that the person's spirit had been washed of any evil spirits and thoughts that might have entered the soul during the night.

This ceremony was explained to me by two men standing nearby. Just then, a young eagle with a fish clutched in its talons flew low overhead, screaming as it was pursued by ravens. "Wow! Look at that!" one of the men said. "I've never seen an eagle with a fish!" I motioned at a line of fir trees in the distance and told him that a pair of eagles were nested there. "Don't point!" he said, shocked. "You should never point at an eagle with your finger. An Indian would point like this"—he cocked his head upward—"with his nose." He didn't explain the reason for this prohibition.

"I was pointing at the trees, not the eagle," I said.

He looked relieved. "Okay."

32.

WE REACHED THE BORDER CROSSING AT SUMAS, WASHINGton, about half past ten that morning.

The reader will recall that I had a .357 magnum revolver to protect me and mine from robbers, psychopaths, rapists, and dognappers, a precaution that had proven totally unnecessary. Carry permits from three law-enforcement agencies, valid in thirty-six states, were in my wallet, but I did not have a permit to pack concealed heat in Canada. Or unconcealed for that matter. The Canadians have strict gun laws. Get caught with an unauthorized, unlicensed pistol and you *will* go to jail. The question was, What to do with the revolver? On the drive up from Anacortes, I phoned Canadian customs and asked if I could store it with them until I returned. No, a woman answered, and referred me to the Sumas police department.

"Well?" Leslie asked when I got off the phone. She thought my taking a gun on the trip had been overkill, so to speak, and was taking some satisfaction in my dilemma.

"I can keep the gun at a supermarket. Bromley's Market."

"You mean supermarket as in grocery store?"

"That's what the cops said. Bromley's holds guns for safekeeping for U.S. citizens going through Canada."

In Bromley's parking lot, I pulled the holstered weapon out from the front door map compartment, unloaded it, and, not wishing to alarm customers and checkout clerks, jammed it into my waistband and covered it with my shirt. Making my way down the cereal aisle and through a double door to the back, I found the store manager in a cramped office, up a flight of dark, creaky wooden stairs. It all had a Dashiell Hammett feel. *I'm goin' inta Canada till things cool off, Max. Keep this for me till I get back.* The manager had me sign a couple of forms, collected ten dollars, put the gun and the bullets in a freezer bag, then stashed the bag in a safe. He said that if I did not retrieve it within a year, the store would dispose of it.

And so, disarmed, we crossed the border and passed through Canadian customs without a hitch. Fred's trip odometer read 5,360.4 miles.

The Alaska Highway, formerly known by its military acronym, ALCAN, for Alaska-Canada Highway, owes its existence to the Imperial Japanese Army and Navy. An overland route to link the Lower 48 with Alaska through Canada was first proposed in the late twenties by the director of the U.S. Bureau of Public Roads, one Thomas MacDonald. The idea caught the fancy of an Alaskan sourdough and fur trapper named Clyde "Slim" Williams. In the winter of 1933, to demonstrate that such a road was feasible, he traveled the route by dogsled. When the spring thaws made sledding impossible, he fixed Model T wheels to his sled and mushed his team of half-wolf huskies on to the continental United States.

For this feat of endurance and guts, Slim Williams became a minor celebrity, but his and MacDonald's dream didn't come close to realization. It required the support of the Canadian government, which saw no point in spending millions for a road that would go from noplace to nowhere. Then Japan's navy bombed Pearl Harbor, its army threatened to seize the Aleutian Islands, and suddenly a highway to Alaska seemed like a good idea to both the United States and Canada.

In February 1942, U.S. Army captain Alfred Eschbad, commanding a company in the 648th Topographic Battalion, received a telegram at his headquarters in Louisiana. It was from Brigadier General Clarence Sturdevant, deputy chief of the Army Corps of Engineers, and it said: YOU WILL TAKE ONE COMPANY OF MEN AND PROCEED TO DAWSON CREEK, BRITISH COLUMBIA, AND THENCE IN A NORTHWESTERLY DIRECTION TO FAIRBANKS, ALASKA, LOCATING A ROUTE FOR A MILITARY ROAD. YOU WILL HAVE THIRTY DAYS TO PREPARE FOR DEPARTURE.

Eschbad and his surveyors got up there in less time than that and began to blaze a trail. They were followed by ten thousand civilian contractors and soldiers, one third from African American construction battalions. Starting on March 9, 1942, they worked seven days a week, sixteen hours a day, bulldozing through endless forests, bridging rivers, skirting swamps and muskeg bogs. They endured winter temperatures of forty below and springtime floods and summer swarms of blackflies and mosquitoes so thick they could actually drive a man insane. More crews were meanwhile proceeding southeastward from Fairbanks. The two parties met up at Kluane Lake, in the Yukon Territory, on October 25, 1942. In less than nine months, they'd built seventeen hundred miles of road through what was—and largely still is—one of the last great wildernesses on Earth.

A two-and-a-half-day drive from the border got us to Dawson Creek and the beginning of the highway. We had passed through the Fraser River canyon, a region that called for a thesaurus of breathless adjectives. *Stupendous. Spectacular. Magnificent. Majestic. Awesome.* Mountains like half a dozen Gibraltars stacked one atop the other, ribboned with rock veins, rose almost sheer on both sides of the canyon, through which the swollen Fraser surged with incalculable power. Cataracts crashed in the narrows; back eddies whipped around the bends with such speed it looked as if two rivers were flowing side by side in opposite directions.

In Dawson Creek, at a roundabout near the Alaska Hotel and Café, stood a whitewashed concrete post about ten feet high. MILE "0" ALASKA HI-WAY, it said. From the Mile Zero marker on U.S. 1 at Key West, we had put on a little over six thousand miles, and I felt a certain shrinking of the traveler's spirit when I looked at the plaque atop the monument. FT. NELSON—300. WHITEHORSE—918. DELTA JUNCTION—1398. FAIRBANKS—1523. Were our ultimate destination on the list, it would have read: DEADHORSE—2018.

We set off on the fabled highway. In her lap, Leslie held our copy of *The Milepost*, a guidebook that is the bible for north country travelers, and at nearly eight hundred pages half as long as *the* Bible. This publication presents a dizzying amount of information about virtually every mile of the twenty-four highways in British Columbia, the Yukon Territory, and Alaska.

"For many people, the Alaska Highway is a great adventure. For others, it's a long drive," read *The Milepost*'s introduction to the AH.

We found it a little bit of both. Driving it used to be nothing but an adventure; it was all gravel when it opened to the public in 1948, and not until 1992 was the last segment of the original road laid under asphalt.

But paving hadn't turned it into an anodyne interstate, either.

"Road conditions on the Alaska Highway are not unlike road conditions on many secondary roads in the Lower 48," the guidebook went on. "It is the tremendous length of the highway, combined with its remoteness and the extremes of the Northern climate, that often result in surprises."

Among those surprises were the gravel breaks that appeared without warning. We'd be sailing along on a smooth surface at fifty-five or sixty miles an hour and suddenly hit a patch of dirt, anywhere from a few yards to half a mile long, pocked with chuckholes. Slamming on the brakes wasn't an option, not with a trailer in tow. Until I could slow down to a reasonable thirty-five or so, Ethel banged and bounced and rocked. When we stopped to refuel in Fort St. John, I looked inside and found the minifridge door flung open, likewise the cabinets and drawers, and tin cans, cereal boxes, and bottles strewn all over. I also discovered that the valve to her main propane tank was frozen shut. Nothing I could do with a pipe wrench and channel locks would break it loose. The gas station mechanic gave it a try, got the same result, and directed me to a propane gas company up the street.

"Never had this happen before," said the service manager there, after he failed to open the valve.

"She's a special trailer. Pretty but temperamental."

"Lotta pretty things are like that," he said. "Gotta take the tank into the shop, pull that old valve off, install a new one."

Fifty dollars and about two hours later, we pushed on three hundred miles to Fort Nelson, a frontier settlement sans power, sans phones, sans running water as recently as the fifties, now with all of the above plus Wi-Fi, a working town that services shale oil fields. Huge trucks, dirt-caked pickups, and earth-moving machinery were everywhere.

In the far northern reaches of the Canadian Rockies, the highway became more like the original pioneer road, narrowing as it climbed through limestone gorges. Guardrails disappeared; more gravel breaks appeared. Black bears ambled at the roadside. Two Stone sheep rams escorted ewes and kids down from an outcrop onto the road. I eased out of the truck to photograph them, and they were so innocent of people they practically brushed me.

At Summit Pass, the highest point on the highway (4,250 feet), we stopped at a gravel turnout to take in the view. If my driving glasses had been as powerful as astronomical binoculars, I would have seen no end to the white spruce forests, reaching unbroken across wide basins, climbing over ridgelines, and so dense it looked as though you could walk across the treetops as easily as you could across a meadow. Bare, rocky peaks thrust up above the timberline, every one snow-covered.

"Okay, this is stupid," Leslie said, "but have you noticed how many trees there are in North America?"

"Back in Nebraska, you wondered where they were. Here they are."

"Sometimes I feel like we're in one of those old movies, driving by a fake backdrop that just keeps repeating itself."

An ancestor of Fred's, a blue, twenty-year-old Toyota truck that looked like it had done a couple of tours in Afghanistan, pulled in next to us. It had Virginia plates. Two unshaven guys were inside. The driver was about thirty, the passenger fifty or so.

"That Airstream is really cool," the younger one said, and asked permission to take pictures of Ethel.

"No problem. She'll be flattered."

"Where you headed?"

"Prudhoe."

"Hey, us, too. So where've you come from?"

"Key West. Been on the road nearly ten weeks. We're going from the southernmost point to the northernmost."

"Man, that is *so* cool."

Feeling pretty damn cool, I asked what was taking them to Prudhoe.

"Just for the helluva it," said the passenger. "Maybe we'll see you up there."

Maybe in italics. When the younger man got back in the truck, it wouldn't start. While his friend took the wheel, he climbed out to push. I gave him a hand. We rolled that aging Toyota about fifty feet before the engine caught. The two men were off again, and so were we, Whitman wishing us well:

> I think whatever I shall meet on the road I shall like, and who-
> ever beholds me shall like me, I think whoever I see must be
> happy.

We followed the Liard River toward the Yukon border. A moose calf browsed in the willows on a gravel bar. Farther up, we saw what we thought was its mother, grazing in the grassy verge between the road and the forest. It turned out to be a woods bison. Another knelt on all fours a few hundred yards on, and then we spotted two more. The woods bison, a subspecies of the American bison, is the largest land mammal in North America, with males weighing in at over a ton—five hundred pounds more than a typical Great Plains bull. These grand beasts once roamed the subarctic forests by the tens of thousands, but there seems to be something about buffalo that excites human blood lust. Like the plains bison, they were hunted to the edge of extinction. Only a few hundred were left in 1900. They have since made a slow, halting recovery; around three thousand can be found in the wild, all in northern British Columbia and the Yukon. To see four in just a few minutes was thrilling. But that was nothing. Half an hour later, after topping a low rise, we came upon a herd of almost a hundred blocking the road: cows, calves, and young bulls overseen by the herd bull, the Boss, standing on an embankment above the highway.

I pulled over at a safe distance, slowly opened the door, and crouched behind it, resting Leslie's camera on the lowered window. A small SUV drew alongside, two toddlers buckled into infant seats in the back, a young woman at the wheel. She also stopped to snap a few pictures, then started off again, a little too quickly for the Boss's liking. He kicked up dust, charged down the embankment, and came straight at her—a Humvee equipped with horns and malicious intent. I couldn't get over how big he was; his hump would have scraped the top of a garage door. I leaped into the truck. The SUV's brakes squealed, and it reversed direction at about twenty miles an hour. Satisfied with the retreat, the Boss turned and plodded back up the embankment.

"Did you see him charge me?" The woman sounded more indignant than shocked, as if the bull had committed a traffic violation.

"Couldn't have missed it. You went too fast. He probably thought you were a threat. Go ahead, but take it slow."

"No, no, uh-uh. I've got kids with me, and he's pissed off."

I offered to ride point, figuring that the bull would have second thoughts about colliding with big Fred, all seventy-five hundred pounds of him. While Leslie kept an eye on the Boss and the SUV hugged the Airstream's rear bumper, I drove up the road at walking speed, behind the confident grin of Fred's steel moose bar. A tap or two on the horn parted the herd, and after we'd gone through the woman threw me a wave and sped away.

An adventure is an undertaking involving danger, unknown risks, and hardship. I'd been on enough adventures to know that our journey didn't meet the criteria. Beyond the chance of being blown off the road by a passing semitrailer, there were no dangers; the risks were predictable; instead of hardships, we experienced mere inconveniences.

Like the fits Ethel pitched on the Alaska Highway's rough patches. Vintage Airstreams have a feature, "the door-within-a-door," which is a small, screened ventilation door set inside the main door. The hinges on ours were worn, and the door flew open when we hit a bump. Next the ceiling hatch locks popped loose and the hatch screen fell out. Without locks, the hatch could be torn off at forty or fifty miles an hour, making the trailer uninhabitable in a rainstorm. I made redneck repairs. Read: duct tape.

In our night campsite at Watson Lake, in the Yukon Territory, the propane alarm, quiescent for weeks, blared yet again for no discernible reason. This at three in the morning in a downpour. Knowing the false alarms were caused by voltage surges, I went outside and disconnected the 110-volt line; when that failed to silence the thing, I threw the master switch inside, shutting off battery power. Quiet at last. Meanwhile, Fred's roof rack continued to leak, and for the tenth or twelfth or fifteenth time, the dogs had to be transferred from truck to trailer.

In *Blue Highways*, William Least Heat-Moon observes that *travel* is derived from the same Latin root as *travail*.

But, as I've said, these were only inconveniences. For sheer misery and self-inflicted torment, no one could surpass the bicyclists of the Alaska Highway. We'd seen them every day since leaving Dawson Creek. Some rode solitary, some in groups of three or four, hunched against rain and wind in foul weather, toiling over mountain passes, their bikes laden with camping gear and bulging saddle bags. No cozy inn awaited them at the end of the day, only a pup tent pitched in a mosquito-plagued wilderness. I admired their grit and fitness, but nowhere near as much as I questioned their sanity.

It rained off and on for the whole four hundred miles between Watson Lake and Haines Junction. Midway, we stopped in Whitehorse, capital of the Yukon, and with twenty-four thousand people the largest city on the highway. After five days of driving through paleolithic land-scapes, it looked as big and sprawly as L.A. Our perishables had spoiled overnight, after I shut off the power to squelch the rebellious alarm. We needed to resupply, and Whitehorse had, yes, a Walmart and supermar-kets and other conveniences. The city got its start in the late 1800s, as a mining settlement during the Klondike gold rush. There is a bronze statue downtown of a stampeder holding a shovel, a malamute at his side. Also faux-frontier saloons where dance hall girls in naughty outfits enter-tain tourists. Jack London, Robert Service, Dangerous Dan McGrew, all that. Like Deadwood, South Dakota, or Tombstone, Arizona, White-horse trades on nostalgia for a raucous, romantic past because in its pres-ent incarnation it's as commonplace as anywhere else. And to that we said, "Thank goodness!" Thank goodness for the Walmart with its meat market and produce shelves.

Then it was into and over the Cassiar Mountains. Approaching Haines Junction, we were confronted by the formidable bastions of the St. Elias Range. Clouds curled over ridgelines like surf atop waves two miles high. Glaciers swept down the valleys. The icy peaks of Mount Logan, second-tallest mountain in North America (19,520 feet), and of lesser mountains speared the overcast. The Yukon Territory! I had been in it many times before, decades ago, sitting in front of a tall, wooden Philco radio in my grandparents' bungalow in Berwyn, Illinois. The theme music, strings and wind instruments suggesting windswept spaces, lifted me out of that quotidian setting. Then the announcer's voice bore me away, into the frozen North: "Sergeant Preston of the Northwest Mounted Police, with Yukon King! Strongest and swiftest lead dog, breaking trail in the relent-less pursuit of lawbreakers in the wild days of the Yukon! Brought to you by Quaker Oats . . ."

The reality matched my boyhood fantasies, even exceeded them. Really, it's impossible to convey the scale and wildness of that country. A popu-lation density of more than one person per square mile would be regarded as congested. Every 100 or 150 miles, a gas station, a log cabin or two, a general store, and a campground or small motel—that does it for human settlement.

We left Haines Junction in a miasma of cold rain and fog. The high-way skirted Kluane Lake, five miles wide and forty long, long enough that we at first mistook it for a river. The weather broke, and in the bright sunlight the waters were as turquoise as the flats in the Florida Keys. We barely noticed. We were glutted on scenery, dazed by it. Our senses could no longer respond to it. Driving through it is like touring a major exhibition at the Metropolitan Museum of Art; you wander from gallery to gallery until you're surfeited with genius and you find yourself standing in front of some grand masterpiece with the mindless stare of a retarded marmoset.

Two roadside signs were displayed at a ramshackle gas station in a place called Burwash Landing. One read NO FUEL NEXT 108 MI.—U.S. BORDER, 128 MI., and the other, in bold, black letters, LONG LIVE THE USA. With Fred's tank just a quarter full, I pulled in. I was also curious. In my travels abroad, I'd seldom encountered outpourings of affection for the United States. True, it's sometimes difficult for an American to think of Canada as a foreign land, or, to turn that statement around, *not* to think of it as a part of the United States that perversely adopted the metric system and eccentric spellings of words like *color* and *honor*: *colour, honour*. Nevertheless, it truly is another country, which led me to inquire of the young attendant, "So who's the big fan of the U.S.?"

"The owner. It's a marketing thing. He figures that sign will pull in Americans."

I said that the warning of no fuel for the next 108 miles would be effective all by itself, but I appreciated the owner's sentiments.

No fuel, but frost heaves all the way. In subarctic and arctic climes, the freezing and thawing of the soil causes it to lift, which in turn cracks pavement and creates dips and rises in a roadway, like ocean waves. We were practically seasick when, six days after leaving Sumas, we reached the international boundary. Beyond the port of entry, we asked another traveler to photograph us in front of a big wooden sign that said WELCOME TO ALASKA. Seventy-two days ago, we'd had our pictures taken at the Southernmost Point. From there to here, we'd come 7,257 miles. Eight hundred more, give or take, lay between us and Prudhoe Bay, and better than half that would be on the rugged Dalton Highway, or Haul Road. But for the first time I felt confident that we were going to get there.

33.

THE SCENIC ORGY CONTINUED ON THE ROAD TO TOK—
pronounced *toke*. In the blue distance, the Wrangell Mountains
blockaded a big slice of the sky, and the clouds swirling among the
peaks lent them the mysterious look of some lost Shangri-la. Well, you
don't go to Alaska to look at monuments, cathedrals, or the ruins of vanished civilizations. What little there is of urban development is undistin-
guished at best.

This was my fourth visit to the largest state in the union, and I was as
awed as I'd been the first time. It shouldn't be called a state, as if it were
in the same league as Montana or Texas; it's a subcontinent, half the size
of India at 572,000 square miles, with fewer inhabitants (686,000) than
Detroit, and more bears of all species (135,000) than there are people in
Fairbanks. I'm not sure those figures communicate its immensity, so I'll
try something else. If you superimposed Alaska on the continental United
States, its northernmost town, Point Barrow, would be in northern Minnesota; its southernmost, Ketchikan, in south Georgia; its eastern bound-
ary would split Indiana down the middle, its western would touch
Colorado, while the Kenai Peninsula and Aleutian chain would arc from
Oklahoma into California.

In Tok, over the line, we tucked the trailer into a tranquil grove of firs,
spruce, and birch. Among Tok's roadside attractions was a log cabin with

a lawn mower on its sod roof. In the morning, we found a trail through the woods surrounding the campground and let slip the dogs. We'd put bell collars on them because we were in grizzly country, and bear warnings were posted at the trailhead. But we saw no sign of *Ursus arctos horribilis*.

Then we left for a town called Chicken. Leslie had found a reference to it in *The Milepost* and recalled that a trucker we'd met in Anacortes told us not to bother going there; the road was in bad shape, and Chicken had burned down in a forest fire. We ignored his travel tip, figuring that since we'd visited Two Egg, Florida, we had to see Chicken, Alaska—if for no other reason than to find out which came first.

In the 1890s, Klondike prospectors working their way into Alaska from the Yukon set up a mining camp on a tributary of the Fortymile River. They hunted ptarmigan, a subarctic partridge, to sustain themselves, and so decided to call their settlement Ptarmigan; but because no one knew how to spell the word *ptarmigan*, they chose Chicken instead.

Chicken was located sixty-seven miles up the Taylor Highway. Our informant was wrong about its condition; it turned out to be in pretty good shape. It climbed and twisted through dispiriting expanses of swamps and black spruce forests. (Not all of nature in Alaska is grand and inspiring.) Even when it looks its best, the black spruce is an ugly tree, scrawny and stunted, and these in their millions did not look their best. Charred by the fires that the trucker said had reduced Chicken to ashes, they were nearly branchless stalks resembling giant pipe cleaners. The pavement gave out; the road turned to mud and gravel and bridged a tannin-browned creek, the Mosquito Forks. Just past the bridge, signs and symbols for food-gas-lodging, identical to those on an interstate, stood at the roadside. One pointed to the right and read: DOWNTOWN CHICKEN. 2/10 MI.

Nearly out of gas, we turned in that direction and came to what looked like a set for a B-grade western: a row of weathered log and frame storefronts with porches supported by rough-hewn posts: the Chicken Mercantile Emporium; the Chicken Liquor Store; the Chicken Creek Saloon; and the Chicken Creek Café. Near the Mercantile, beside four outhouses, called "the Chicken Poop," was a single gas pump. We filled up, and having determined that the trucker had been wrong again we had a look around.

Whether or not it came first, Chicken's grip on existence is tenuous.

Its population, four hundred in its gold-rush heyday, hovers at around fifty in the summer and nine or ten in the winter. It's still a gold-mining town, mostly recreational panning in the creeks nearby, but its life depends on motorists who come up as we did, or from Dawson City in the Yukon, by way of a tricky mountain road, the Klondike Loop. This is what Chicken has, in addition to the establishments and fuel pumps already mentioned: a post office, two trailer parks, and a resort with cabins, the Chicken Gold Camp and Outpost. This is what it doesn't have: paved streets, sewers, city water, phones, or electricity (water comes from wells; power from generators). It is a libertarian's dream come true because it also does not have a mayor or town council, no government whatsoever. Law enforcement is provided by the state police or the fish and game department, whose officers drop in now and then.

Our self-guided walking tour completed, we retreated to the Chicken Creek Saloon, which had the only liquor license for a radius of eighty miles. That wasn't too remarkable, as there was nothing around but trees and muskeg for a radius of eighty miles, and they don't drink. License plates and business cards papered the walls; countless baseball caps, left by travelers, hung from the ceiling, along with shredded ladies panties. When things get to rocking in the saloon, women take off their underwear and ram them into a small salute cannon kept in the bar. The artillery piece is then charged with gunpowder, wheeled outside, and fired, blasting Victoria's Secrets (and more conventional undergarments) all over the parking lot.

Things were not rocking when we walked in for a drink with the ruler of the roost in downtown Chicken, Susan Wiren, proprietor of the saloon and the other three businesses. The only patron besides ourselves was Shannon, a Canadian woman of fading good looks. Although she'd started Happy Hour early, Shannon wasn't near tipsy enough to bombard Chicken with panty shrapnel.

Meanwhile, we talked with Wiren. She was fifty-six years old and didn't fit the mold, if there is such a thing, of the pioneer woman. She had a degree in art, an aristocratic look—finely chiseled features, frosty blonde hair, glacial blue eyes—studied French, and pursued upper-class hobbies like tennis, sailing, and riding. If she'd been in a summer dress instead of a fleece vest, denim shorts, and hiking boots, she would have looked right at home at a garden party on the Philadelphia Main Line.

Her journey to Chicken began not far from there, in New Hope,

Pennsylvania, where she was bored to death until she met and married a sailor and adventurer named Greg in 1988.

"He was an extremely interesting person. If I'd interviewed him properly, we probably would never have gotten married. But there was a lot of chemistry going on. We really loved each other."

Enough chemistry that when Greg later took a notion to search for gold in Alaska, Wiren followed him with their two small sons, Max and Wolfgang. They lived in Eagle, which is even more remote than Chicken, a Yukon River town at the end of the Taylor Highway. Wiren found herself looking after two kids in a wilderness cabin without electricity or plumbing, while Greg sought nuggets in the creeks and streams. He didn't find any, but when he and Wiren learned that four shops in Chicken were in bankruptcy they took a flyer, made a lowball offer, and bought them from the bank.

"That's how we got here, and then Greg . . . Greg has a short attention span, . . . and left. He ran around on me, and eventually I divorced him. I looked at my life and I thought, *This is actually pretty good*, and I substitute taught for a while in Fairbanks, and I bought him out."

Now, fifteen years later, the businesses were thriving and employed seven people. The mercantile sold clothes and gifts, the café offered salmon burgers, hamburgers, and of course chicken, as well as potato salad and pies Wiren baked herself. She was doing well enough to foot the bills for younger son Max, in med school in France.

"I never imagined I'd be doing this, but I really love my job and I really like it here. With Max in med school and with cash flow, I'll probably have to do this for five more years before I can retire."

Where would she retire to? Leslie asked. Wiren answered that she'd always imagined buying a houseboat and living in Wrightsville Beach, North Carolina. Except her boyfriend didn't like boats. He had a house near Las Vegas, forty minutes from the strip and a ten-minute walk from the desert. That was where Wiren spent her winters, and she loved it, too. Like Alaska, the desert was an extreme, and she was drawn to extremes.

Shannon spun on her bar stool and jumped into the conversation. "So where am I going to visit you next?"

"Lake Las Vegas," Wiren said, her expression and voice going flat. She didn't like being interrupted. "It's right by Lake Mead, and it's beautiful."

"So you gonna cook for me there?"

"Ha! Don't you wish."

"The food here is amazing!" Shannon said.

Wiren warmed to the endorsement. "We do have awesome food. I make the salmon burgers from scratch. Know what I just learned, studying French on Rosetta Stone? There is honor in every profession. I used to fall into the trap where you have to have a college degree and all that, and we have to do something important. That is bullshit! In Rosetta Stone, the little girls pretending to be waitresses. What's wrong with that?"

"I have to laugh," Shannon said. She'd plunged deeper into Happy Hour. "Because I've always worked two or three jobs, right? So I deliver mail during the day, and I clean at a school nights in B.C. I've worked in bars on weekends, right? So I bought another house on Vancouver Island, and so I've been . . . I'm like up there in age, right? And so I said, *Well I don't want to do this other second job cleaning the school, so I'm gonna work in a bar.* So my friend Pat, she says to me, she goes, 'Well, aren't you a little old?' So I thought, *I'm gonna check this out.* And you know what? I go to the bars, and I'm tellin' you, some of the women are grandmas. We're talkin' good waitresses. The Dinghy Dock Bar, which is where I would really like to work, was all young people. I'm tellin' you, and I—tip—good. And you know, the service was so shit, and if they left with a buck . . . You know what? They were ignorant. They weren't *fun.* They weren't . . . You know, I was kinda doin' the, like, you know, the needs. Do you need . . ."

I watched Wiren's face throughout this train wreck of an oration, her brows knit at first in concentration, trying to figure out where Shannon was going, then, upon realizing that she wasn't going anywhere, putting on a look of pained forbearance that said she didn't suffer fools gladly but often had to suffer them regardless.

"I think Susan's point," I said, hoping to rescue her as well as ourselves, "is that there's a dignity in what a lot of people do."

"A dignity," Wiren said. "I never realized that until I started studying Rosetta Stone. I'm much more proud of myself than I ever have been before with the lowly job of baking pies."

Wiren had begun to study French because Max spoke French like a Frenchman, and she expected to someday have French grandchildren.

"I think it's the self-improvement thing we go through in our fifties."

I said, "I've got to display my ignorance. You said you've been studying French on Rosetta Stone. I don't know what that is."

Wiren twitched, taken aback. "I'm surprised you don't know that."

"I missed out on the self-improvement thing."

It was, she informed me, an online language course. The little girls pretending to be waitresses she'd referred to were virtual figures, with whom one practiced ordering meals. Wiren now spoke French fluently enough to carry on conversations with Quebecois who pass through Chicken.

"But I guess my real gift is merchandising and schmoozing with tourists," she said. "But I get tired of it."

"Of merchandising or schmoozing?"

"I get tired of the mundanity of humanity sometimes."

She was usually out of bed at three in the morning, in the kitchen before four, her hands buried in dough. Pie dough. Cookie dough. And, I was happy to hear, dough for cinnamon buns. She timed the baking so the goods were warm when the first customers came in, and sometimes that produced, she said, stupid questions.

"They'll say things like 'Did you bake these here?' The stupid, obvious questions, like 'What do you in the winter?'"

Her scorn for fatuous interrogators made me cautious about the questions I put to her. I decided to throw out one I hoped would meet her standards, telling her that we'd been traveling the country to find out what held it together, and what were her thoughts about that?

She pondered for a few seconds, attempted an answer, and gave up. "That's a difficult question," she said finally. "I've had three glasses of wine, and I'm just a pie baker trying to get a kid through med school."

Besides the three glasses of wine, she'd had very little sleep. A bear prowling around her cabin had kept her awake most of the night, and it was a big bear.

"I brought my seven-millimeter out of the case, and it's sitting in the bedroom right by the door."

This wasn't a new experience. She remembered one bear that she'd encountered eleven years ago. It, too, had been hanging around the cabin and had frightened the horses Wiren then kept in a corral nearby.

"My friend Cassie was here. She had Greg's old thirty-aught-six. So one night it was cold in April, and the kids and I and Cassie were walking up to get some wood. We were thirty, maybe forty feet from the house, and this black bear charged us. Cassie dropped him in one shot, and the bear was grunting in death, and my reaction was 'Shoot him again!'"

The two women then dragged the carcass to Wiren's driveway, rolled it onto a tarp, and skinned it out. The next day, they cooked the meat in red wine, and Cassie kept the hide for a rug.

Some humble pie baker, I thought. Alaska's nickname, "the Last Frontier," has more truth in it than most state nicknames, and Wiren, her merchandising skills and Internet connections aside, saw herself as part of a tradition of frontier women.

"I actually am an icon," she said, with a smile to show that she was joking. Well, sort of joking. A few years earlier, two friends of hers had driven up to Chicken on a motorcycle and given her a book about women in Alaska's early days.

"It had a terrible ending, but one thing I got out of the book was that in Alaska women have always run these roadhouses. It's a way to make a living, and I realized right then that I was an archetype. Really. You can make a living. You don't have to have an education. I happen to have one, but you don't need one. Know how to bake pies and [serve] cold beer, that's all you need."

Leaving her wineglass half full, she went home to rest up for another day that would begin at three in the morning.

It was now seven in the evening. We dined in the café, Leslie on the salmon burger, I on barbecued chicken, mostly to prove that there were chickens in Chicken, there having been no eggs in Two Egg, nor any Two Egg.

34.

O N A FINE MORNING, BROILING BY ALASKAN STANDARDS—
seventy-two degrees—we arrived in Delta Junction, end of the
Alaska Highway. To the southwest, visible at a distance of one
hundred and fifty miles, Mount McKinley punched into altitudes where
airliners cruised, peaking at 20,320 feet: the roof of the continent, buried
in everlasting snows. The Koyukon Indians called the mountain Denali
(the Great One); it was renamed in 1896 in honor of President William
McKinley; in 1975, the state of Alaska recognized its original name and
petitioned the federal government to do likewise but, because nothing
can be done in this country without political interference, a senator from
Ohio—McKinley's home state—blocked the move. Personally, I prefer
Denali. The mountain *is* great, awesome, magisterial, qualities that do
not describe President McKinley.

We rolled into Fairbanks, named for another politician, Charles Fairbanks, Theodore Roosevelt's vice president. A good thing for him, because
nobody ever remembers a vice president.

But for low water and an Italian immigrant and prospector, Felice
Pedroni, there probably would be no Fairbanks today. In the summer of
1901, one Captain E. T. Barnette was traveling down the Chena River in
a steamboat, with the intention of establishing a trading post on another
river, the Tanana. The steamer ran aground, and Barnette and his party
were forced to disembark. Pedroni and his partner, Tom Gilmore, pros-
pecting in the hills nearby, spotted the steamer's smoke and came to the

aid of the stranded passengers. They convinced Barnette that he would be better off building his trading post right there, and that's what he did. Pedroni and Gilmore were his first customers. They bought supplies and headed back into the hills. Less than a year later, Pedroni hit pay dirt near the Chena, and another gold rush was on. A thousand miners flocked to Fairbanks, and by 1908 it was the largest city in Alaska.

Nowadays, it takes a distant second place to Anchorage. A little over thirty thousand people live inside the city limits, and a little under a hundred thousand in the metropolitan area, Fairbanks North Star Borough.* Still, stoplights and traffic and urban noise hit us like a zap from a cattle prod. In Pioneer Park, where we picked up city and state road maps, tattooed soldiers from Fort Wainwright, in high and tight haircuts and gray army T-shirts, were tossing a football in the parking lot while a rap about a hot little mama doing a *thang* with her ass thundered from their car. We could feel the sound waves on our eardrums. And so, after the immense solitudes, after the deep silences of the timeless wilds on the Alaska Highway, we were yanked back into our present century.

Our campground on the Chena, not far downstream from where Barnette's steamboat hit the rocks, was as crowded as a mall parking lot on a Saturday afternoon, and our site looked as narrow as a mall parking space. My improved backing-up skills were presented with a new challenge. Leslie got out of the truck to direct me. As I turned the wheel and eased into reverse, she yelled, "No! You're going to hit the tree!"

It was past ten in the evening, broad daylight that far north, but I saw no tree in the sideview mirror.

"The tree on the right," she said.

"So more left?" I called out the window.

"Right, I mean, yes, more left."

I turned the wheel to the right, which, theoretically, was supposed to make the trailer go left.

"No! No! Now you're going to hit the picnic table!"

"I don't see the table! *Please.* Stop pointing out all these terrain features and just tell me right, left, or straight."

---

* Counties in Alaska are called boroughs. There are twenty, and some are larger than the states in the Lower 48. The Unorganized Borough, for example, could accommodate all of Texas.

"Let me try it. I can't do any worse."

We were both tired and hadn't eaten a thing since breakfast. At this point, a neighbor took pity on us. He was an older gent from Oklahoma, and he used to haul stock trailers for a living. He stepped up to me and said in the quiet voice of command: "You have to start over. Now pull out, turn hard right till you've got your truck and trailer in a straight line. Then do exactly what I tell you to do."

I followed instructions. With Fred and Ethel lined up, he directed me to go in reverse, swing the trailer slightly to the right, then slightly left, then to pull a little forward.

"Okay," said Oklahoma. "Now straight back, slow. If she starts to jackknife, don't turn the wheel too much, a little at a time is all it takes."

And Ethel slipped in, neat as could be. I thanked Oklahoma and gave Leslie a triumphant grin. "See? No trees, no picnic tables. Just right, left, straight."

"Next time, let me try it," she said. "You depend too much on the kindness of strangers."

She made cheese sandwiches, we broke out the camp chairs, the scotch and vodka, and under the almost-midnight sun celebrated our arrival in Fairbanks. Why quarrel about backing up a trailer? About anything? We'd made it this far without running into nasty marital weather. Nothing worse than a couple of brief squalls. We were still road buddies, still comfortable in our own company.

We spent the next two days restocking the cupboards and preparing for the final push to the Arctic Ocean.

A duffel bag stuffed with waders, hip boots, and fishing tackle was hauled off the rooftop carrier and stowed into the truck bed with the dogs' stuff, a second spare tire for the truck, two spare trailer tires, and a tool bag containing jacks, lug wrenches, emergency flares, and extra lug nuts. Add rain gear, insect repellent, and headnets—the mosquitoes and blackflies in Arctic Alaska are not merely troublesome; they're savage and as numberless as the stars.

At the Bureau of Land Management office, a ranger handed us two pamphlets, one titled *Driving the Dalton Highway*, the other *Bear Facts: Essentials for Traveling in Bear Country* (the brown bear on the cover was slightly smaller than a dump truck).

"The highway is narrow with soft shoulders that drop off steeply on either side," read the first publication. "Hills can be long and in excess of 12% grade . . . You may encounter slick mud, clouds of dust, or snow and ice—even in summer. Flash floods and uncontrolled wildfires may create extreme hazards."

"SERVICES ARE LIMITED," it warned. "Gas is available at Yukon Crossing (mile 56) in summer, Coldfoot (mile 175), and Deadhorse (mile 414) year-round. There are **no medical facilities**, grocery stores or banks . . . There is **no cell phone coverage** outside of Fairbanks and Deadhorse."

A sixteen-point checklist followed: "PREPARE FOR THE LONG HAUL . . . Inspect all tires and have them properly inflated . . . Empty your RV holding tank and fill water tank . . . BRING FOR YOURSELF . . . First aid kit and necessary medications . . . Camping gear, including sleeping bag."

Cheechako is Alaskan slang for a tenderfoot, and a cheechako is anyone who hasn't wintered over. In that sense, we were cheechakos, but we weren't when it came to bears. Leslie had joined me, my son Marc, and two other people for part of my first journey to Alaska in 1995. We had close encounters with fourteen brown bears, only one of which was mildly threatening. Leslie was cooking pancakes and tossing rejects aside—bad idea—when a young male ambled into our camp, wanting a seat at the table. We drove him off by banging pots and pans.

Having survived that encounter, we were interested in the bear pamphlet's counsel. Most black bear attacks are predatory, so fight back, it advised; most brown bear attacks are defensive—the animal is protecting a kill or its cubs, so roll onto your stomach, cover the back of your neck with your hands, and play dead. Typically, the bear will stop once it sees you are not a threat. So far, so good. Then came this: "If, however, the brown bear begins to feed on you, fight back vigorously."

Leslie chortled. "Oh, sure. He bites off your left arm, so whack him with a right. But what if he's noshing on your liver?"

A sporting goods store downtown supplied us with bear spray, ready-to-eat meals, fishing flies, and licenses. Leslie bought a blue plastic gold pan that could double as a salad bowl if her search for ore didn't pan out.

Nick Stepovich was putting on a show for his customers in Soapy Smith's Pioneer Restaurant when we walked in for a lunch. A waiter guided us to a table on a platform in the rear, and from that vantage point we watched Big Nick entertain the crowd. An Alaskan's Alaskan of Alaskan dimensions—figure six-four and 250 pounds—he was dressed for Florida in a T-shirt, plaid Bermuda shorts, and sandals as he roamed among the tables. In a voice to match his size, he told tales of the gold rush and delivered oral histories of the state and his family's exploits in it, while flinging his long arms at the walls, nearly every square inch plastered with photographs ancient and recent, wanted posters, gold pans, pickaxes, and framed covers of *Time* and *Life* magazines commemorating Alaska's admission to statehood in 1959.

We all learned about Soapy Smith himself, the frontier con man and gangster who made a fortune bilking miners during the Klondike gold rush and died in a shoot-out in Juneau. We learned about Nick's grandfather "Wise Mike" Stepovich, an immigrant from Montenegro who came to California in the 1890s and drove a team of twelve oxen up the West Coast to Alaska and struck gold on Fish Creek, north of Fairbanks.

"And the oxen all lived!" Nick boomed.

And so did the five children born to Wise Mike and Olga, a Montenegrin woman he wed in an arranged marriage. She was thirty years his junior. One of those children, also named Mike—Nick's father—grew up to become a fine minor league baseball player. He was picked up by the Boston Red Sox and would have had a career in the majors if his mother hadn't intervened.

"My grandmother told him, 'You're not going to be some goofy ball player. You're going to Notre Dame law school.'"

And young Mike went off to Notre Dame, returned to Alaska, and forged a career in politics. Along the way, he found time to get married and father thirteen children.

"He was our territorial governor!" bellowed Nick over the buzz of conversations, the clatter of plates, waiters taking orders. "He lobbied all over the country to get us admitted to statehood." He strode to a photograph of his father holding a newspaper from 1959. WE'RE IN! the headline shouted. "And that's my dad right there with President Eisenhower!" Pointing at another photo.

Nick turned to some of the objects in the place. "Look at that!" He gestured at a length of twisted wood five feet long. "Anybody know what that is?" "A big stick," a customer answered. "No! It's Paul Bunyan's toothpick. A diamond willow, actually. Can't get it anywhere else. You'll walk a hundred miles through the woods and not find one." He waltzed back to the center of the room and towered over a table. "Sarah Palin sat right there!" Oohs and ahhs from the customers, mingled with a smattering of derisive hoots. "But you know what they say, Never mix politics with silverware. So let's talk about religion!" Laughter. Then Nick wound up. "What counts is, you leave here with a little bit of Alaska in you. You've been a local all day today. If you can't come back, spend more! Thank you, very much." Applause.

There are only 680,000 people in Alaska, and most come from somewhere else and are as shallow-rooted as tundra shrubs—Inupiats, Inuits, and Athabascan-speaking Indians excepted. Third-generation Nick was the equivalent of a *Mayflower* descendant. I wasn't likely to meet a more authentic native, so I sat down with him after his performance. A big bundle of nervous energy, he didn't do much sitting but constantly hopped out of his chair to run into the kitchen or to the register or to give orders to his wait staff.

Restaurateur Nick had mixed politics with silverware when he served as a Republican state representative from 2002 to 2004.

"The funny thing is half the guys on the legislature went to jail," he said. "That's why I tell people serving in the legislature is no big deal."

He didn't say what had put his fellow representatives behind bars. He might have been referring to the "Corrupt Bastards Club," a band of Alaskan senators and congressmen who mixed politics with oil by taking bribes from oil company executives, who also went to prison.

On the last frontier, oil and other natural resources *are* politics. Big Money and Big Government are joined at the hip. The state government runs on its share of revenues from companies like British Petroleum and Royal Dutch Shell, and pays annual dividends to Alaskan citizens simply because they live there. A ceremony more revered than the Fourth of July occurs each year, when the governor stands before TV cameras to open a gold-colored envelope and reveal the magic number. It can be anywhere between eleven hundred and thirteen hundred dollars for each resident, which doesn't go far in a state where a gallon of gas costs seven bucks, but is, nevertheless, as close as anyone can come to picking money off a money tree.

To Nick, grandson of a Klondike stampeder, this corporate-subsidized welfare state is a form of socialism that's sapping Alaskans' frontier spirit of individualism and self-determination.

"We used to say, 'Come to Alaska. America's favorite colony,'" he said. "We're the freezer for the rest of the country. Put some away, take it out when you need it, and it's as good as the day when you got it. Our oil, our fisheries, our minerals. Our state constitution calls for the highest possible yield with any resource. Well, is the highest yield what you can sell to a multinational or a conglomerate? Or is it to get the people of Alaska involved where they can double or triple that through the economy and the capital stays here?

"We don't have libraries and movie stars and beaches and hot weather and opera houses. We have resources. I don't think everyday individual Alaskans have made out on resources. Look at Fairbanks. We should be looking like the finest neighborhoods in Philadelphia with the wealth that's come out of here. *Eight hundred billion dollars* have come off the North Slope, but we've never had a J. R. Ewing, a billionaire off oil who lived here."

Nowhere were Big Government and Big Business partnered as they were in the biggest state. The federal government, he said, was "a security agency for the oil companies."

But Nick wasn't going to bite the petroleum hand that fed his state. Right out of high school in 1975, he'd gone to the North Slope as a welder's helper on the construction of the Trans-Alaska Pipeline. He made enough money—forty-five thousand dollars—to pay his way through college in Seattle and later in Oregon.

"And I paid my tuition in cash." He laughed. "They didn't know what to make of that."

Nick fidgeted—even when seated, he was in motion—and his glance flicked to two customers who'd just entered. "You can sit over there," he said, motioning at an empty table. Then, turning to me: "I'm the host, too. I do a little bit of everything."

I figured that his brief tenure in the state legislature qualified him as a political figure; and having asked one—Florida Speaker of the House Dean Cannon—my Big Question, I presented it to Nick Stepovich of Alaska.

"I think what holds it together is that there's enough room for each person to live their life and their dreams, according to the land, not according to man-made things, our government and all that. You want to come up here and gold-mine or build stuff, there's room for that. An Italian, a Serb, a Russian, a Jewish person, anybody can come up here and make their way. That's the way this country was built. But I think we've lost a lot of that by uniform requirements, uniform regulations, that's where we have trouble. But give a man his acreage, put land in a man's hands, doesn't matter who he is, and he can make it."

If some of this was familiar—the Gulliver of American enterprise pinned down by the Lilliputians' regulations—some of it was not. What I found interesting was Nick's mention of land, of room to realize your dreams. In the rest of the country, the idea that there was a connection between room—not metaphorical room but real, physical space—and the opportunity to build a better life had vanished more than a hundred years earlier. Nick's language was language only an Alaskan would use; it was the language of the frontier.

But he'd had enough of mixing politics with silverware. He bounded out of his chair to snatch an album of family photographs: his grandmother Olga on the day she arrived in Alaska, wrapped in furs on a dogsled in what looked like ten feet of snow; his father throwing out the first pitch of the season for the Midnight Sun League, which, Nick added, had produced a roster of great major leaguers from Tom Seaver to Darryl Strawberry to Barry Bonds.

Had he played baseball? "No. Basketball," he said, and continued his boosterism. "The lakes are spring and glacier fed. You can see fish from the deck of your cabin. And we've got great skiing. It's like Peter Pan. The men never grow old."

I forgot to ask what happened to the women.

35.

I N *THE OREGON TRAIL*, PARKMAN WRITES THAT WAGON-TRAIN EMI-grants described departure from the frontier at Fort Leavenworth as "jumping off." There is a little bit of that feel when you leave Fairbanks for the Dalton Highway. Milepost Zero is where the pavement ends, eighty-four miles north of the city.

Just before reaching that point, we pulled off at the Colorado Creek trailhead to give Sage and Sky a run. They'd been cooped up in Fairbanks, and English setters get a little crazy if they don't cover, oh, ten or fifteen miles a day.

We set off, ignoring an advisory that it was a winter trail unsuitable for summer travel due to boggy conditions. It was easy going for about half a mile on hard ground. Beyond that, the terrain turned into stinking muck cobbled with tundra tussocks. Walking on them was like walking on bowling balls laid atop a water bed. Four legs better than two, the dogs made out better than we. In a moment, they fell into stalking mode. Bellies low to the ground, necks extended, they crept a few yards, paused, crept a little farther. As always, I was mesmerized by their transformation from pets into predators. I could see the wolf in their movements, in the total concentration in their eyes. A flock of sandhill cranes, scouring the marshes for frogs and insects, had captured their attention. Sensing danger, the cranes scuttled away, uttering their prehistoric, rattling cry, and flew off, slate-colored wings spanning six feet.

Sage bolted after them and once again got herself into trouble. She leaped into a mire, burying herself up to her chest. She tried to paddle her way out, but she might as well have tried to swim in a tar pit. My mind flashed back to the ducks in that Texas river, and to other fixes she'd gotten into in the past, like the time when she'd jumped into the Delaware River in Pennsylvania and was nearly swept away. Or when she'd ranged too far in the Arizona mountains and got lost for two hours. Hopping from tussock to tussock, I waded into the bog, then reached out, snatched her collar, and hauled her to firm footing. She was now a two-toned dog, white on top, coated in jet-black goo below.

"Bad dog! When the hell are you going to learn that you're too damned old for these stunts?" I scolded, fixing a lead to her collar.

She gave herself a good shaking and me a look of indifference. We walked her and Sky back to the truck on lead, washed them off in the creek, and headed north on the Dalton. Alongside it snaked the Trans-Alaska Pipeline, the main coronary artery of the Alaskan economy, eight hundred miles of welded steel cylinders, four feet in diameter. Seventy-two days had passed since we'd started up the Overseas Highway, America's southernmost road; now we were rolling up the northernmost. It was amazing to think that the two were in the same country; as we looked at the boreal forests, the tundra fells sweeping away for as far as the eye could reach, the palm trees and green and azure waters of the Florida Keys seemed impossibly distant.

A flagman stopped us before we'd gone two miles. Road repairs were under way. The Dalton takes a beating from the climate and the twenty-four-seven truck traffic. (That morning, I'd taped cardboard across Ethel's front window to keep flying rocks from damaging it.) Three bikers, in Darth Vader getups, rumbled up behind us as we waited. One dismounted and tapped on my window. I lowered it while he raised his tinted visor, revealing a stubbled, middle-aged face.

"Hey, where can we get some gas?"

"Yukon Crossing. About fifty-five miles up the road."

"You mean there's no gas till then?"

"Nope. None."

"That's crazy!"

"Maybe. But that's how it is."

"They told us in Fairbanks we could get gas, so we didn't fill up."

Seriously dumb, I thought. The greenest cheechako would have known better.

"I've got ten gallons up on the roof if you guys really need it."

Apparently the pilgrim didn't think they did. He ducked behind the visor and remounted his Harley, and when the flagman waved us on the trio blasted past us.

A little more than an hour later, we bumped across the Yukon River bridge. A humorist had painted a wooden sign to look like one of those electronic readouts that tell you how fast you're going. YOUR SPEED, it said, 10 MPH. Below, one of the great rivers of the world, two thousand miles long and half a mile wide, glittered like a band of burnished steel. It slipped quietly along toward the western ranges and its mouth in the Bering Sea. At the roadhouse on the west side of the highway I topped off Fred's tank at the single pump. By the price, you would have thought I'd filled a twin-engine Beechcraft. On my way inside to pay, I saw the three bikes parked in the dusty lot. The pilgrims had made it.

We put up on a swath of bare dirt at Five Mile Camp. Seven hundred and fifty workers had lived there when the pipeline was under construction. Their prefab barracks and Quonset huts were long gone, replaced by a motel built of corrugated steel and a funky little truck stop, the Hot Spot Café, which boasted a best food to join our roster of salmon burgers, grouper sandwiches, cinnamon buns: "best burgers in Alaska."

Our first night on the Dalton was a wet one (*night* is merely an expression; the sun set about one in the morning and rose at three), and it was still pouring when we woke up, the campground a slough. Before going to bed, we'd stashed our muddy hiking boots under the trailer to dry, and even there they'd gotten soaked. Likewise Sage and Sky's bed, likewise Sage and Sky, who shivered in the chill morning wind. We splish-splashed to the Hot Spot for breakfast and information about road conditions. The maker of best burgers told us that when it rains, the calcium chloride maintenance crews lay on the road to keep the dust down forms a slick layer.

"It's okay if you take it real slow."

We took it real slow, and sailor-girl Leslie said it was like leaving a safe harbor in bad weather. The Dalton had been all dirt the first time I drove it; now portions had been paved with chip seal, a mixture of crushed stone and bitumen. On those stretches we hit thirty miles an hour; otherwise, twenty. The gumbo caulked the tire treads, and the thin layer of mud, with hard surface underneath, was as treacherous as black ice.

The rain diminished to a drizzle. We parked in a turnout and hiked up a granite tor called Finger Rock because it's a rock that looks like a giant finger poking out from atop a low, rounded hill. All around, alpine tundra undulated, much like the Great Plains, toward the Endicott and White mountain ranges. Ten thousand years ago, when woolly mammoths and prehistoric bison and saber-toothed cats roamed the land, paleo-Indians had stood where we stood, scouting for game.

At a little past noon on August 5, we reached a significant landmark and asked two BLM rangers, sheltered in a tent at the wayside, to take our picture in front of a signpost that declared: ARCTIC CIRCLE. NORTH LATITUDE 66 DEGREES, 33 MINUTES. We were pretty puffed up, though our egos had taken a hit a few minutes earlier, when we'd seen two mud-slathered riders on a mud-slathered motorcycle with mud-slathered gear piled on its rear fender and a sign bearing a two-word message: BRASIL–ALASKA.

"We're amateurs," I said to the ranger.

"It's an accomplishment to make it this far. Not many people do it," he said, trying to make us feel better.

And then he tried to make us feel worse, telling us about a Frenchman who'd passed through about a week earlier. This Frenchman had driven to Alaska from Tierra del Fuego, at the southern tip of South America; he'd picked up a custom-built sailboat, equipped with retractable skis, towed it up the Dalton, and launched it into Prudhoe Bay. He intended to sail across the Arctic Ocean, and when he reached the polar ice cap, he was going to lower the skis and ice-sail to the North Pole.

Actually, this story did not make us feel worse; we felt superior to the Frenchman. He was obviously insane.

The sun broke through the clouds, and though we'd traveled only sixty miles, we decided to camp at the Arctic Circle campground to dry out our boots and belongings. It was a primitive camp—no water or power—but the aspen and birch and white spruce were pleasing, and the weather was cool enough to keep the mosquitoes and blackflies at bay. I built a fire, and we set our boots next to it, and lay the dog bed in the sun.

In the evening, we broke out waders and fly rods and tried our luck on Fish Creek. It was misnamed.

I'm a good fly fisherman. It was shameful not to catch a fish *in Alaska*, so, come morning, we tried another river, the Jim. Speaking loudly to avoid alarming any lurking grizzlies, we tramped through the woods and came to a gravel bar jutting into a deep pool below the tail-out of a dancing riffle. The Jim is a beautiful, mostly placid, inconsequential river, but it occupied a dark corner in my memory. Sixteen years earlier, it had almost killed my younger son.

Marc and I, with a photographer named Tony Oswald, had been fishing the Jim from one-man rubber rafts that floated on pontoons. Approaching a sharp bend, Marc got caught in the swiftest part of the current. It carried him into a row of "sweepers"—fallen spruce. The pontoons rammed under a tree, and the raft flipped end over end, throwing Marc into the river. He grabbed the trunk and clung to it. If he hadn't done that, his heavy rubber waders would have pulled him under, into a web of sunken branches. Although he was a strong, athletic twenty-one-year-old, he couldn't pull himself out; his waders had filled with water, and it was thirty-eight degrees.

At that temperature, water kills in fifteen to twenty minutes. It took Oswald and me ten minutes to rescue him. With a long rope tied into a loop in my hand, I walked out onto the downed tree like a gymnast on a balance beam, one that swayed and bobbed underfoot. Oswald, on the bank, held the other end of the rope. When I got to the end, I saw that Marc's fingers were blue. His face was turning the same color as blood flowed from his brain into his body's core. He looked up at me and cried out, "Dad, I can't feel my hands! I'm going to let go!" And I shouted, "No! You'll drown!" It hit me then like a punch to the solar plexus: *My boy is going to die if we don't get him right now.* Somehow, I got the loop around his chest and under his arms, cinched it, and Oswald and I hauled him ashore.

He was already in second-stage hypothermia: complete numbness in his extremities, uncontrolled shivering, confusion, slurred speech. While Oswald got a fire going, I stripped Marc of his flooded waders and wet shirt, pulled my shirt off, and embraced him, bare torso to bare torso, to transfer my body heat to him. A couple of times, he almost lapsed into unconsciousness. I shook him out of it. Mosquitoes swarmed on us. Much later, I counted the bites on Marc's back and stopped at sixty. When the fire blazed up, we turned him around and around in its heat, as if we were roasting him for dinner. The shakes diminished, but he was groggy and not out of danger. We had to get him into dry clothes, so we recovered his raft, lashed it behind mine, put him on it, and then rowed to camp.

I don't recall how long we were on that river. What I do remember was looking over my shoulder every few minutes to make sure Marc was still conscious. I remember the forests sliding by, empty and silent, and a bald eagle on a gravel bar, watching us with an alert serenity as we floated past. And I remember thinking: *If my son dies, nothing here will change, nothing here will acknowledge what to me and his mother will be an unbearable loss. The forests' calm will not be disturbed; the eagle will fly to its nest as if nothing happened.* Never before and never since has the otherness of nature, its complete indifference to human fate, been so impressed on me.

Now, as I waded out into the river with Leslie, those memories made my skin crawl. I tried to evict them, focusing on the task at hand. Tying a gold-ribbed hare's ear to her line, I gave a little lecture on nymph fishing. Cast upstream at a forty-five-degree angle, mend the line, drift the fly downstream till the line begins to straighten, give the rod a couple of twitches to simulate a nymph struggling to the surface, then retrieve and cast again. The tutorial was followed by a demonstration, and on my first cast I caught a fifteen-inch grayling. I released it, certain we would reel in enough for dinner. We didn't. Working upstream and down for the next two hours, we failed to stick another fish. My shame was complete.

"Enough of this," Leslie said. "Let's see if we can find gold."

We drove fifteen miles to the South Fork of the Koyukuk, which, a booklet promised, had "high potential placer gold values," meaning an average of twelve dollars per cubic yard. We trekked some distance up that river, Leslie stopping every few minutes to dip the pan into the sand and gravel, swish out the water, remove the large stones, and then sift through the remains for color. Two hours of this produced as much gold as two hours of fishing had produced fish.

"It's this cheesy-looking plastic pan that's doing it," she said. "We should have gotten a metal one." She paused to reconsider. "I guess it's just been a day to adjust our expectations."

36.

N THE SUMMER OF 1900, A WAVE OF STAMPEDERS WORKING THEIR way up the Middle Fork of the Koyukuk reached a mining camp at the mouth of a tributary, Slate Creek. The green prospectors took one look around, got cold feet, and turned back. From then on, the camp was called Coldfoot. So reported Robert Marshall, explorer, forester, and naturalist, in his 1933 book *Arctic Village*. By 1902, Coldfoot had grown big enough, with a gambling den, two roadhouses, two stores, and seven saloons, to rate a post office. It closed ten years later, as the gold rush receded into history. The settlement was virtually abandoned, not to be revived until the discovery of black gold in Prudhoe Bay. It boomed as a construction camp for the Trans-Alaska Pipeline in the midseventies and is today a stop for the Dalton Highway's long-haul truckers, as well as travelers like us. With a permanent population of exactly ten, it consists of the following: a post office (recommissioned in 1984), a diner and saloon, a BLM visitor's center and ranger station, an airstrip, and the Slate Creek Inn, which, like all the hostelries in the far North, looks like a giant shipping container.

It was early evening when we pulled in, filled Ethel's water tank and Fred's gas tank, then checked in at the BLM office to ask about conditions in the Atigun Pass. That is the most dangerous stretch on the Dalton: a long, winding climb up into the Brooks Range, followed by an equally long, winding drop to the Arctic coastal plain. A gradient of

6 to 8 percent is considered steep on most highways; in the Atigun Pass, it's 12 percent, meaning that for every one hundred feet of run, the road gains twelve feet in altitude. A ranger advised us not to tow our trailer over the pass. There were no guardrails up there, it was snowing, and we could expect ice and mud. It was for professionals only, he said, making it plain that he knew we weren't.

Outside, in the parking lot, we spotted a familiar, battered blue Toyota truck and the two men we met in British Columbia nearly two weeks before.

"Hey," I called. "So did you guys make it to Prudhoe?"

"Not yet," answered the younger man, Levi Mason, the one who'd admired Ethel. They'd been to Denali, where they'd hiked for five days. Levi was from West Virginia and married to his buddy's niece. His buddy was Don Golliday—the name at first sounded to me like Doc Holliday—and he was a commercial roofer. He and Levi were dedicated backpackers. Together they'd tramped the Appalachian Trail and the mountains of Colorado and Utah. For twenty years, Don had dreamed of putting his boots down in Alaska.

"What made you decide to make the drive? You could've flown here."

"I wanted the experience," Don drawled. "I wanted to see the whole territory, all the way across. It's all about the experience for me. Canada was absolutely wonderful."

"Wasn't that something?" I said.

They broke into grins. "I had no concept until we drove across it. Every day, I thought, *Well, it's over, we're right there,* and then we got to British Columbia and Yukon, and I thought, *Oh, my God!* Fell in love with the place. We kept using the same words over and over. *It's awesome, it's magnificent, mind-boggling.*"

"So what was it like on Denali," I asked Don, "trying to keep up with a younger man?"

"He put me through the ringer up in the high country. But I got through with my own pack."

"He's a tough, tough man." Levi took out his camera and clicked on a shot of Don humping a pack across a glacier. "We made over thirty miles in five days. Went over several passes, six thousand feet, seventy-eight hundred, right across the top of a glacier. Don just kept chuggin' along. He's unbelievable for fifty-six."

"Fifty-five," Don corrected.

Levi was going to fly home when they returned to Fairbanks—"I made a wrong turn and acquired a mortgage, a wife, and a job," he said— but Don planned to meet up with his brother, who would be coming in by plane, and wander Alaska for another two months.

"Did you retire to get all this time off?"

He shook his head. "I got a story. You wanna hear the story?"

"Sure."

"In 1974 I bought a 1970 Mach One, and I've had it ever since. I blew up the engine and had it in storage for ten years at my daughter's. I sold that Mustang to my other daughter. She and her man are gonna restore it. That's how I got the money for this trip. *I had to do it.* It was the time. I'm at the age where I needed to go. I'm still in good shape for my age, and I decided this was the year, chips fall where they may."

"You mean you quit?"

"Well, sort of," he answered. He'd told his boss he was going no matter what. Maybe he'd have a job when he returned, maybe not. Meanwhile, he got another offer for a supervisory position with a roofing company based in North Carolina. Don told the firm he was interested but that he was bound for Alaska and wasn't going to back out. If the job was still available in October, he'd be home by then. The company didn't go for that. Don hit the road. When he and Levi got to Edmonton, Alberta, he was surprised to receive a call from North Carolina. The company still wanted to hire him. An employee would interview him later over the phone.

"He actually blew off the interview because we didn't have cell service," Levi interjected, in tones of admiration. "We had a choice to hang around in Edmonton or go on, and we went on."

"We went right through B.C. and didn't have no coverage for two days. So when I called the guy"—a low laugh trickled into Don's voice— "I think that was the end of it."

"Ballsy," I said. "We're in a recessed economy, everybody crying for a job."

"Oh, I've gone for a long time with no job. I've lived on lean means. Yes, I have. I know what it's like."

"And you still said the hell with it."

"I did. I did," he said, and with no remorse.

I'd liked them when I met them. I liked them even more now. I've always had a weakness for people who refuse to do the sensible thing, or what the world considers sensible, and follow the wisdom of their own hearts.

As Golliday climbed back into the unreliable Toyota, I could hear Dylan's raspy-voiced "Let Me Die in My Footsteps." And I could hear lines from Whitman's "Song of the Open Road":

> You but arrive at the city to which you are destined, you
>   hardly settle yourself to satisfaction before you are call'd
>   by an irresistible call to depart . . .
> You shall not allow the hold of those who spread their
>   reach'd hands toward you.

We pressed on to Marion Creek, about four miles up the road. Apparently the highway sign outside Coldfoot—NO SERVICES NEXT 240 MI.—affected travelers in the same way Coldfoot affected the prospectors whose timorousness inspired the name. We had the campground all to ourselves.

Cold was the operative word, cold for August anyway, temperatures in the low forties. With no heat in the trailer (the wood-chip stove had been removed to make room for a dresser), I'd borrowed a small space heater and an inverter to run it, and had discovered, too late, that it drew more power than the inverter could supply. Along with no heat, we had no hot water. The propane water heater wouldn't light; dust had clogged the valves. I'd tried bleeding the system, to no avail. We hadn't bathed in four days.

A night on the town was called for. We had a drink in the Coldfoot bar—a beer set me back five and half dollars—followed by dinner in the roadhouse. One room with a satellite TV and a long table was reserved for truckers. They'd been granted dispensation from the no-smoking ban because they were the folk heroes now, as the trappers and prospectors had been a century ago, and they were watching their fellow folk heroes on the TV. It was showing—I'm not making this up—an episode of *Ice Road Truckers*.

So how real was the reality show? Out on the back deck of the Coldfoot roadhouse, we spoke with Keith Mitchell, an ice-road trucker's trucker. He was fifty-eight years old and had been hauling freight on the Dalton for thirty years, almost as long as there had been a road. The TV show, he said, accurately portrayed the hazards drivers faced, but their conflicts and arguments were exaggerations, ginned up to make the series a kind of transportation soap opera.

"I think if they want drama, they're gonna have drama," he said, flashing a toothpaste-commercial smile.

Mitchell, a Flathead Indian from Montana (although with his fair complexion and light brown hair he looked less Indian than I did), remembered the days when the highway was much narrower, paved with river rock that made the five-hundred-mile trip a jolting, teeth-rattling ordeal that took twenty-four hours. The average running time is more like fifteen hours today, twelve in the winter, when snowpack acts as nature's road-repair crew, filling in ruts and potholes. Mitchell drove for an outfit that delivered all sorts of cargo.

"You name it, we haul it," he said in a cowboy drawl.

This trip it had been diesel. He pointed at his rig, a tanker parked among flatbeds and tractor-trailers in a muddy lot big as a baseball field and cratered with pond-size chuckholes. He'd picked up the fuel at a refinery near Fairbanks, offloaded in Deadhorse, and now he was heading back empty. He made the run twice a week all year round.

Talking to Mitchell was a little like talking to a fighter pilot. He was all "right-stuff" laconic, playing down the dangers. Still, the Dalton was more stimulating to the adrenal glands than the highways in the Lower 48. He'd tried hauling freight out of Seattle and got so bored that he was back on the North Slope within six months. He preferred driving in the winter, despite cold that seemed to belong to interstellar space.*

"You get better traction on the snowpack, except when it warms up to thirty degrees and your tires overheat and melt the snow. It's better truckin' when it's ten below."

"Have you ever almost fallen asleep?" Leslie asked.

"Oh, yeah. You get used to the route. Same old rock, same old tree. But the Atigun Pass has a way of wakin' you up. Gets your heart rate goin'. It's a long way to the bottom. The pass can get pretty gnarly. Makes its own weather up there. You've got snow, wind, rock slides, avalanches."

The worst hazards were the winter storms and whiteouts on the coastal plain.

---

* The lowest temperature ever recorded in the United States, eighty degrees below zero, was in 1971 at the Prospect Creek Camp, south of Coldfoot.

"If it's blowin', you can stay out there for three days. And you're alone, and it's pretty stressful. You're constantly thinkin': *Do I have enough food? Do I have enough water? Do I have enough clothes?* Cuz nobody's gonna come out and get you."

The Dalton had been an industrial, trucker's road until 1994, when it was opened to ordinary motorists. Mitchell's dismay with what he termed *civilian traffic* came as no surprise.

"Too many people with too little common sense, riskin' their lives. They don't know what they're gettin' into up here. You're completely on your own." (We hoped he didn't mean us, but he might have.) "Take these motorcyclists. One of 'em died just two days ago. Fishtailed in the mud south of Yukon Crossing, and that was that."

And then there were the amateur truckers who thought they were pros. Like the one he'd rescued during a whiteout near the Franklin Bluffs south of Deadhorse.

"I had to stop. I couldn't see the reflectors at the side of the road. Saw another trucker who stopped and asked what was up ahead. I said, 'I can't go any farther.' He said he was going to chain up and go on. So he did that, and all he's got on are lightweight clothes. Didn't put on his arctic gear, so when he got back into his truck, he had wet clothes. And all he had was a nylon sleeping bag, and that had got wet, too. So he passed me and went on up the road. But then he stopped. Plowed right into a snow-drift. He radioed me and said his engine had sucked in snow. His truck was dying, and he asked me, 'Can you help?'

"And I said, 'I don't know where you are.' I had no idea how much farther he'd gotten. But I got on my arctic gear—it took about twenty minutes—and I got out and tied my air hose to a hammer and wrapped it around my front bumper for a lifeline. Got to the end of it and still couldn't see him. I went another twenty feet and reached his back bum-per and got him out and into my truck. We spent three days in there. He knew better. He quit haulin' after that."

"Let's go to church," Leslie said.

This was an unusual summons from my lady, who is more likely to worship in the temple of Voltaire and Richard Dawkins. I wondered if the prospect of crossing the treacherous Atigun Pass had put the fear of God into her. Actually, she was just curious. She'd picked up a flyer in

Coldfoot inviting travelers to attend Sunday services in the Kalhabuk Prayer Chapel in the town of Wiseman.

I was all for the religious exercise. By the doctrines of the Catholic Church, I'd sunk deep into mortal sin on the trip, having missed Mass for eleven Sundays in a row. The service was advertised as "nondenominational Christian," which wouldn't qualify as a Mass in the Vatican's eyes. Still, I reasoned that attendance might win me some points and a reduced sentence should I plunge off the Atigun Pass, say a long term in Purgatory.

We crawled out of our warm sleeping bags into the shivers of a rainy morning and tried to make ourselves presentable. I shaved in cold water. We took icy sponge baths, combed our hair, put on our cleanest dirty clothes, and drove to Wiseman, three miles off the Dalton down a miry road running through soggy woods. I doubted it had changed since it was established in 1907. *The Milepost* described it as picturesque: unpaved lanes, a trading post, a lodge, a few log cabins scattered helter-skelter in the woods. Whitened antlers hung above doorways, smoke drifted from stovepipes poking through the rooftops; sled dogs barked in their kennels.

A town map with some curious landmarks—"Public Outhouse," "Moose horn pole"—guided us to the Kalhabuk chapel, a tin-roofed log shack no bigger than an average bedroom.

Inside, we were welcomed by the warmth of a wood-burning stove and by the minister, a small, white-haired woman named June Reakoff. Her congregation consisted of Wiseman's entire population, eight people, and three of those were her son, her daughter-in-law, and her grandson.

The service was the soul of simplicity and informality, the diametric opposite of a rococo high Latin Mass. I imagined it was like a gathering of believers in the early years of Christianity, before bishops and priests laid down the law: let's have some structure to our assemblies; let's have some ceremony and gold chalices and candles and bells and incense. June led us in hymns for about half an hour. She had a good voice; so did a BLM ranger, Greg Robbe. I can carry a tune fairly well if the only voice I hear is my own; in groups, I am consistently off-key and wander at random from note to note. In big cathedrals the voices of hundreds drown out my squawks, but I couldn't get away with it in that tiny room. I lip-synched.

Seated at the front of the room, June opened her sermon with a long, homey tale about a rusty kettle she'd found and how she'd restored it by heating it in the coals of a woodstove, scrubbing it inside and out with a wire brush, and polishing it with vegetable oil. After five minutes, she appeared to sense that we were wondering where she was going with this household parable.

"This must seem like a shaggy dog story to you," she said, and then came to the lesson. "It took the fire, and it took abrasive brushing, and it took oil to make the kettle clean. We can equate that spiritually in our lives, too . . . God has to pour out the oil of the Holy Spirit to bring out the luster in our lives . . . Thinking about the rusty kettle, I thought of how God designed us in a certain way for a certain purpose, but things happen in our lives and we become dirty and unusable for the master's use. But [she fell into a near whisper] we have someone who can clean us up."

Catholic guilt is different from Jewish guilt, but they bear this similarity: they are woven into the bearer's DNA. Nonetheless, June's homily perked me up. A Catholic priest would have stressed God's judgment. She emphasized his mercy and forgiveness. When we came to the recessional hymn, I belted it out without caring if I sounded like a seal with a sore throat.

After dismissal, June invited us to her house for coffee and hot chocolate, and there I committed . . . let's call it a secular transgression. I happened to sit next to June's son, Jack Reakoff, a wiry man with a movie star's bone structure, deep-set, penetrating eyes, and a quiet intensity. The buzz of small talk filled the room, but he wasn't a small-talk kind of guy. Born and bred in the Alaskan bush, he had a passion for wildlife conservation. He chaired a commission that advised on the management of subsistence hunting and fishing on federal lands and was vice chairman of an advisory board to the state Department of Fish and Game.

While the others turned their attention to Cracker, a small bunny a young woman had taken to church and brought into the house wrapped in a blanket, Reakoff began to tell me about the decimation of Alaska's caribou through overhunting. He blamed Fish and Game's policies.

"They took the Mulchatna herd in southwest Alaska from two hundred thousand animals in 1995 to twenty-eight thousand in twelve years," he said with barely suppressed outrage. "Trophy hunting wiped out the bulls. They let the hunters annihilate the herd."

"This is important," his mother interrupted, looking at me. "You should record this."

Everyone fell silent. I took my digital recorder out of my pocket. The device spooked Reakoff's wife, sitting across the room. She stiffened and said, "I wish you wouldn't."

I glanced at Reakoff, who motioned for me to go ahead, and I turned the recorder on. Journalists aren't the nicest people in the world.

Now, he continued, the central arctic caribou herd in his part of Alaska—sixty-seven thousand animals—was about to get whacked. Fish and Game had extended the hunting season, upped the bag limit to five animals per hunter, and permitted shooting cows as well as bulls.

And why was this happening? Despite the billions Alaska took in from oil revenues, its Fish and Game budget—about thirty million dollars—was funded from the sale of hunting and fishing licenses. The more out-of-state licenses it issued, the more money it took in. The irony was hardly subtle: generating income for wildlife conservation depended on destroying wildlife.

"In fifteen or twenty years there won't be any wildlife resources left in Alaska."

I said that it sounded like the Great Plains buffalo all over again.

Reakoff nodded. Exactly what he'd called it many times: "The bison syndrome." He was growing more heated, and his wife more upset, pursing her lips, frowning. When he described certain Fish and Game officials as "absolutely bloodthirsty," she snapped, "Jack! Stop talking!" and stung me with a look that said, "And you stop recording him."

Of course, I should have shut the recorder off right then, but June looked on serenely and Reakoff wasn't in the least fazed by his wife's anger. She stomped out, and he resumed his jeremiad, prophesying an Alaska in whose forests no wolves would howl, nor bears prowl, nor caribou migrate in their thousands.

"It won't get any better. The outlook is a black cloud on the horizon. It won't get any better until Alaska stops being a cheapskate state. We've constantly got our hands out to the federal government. Oh, we hate the feds. You hear nothing but that the state of Alaska hates the feds, the feds, the feds. But we've got our hand out at every turn for federal funding for wildlife management, federal funding for road maintenance. I was born in the territory of Alaska! I've got the full right to tell you for a fact that we've got the biggest bunch of hypocrites you've ever seen in your life in Alaska! We're banking money and killing our resources. We're killing *your* resources off, too, as Americans. Two-thirds of Alaska is federally owned. This is *your* land, *your* resources that are being wiped out as a funding source for the state of Alaska."

After we left, I was feeling depressed about the coming slaughter and guilty about contributing to marital discord.

"Couldn't you tell that she didn't want you to record him?" Leslie said.

"Of course I could. I'm not that stupid."

"Then why did you?"

"Because his mother was right. What he had to say was important. It's like we haven't learned anything in this country in a hundred and fifty years."

"He's going to go home right into an argument."

"Let's us not have one, okay?"

"Okay."

37.

THE PROPANE ALARM WAILED US AWAKE AT SEVEN IN THE morning, prompting Leslie to cover her ears and me to silence it in the usual manner—by turning off the battery power. Heeding the warning not to take Ethel over the Atigun, we were leaving her behind. She looked rather forlorn, all by herself in the wild woods. But we were relieved that we wouldn't have to deal with her issues for the next two or three days.

We swung south to Coldfoot, which had the nearest functioning phone, and tried to reserve a room at one of the hotels in Deadhorse. All were full up, mostly with oil field workers. We left regardless. If we had to, we'd roll out our sleeping bags and snuggle up with the dogs in the truck.

Past the marblelike spires of Sukapak Mountain, which by tradition marks the boundary between Eskimo and Athabascan Indian territories,* the boreal forests grew thinner. The trees, pruned by cold winds and starved for sunlight half the year, were seldom taller than fifteen feet, though some were a few hundred years old. At Milepost 235, indicated by a sign, stood the FARTHEST NORTH SPRUCE. Vandals had hacked into it with axes, killing it, but nature had triumphed over human idiots: a new tree sprouted a few yards to the north.

Now the tundra reigned—lichens, berry bushes, shrublike willows.

---

* Athabascan is the language spoken by the tribes of interior Alaska. Curiously enough, the Navajo and Apache of the Southwest speak a dialect of Athabascan.

The mile-wide Chandalar Shelf stretched before us, split by the Chandalar River; on its far side, the rise of the Brooks Range, the northernmost mountain chain in the United States, looked as abrupt as the rise of Manhattan's skyscrapers from the Hudson. In the mid-1800s, those far-ranging, ubiquitous French fur trappers had penetrated this far north and called the Gwich'in Indians inhabiting the region *gens de large*, meaning "nomadic people." Over time, the word was anglicized into *chandalar*. I had hiked there years ago and vividly remembered the silence, far off the highway. It was dense, primeval, older than history, a silence never broken by traffic or airplanes or chain saws or by any human sound save the yells of Gwich'in hunters driving their dogsleds.

When we began to climb the pass, my GPS measured our altitude at twenty-seven hundred feet, and Fred's thermometer read forty-two degrees. The road was as rough and slippery as advertised. The few guardrails had been mangled by rock slides and avalanches. We went on up, the temperature falling, and we were soon driving in wind-whipped flurries. A flock of Dall sheep, white enough to be mistaken for patches of snow, clung to a ledge on the west side of the road. The gorge opposite plunged two or three hundred feet straight down. I was the soul of both-hands-on-the-wheel, both-eyes-on-the-road concentration when a south-bound flatbed rounded a curve ahead. If it was a bit nerve-wracking, it was also exhilarating. The pass topped out at forty-eight hundred feet, and there the snow thickened, the falling flakes mingling with the vaporous sheets scooped from the cirques by the wind and flung across the road.

We pulled into a wide turnout and got out and stood looking down at the silver braids of the Atigun River. The wind blew hard and tore the clouds apart for a while, and a rainbow, like a fallen arch, appeared to be lying flat on a bare mountainside.

"There's a land where the mountains are nameless," wrote Robert Service. "And the rivers all run God knows where." Though we know now to where the rivers run—the Brooks Range forms the northern continental divide, and they run to the Arctic Ocean from its north side, south to the Yukon drainage from the opposite side, thence west into the Bering Sea—almost all its peaks remain nameless. They're runts compared with the summits in the Wrangells and the Rockies—the highest reaches barely over nine thousand feet—but, except for the Dalton and the pipeline, they're as wild and unpeopled as when the first fur-clad migrants crossed the Bering land bridge into North America twelve thousand years ago. Their glacial valleys and shrouded crags lure the traveler to come, come and find what you're looking for—gold or beauty or a world with the dew still on it—at the same time that their shale slopes and fearsome gorges repel, shouting to the stranger, "Keep out! You don't belong here!"

I shifted to low gear, and we began the descent. Leslie was delighted; crossing this divide provided the drama she'd missed on the western divide in Montana. Down, down, the road wringing itself around the mountainside, down into the Atigun River valley. Groups of caribou trotted in the distance, stalked by camouflaged bowhunters, whose tents filled every turnout and campsite. For obvious reasons, rifle hunting is prohibited within five miles of the highway and pipeline. Stopping at an overlook above the Atigun River Gorge, we watched an archer sneaking through a creek bed toward a bull caribou with a rack so tall and wide we wondered how he could hold his head up. Three other hunters advanced down a hillside in full view of the bull, trying to push him to within range of their companion. I looked around for TV cameras; it was as if we'd stumbled into an episode of a show on the Outdoor Channel.

"That's a beautiful animal," Leslie said. She must have been thinking about Jack Reakoff's forecast of the coming caribou holocaust. "If that guy tries to kill it, I'm going to be really tempted to jump out and wave my arms and scare it away."

I told her to resist the temptation; she might get shot herself.

The bull proved it didn't need her help. He lifted his nose, didn't like what he smelled, and loped onto the road, where he posed for a few seconds, his antlers like branched lightning, his cape showing dull white in the sun. Then, startled by an oncoming truck, he leaped down the embankment on the opposite side and ran full tilt over a hill.

We drove on, were held up for twenty minutes by a road repair crew, and then blew a tire, the first in all the miles we'd covered. The left rear was pancaked. Changing a tire on the Dalton, with truck traffic and two lanes and ten-foot dropoffs on both sides, can be hair-raising, but Fred chose a spot near a pull-off. Forty-five minutes later, we were on our way again. Score one for the anal-retentive guy who'd brought two spare tires.

Past Galbraith Lake, the road made a gradual descent onto the coastal plain, the very definition of desolation. It's actually a desert, annual precipitation of less than eight inches, a desert that rests upon an immense bed of subterranean ice two thousand feet deep in places. The coastal plain is called the "North Slope," though there is no slope anywhere. The utterly treeless, shrubless flatness stretched out to infinity, fractured into a mosaic of irregular squares and rectangles and wedges by seasonal freezes and thaws. The only relief from the horizontal was cone-shaped hills called pingos, spaced miles apart, and the occasional low, ice-cored mounds pushed to the surface by permafrost. Here and there, thaw lakes glittered like shards of broken glass.

Always there was the pipeline, snaking over the tundra on its vertical supports, sometimes vanishing underground. Curiously, it did not mar the natural landscape but somehow seemed to be part of it.* Even the warehouse-like pump stations blended in; the sheer scale of Arctic Alaska dwarfed anything humans could build.

Off to our right, parallel to the road, the Sagavanirktok River rushed toward Prudhoe Bay, its glaciated waters the color of liquid cement. The river is commonly called "the Sag," as its full name (an Eskimo word meaning "strong current") trips up the most agile tongue. The Franklin Bluffs, a sandstone escarpment resembling the Dakota Badlands, walled the Sag's eastern bank. Peregrine falcons nest in the bluffs. We saw a northern goshawk gliding over the tundra, but no falcons. Not that we looked all that hard. We were bone-tired after nearly ten hours on the Dalton. At last we came to the end of it, the end of all roads in America, Milepost 414, and entered Deadhorse. We'd made it from Key West in seventy-nine days. The reading on Fred's trip odometer: 8,314.

Deadhorse is the strangest and ugliest town in the country, so unabashedly, unapologetically ugly that it's fascinating. It's not really a town at all. It has its own post office and zip code, but there is no municipal government, no fire department or police department, no houses, parks, sidewalks, churches, schools, cemeteries, or bars, and no citizens, unless you count the four people listed as permanent residents. The rest of the population, which averages six thousand, is temporary, rotating in and out on two- to three-week stints. All are employed by the oil companies or any

---

* Like the Alaska Highway, it's an engineering marvel, built in three years, in the most difficult conditions imaginable, by tens of thousands of workers, thirty-two of whom died in its construction.

one of the two hundred contractors operating in the Prudhoe Bay field—engineers and technicians, fire-control experts, mechanics, welders, electricians, roughnecks, pipe fitters, truck drivers, heavy equipment operators, pilots, cooks, dishwashers—and they live in sprawling dormitories or in hotels that look no more like hotels than Deadhorse looks like a town.

There isn't a structure or an object made of anything but metal: steel-sided warehouses and welding shops, nests and stacks of drill pipes, yards filled with shipping containers. In place of, say, cathedral spires, drill rigs dominate the skyline. As for vegetation, you're as likely to find a blade of grass on the moon as in Deadhorse, where the word *plant* is used only in its industrial context: the manifold plant, the compressor plant, the seawater treatment plant, the seawater injection plant. Such is the unsightliness of the architecture that one hotel attempts to make a virtue of it: "Overnight in camp-style rooms consistent with the industrial heritage of the region," reads its ad in *The Milepost*. Translation: your room looks like a dumpster with a window.

But even a dumpster was preferable to spending a cold, miserable night in the truck. We drove around, looking for a place to stay. It was hard to see anything. A thick fog billowed in from off the bay. Like gigantic torches, tall stacks burned off waste gases from the wells, the orange flares eerie in the gloom. I felt as if we were on the set of a sci-fi movie, an outpost on some forsaken planet, Deep Space Station Nine.

We couldn't find a room, not at Deadhorse Camp or Sourdough Camp or the Arctic Caribou Inn. The clerk at the last place suggested we try a new hotel, the Aurora.

This massive building—it had 378 rooms—stood on the bleak shore of a thaw lake, Lake Colleen. In keeping with the prevailing aesthetic, it looked as if it had been constructed of about a thousand semitrailers stacked three stories high; but its yellow paint was cheerful, in comparison with everything else. Dozens of grimy pickups lined the parking lot, nose to nose at rails with electrical hookups to keep engines from freezing in the winter.

The Aurora had a room! With free laundry and three squares a day, it would cost us $275. After crossing the Atigun Pass and blowing a tire and five days without a shower, we would have shelled out twice that. And we did, booking two nights. (There was another reason for the extravagance. For security reasons, access to the Arctic Ocean—our ultimate goal—was restricted to commercial tours, and we'd reserved two seats on one leaving the next day.)

Because the Aurora was not a pet-friendly establishment, the dogs couldn't share in our happiness with staying there. They seemed a little bewildered as I walked them along the sooty, gravelly shore of Lake Colleen. Noses to the ground, they tried to pick up a recognizable scent and failed. Nor could they see much in the fog, and what they could see was unfamiliar to their field-dog eyes. Sage squatted, peed, and looked at me as if to ask, "What is this place you've brought us to?"

"Hey! Are those English setters?"

The voice belonged to a young, dark-haired guy at the wheel of a pickup, with British Petroleum's sunburst logo on its door panel. I confirmed the accuracy of his identification.

"We don't see many dogs up here."

"And I can see why. Not a dog-friendly kind of place."

"Not real people-friendly, either. But I like it well enough. Two weeks on, two off. Leaves me a lot of time to hunt and fish. You hunt those setters?"

I said that I did, and we talked bird dogs for a while.

"So what do you do for BP?"

"Dusty," he said, giving me his name. "I'm an AFG technician. Automated Fire and Gas. Systems that monitor natural gas migrating into a wellhead and shut everything down. Otherwise, you get a catastrophic explosion."

"You mean like what happened to that Deep Water Horizon rig in the Gulf of Mexico?"

"Yeah. Like that. We're upgrading the systems right now."

"Sounds like a good idea."

"Oh, yeah. Good lookin' dogs you've got. Don't let 'em off lead around here."

"Don't intend to. All these trucks and machinery."

"Bears. I was thinking about the bears. We get grizzlies walk right through camp like they own the place. Maybe they do. They were here before us, anyway."

I thanked Dusty for the tip and, keeping my eyes peeled for a hulking quadruped in the fog, took Sage and Sky to the truck. I gave them each a good-night treat, then went up to our room, where Leslie had been helping plan a report on mislabeled fish and doing laundry. Clean clothes. Clean, crisp, white sheets. A hot shower.

———

On a perfect summer's morning in Deadhorse—cold and dismal like the day before—we breakfasted in the Aurora's cavernous dining hall. It was packed with workers in the standard uniform: coveralls, work boots, baseball caps. Leslie liked Deadhorse, the organized busyness of it, people focused entirely on their jobs. The atmosphere, she said, reminded her of a big general hospital on one of those TV medical dramas, which I found an odd comparison. "Maybe I'll stay here, find a job."

"You don't know anything about the oil business," I said, sensibly. "What could you do?"

She surveyed the tables, filled with men.

"Prostitution," she said.

I was going to suggest that at fifty-seven, even a well-preserved fifty-seven, she might have trouble finding a clientele, but thought better of it.

"Uh, maybe you'd do better as a madam?"

"Okay. Madam sounds good."

"I'll recruit the girls," I said. "And I'll want fifty percent of what you take in."

She forked her scrambled eggs, thinking things over. "Oh, no. You're not going to be my john."

"Sweetie, I think you mean pimp. A john is the customer."

She laughed. "Guess I'd better get the terminology down right. Maybe I could wash dishes."

The issue of her future employment settled, we drove to the offices of Tatgaani Tours in the Arctic Caribou Inn. There, we and a handful of other pilgrims were held captive in a small room, required to watch a twenty-minute propaganda film produced by British Petroleum. We were model prisoners. No one remarked that after the Deep Water Horizon disaster it would take more than a movie to get BP off the log upon which it was a four-letter word beginning with s. After serving our sentence, Branden Goulet, our guide and minder, herded us outside and into a minibus for the trip to the Arctic Ocean.

Tall, hefty, garbed in blue coveralls, Branden was one quarter Inupiat and had another job besides escorting tourists: animal control officer. Animal control in Deadhorse and environs did not involve nabbing rabid raccoons or stray dogs but more challenging work, like shooing caribou off the roads and keeping track of grizzly and polar bears. It was in that capacity that he began the tour with a prohibition: we were not going to be allowed to wade into the Arctic Ocean, as was customary for visitors, because polar bears had been sighted prowling the shore. Branden's fellow workers were monitoring their movements and would keep him informed by radio. He passed out photocopies of a news story about four people who'd been killed in Norway by a polar bear. I guess he did that to convince those who'd seen cuddly photos of polar bears on Sierra Club calendars that they were dangerous.

"I've never lost anybody to a bear," he said, reassuringly. "I guided twenty-seven hundred and fifty tourists last year, and I brought twenty-seven hundred and thirty-nine back." A dramatic pause. "The other eleven, five children and six adults, were lost to mosquitoes. They saw the mosquito clouds—I warned them, but they didn't listen—and they were carried away."

His delivery was so deadpan that a few passengers didn't realize he was kidding.

And then he donned a headset and mike, got behind the wheel, and took us through a security checkpoint, designed to keep out civilians and terrorists intent on disrupting America's oil supply. Branden pointed out the natural and man-made wonders of the oil fields, mostly the latter. He had far less to work with than a tour guide in Rome or Paris. The Manifold Building—surprise, a big steel box—was no Colosseum, the Flow Station no Louvre. Some attractions were impressive, like the drill-rig hauler, an enormous vehicle that ran on tires twelve feet in diameter, each one weighing five hundred pounds (try changing that), but the fog made Branden's job all the harder. "Over there is Pump Station One," he said. "You'd see it if it wasn't so foggy."

He had an awesome command of oil field operations. Trouble was, his commentaries were incomprehensible to anyone lacking a degree in petroleum engineering, and that described all of us. But he tried his best, lacing his discourses with mind-boggling statistics: twenty-six oil fields extending along 150 miles of shoreline; fourteen hundred wellheads; peak production of 2.1 million barrels a day, providing 10 percent of domestic demand; construction of the pipeline, the road, and support facilities cost eleven billion dollars.

Now and then, he injected some wit into these recitations to hold our attention. When we passed a rank of suspended pipelines, a woman asked, "What are those things hanging from the pipes? Those long, squiggly steel things? They look like giant corkscrews."

"Wind dampers," Branden replied, then gave one of his theatrical pauses. "Actually, those are how you distinguish male from female pipes."

Wildlife, however, was his forte. Driving by a thaw lake, he pointed out white-fronted geese and tundra swans. Pacific loons swam on another lake. Spotting a couple of caribou, he told us that last year one of his tours was held up for twenty minutes when five hundred animals blocked the road. Then he stopped and pointed out the window. "Look, over there. A snowy owl." A shifting of bodies to the left side of the bus. There it was, roosting on the tundra about fifty yards away, a tiny blob of white in the gray mists. "Saw two of them yesterday, one with a lemming in its mouth." Farther on, he hit the brakes again. There was the second snowy owl, still as a decoy. Branden opened his window and imitated the whistle of a ground squirrel to get it to fly. The mimic sounded perfect to me, but the owl wasn't buying it.

After an hour of looking at drill-rig haulers and snowy owls, we crawled up a sandy stretch of road and stopped above a rocky, brownish shoreline, where chunks of bleached driftwood were scattered like bones. The Arctic Ocean, surfless and gray, stretched away into a curtain of fog.

Branden turned to us. "Stay inside, folks. I'm calling my dispatcher to find out where the bears are."

While we waited for word, he lectured on how polar bears hibernated and stayed warm.

"Polar bears are losing population because of decreasing sea ice," he said, not mentioning that global warming was shrinking the sea ice, or that global warming was linked to the burning of fossil fuels. "They have to swim up to two hundred miles to get here in the summer. Last year, we saw one, a female, that slept for three days after making that swim."

The dispatcher called back. Two polar bears *and* a grizzly were still in the vicinity. Branden scanned the beach with binoculars.

"Don't see them. I can let you out for five minutes, no more. And please don't go into the water. You'll get your certificates anyway." These documents, attesting to membership in the Polar Bear Dippers Club, were normally awarded only to those who take off their shoes, roll up their pants, and wade out up to their knees. The proximity of bears not being our fault, we were granted an exception.

We filed outside. "If you see a bear, don't run unless you really want to," Branden said.

A ruffle of nervous laughter.

The pilgrims beachcombed, picking up souvenir rocks and driftwood. Leslie and I dipped our hands into the water, cold, of course, but not numbingly so, and stood for a moment or two, gazing out across the lead-colored expanse. We'd started seventy miles north of the Tropic of Cancer; we'd finished twelve hundred miles south of the North Pole. I performed my ritual. Disobeying orders somewhat, I waded in up to my ankles, took out the bottle filled with waters from three oceans, dunked it, and added the waters of the Arctic Ocean.

Leslie put her arms around me. "Three yays for us. We got here."

But it wasn't getting there that mattered; it was *the* getting there, what Kerouac called "the purity of movement." On the road, I liked imagining what I would see at the next turn or over the hill just beyond, whom I would meet in the next town and what they would have to say and what their lives were like. The discovery, once made, did not always meet expectations. It was the unexpected that created the real magic, as when we'd come upon that herd of woods bison in the Yukon, the great shaggy beasts suddenly appearing, like a shaman's vision come true. Or meeting someone like Ansel Woodenknife, who'd opened up new perceptions, stirred emotions not anticipated. In the end, though, the journey had been the destination. It had never been anything else.

EPILOGUE

Emotionally, it was over for us but, of course, it wasn't over. Ethel had to be returned to her owner, five thousand road miles away in Texas, and then we had to get home.

In the afternoon, I brought Fred to a garage, where a cheerful repairman named Rick patched the flat tire and hinted that we might want to get a move on.

"Weather changes fast up here. Spring, summer, fall are crammed into about two months. It'll be snowing in a few days. I've seen it snow in July. Winter's fast here, it comes on real fast."

The return trip began on August 10, and Rick was right. Autumn arrived overnight, the tundra shrubs and bushes turning burgundy and orange, and we climbed the Atigun Pass into a snowstorm. Arriving back at Marion Creek Camp, we reunited Fred with Ethel, built a fire, and feasted on baked beans and brown bread.

Our breath made plumes inside the trailer in the morning. A north wind pushed clouds and rain squalls down from the Brooks Range, persuading us not to tarry. It took seven or eight hours to reach Fairbanks. The moon rose, and a reasonable facsimile of night fell at around 11 p.m. It was dark enough to see the Northern Lights if they made an appearance. But they stayed offstage, as the Southern Cross had in Key West.

After blasting the filth off the truck and trailer with a high-pressure hose and making minor repairs to Ethel—she'd taken some hard knocks on the Dalton—we got off on the thirteenth. An eagle flew with us across the border into the Yukon, circled, and flew back to his nest in Alaska. He didn't need a passport or to make any customs declarations. We retraced our route as far as Watson Lake, where, to avoid further backtracking, we followed the Cassiar and Yellowhead Highways to the Lower 48.

The drive took five days and featured our second, and last, quarrel. As we were passing Kluane Lake, a grizzly crossed the road ten yards in front of the truck. He was a brawny young bear with light brown fur that was almost blond in places. I stopped to photograph him, but by then he'd disappeared into the brush. A Canadian camped close by told us that grizzlies were all over the place, fattening up on the berries growing in profusion on the lakeshore. "Cruise around, you might get a picture of one," he said.

In cruising, I drove Fred and Ethel down a two-track running along a ten-foot embankment and realized I'd gotten us into a fix. If I kept going and the two-track dead-ended, I'd have no way to turn around. But to get back on the highway, I would have to pilot Fred and Ethel down the bank and at an angle, risking a rollover.

"I'll scout up ahead to see if this road goes all the way to the highway," Leslie volunteered.

While she was gone, I managed to ease the rig down the slope and up the other side, my heart flailing my ribs and my fingers frozen to the wheel. Leslie was nowhere to be seen. I headed on down the road, terrified that she'd bumped into a grizzly, and spotted her a few hundred yards away, near the junction of the highway and the two-track. Had I stayed on it, I would have found my way back to pavement and safety with no trouble. She'd walked almost a mile through grizzly country to discover this and was on her way back to report it to me.

She climbed inside, slamming the door, and said nothing. Of course, I was immensely relieved, but I listened to some gremlin in my brain that told me the best defense was a good offense.

"Why the hell did you go so far? You had me worried sick."

No response.

"I thought you were going just a little way, not all the way down the—"

"Listen," she interrupted. "I did it because you didn't think you could get down the embankment without tipping over. Do you know what I was doing? Sweating bricks! I was going, 'Hey bears. Any bears? I'm coming through.' Like you're supposed to so you don't surprise them.

Next time you make a stupid decision, you can figure your own way out of it!"

The gremlin prodded me to remind her that I *had* figured my own way out of it. This time, I didn't listen. After fifteen minutes of sullen silence, I spoke the only two words Leslie wanted to hear and thwarted Harry Wade's forecast once again.

In Sumas, Washington, I retrieved my revolver from Bromley's Market. We picked up I-5 to Everett, then went east on U.S. 2, reaching the crest of Stevens Pass in the northern Cascades. Leslie paid homage to her great-great-uncle John Frank Stevens, who, before Theodore Roosevelt appointed him to build the Panama Canal, had served as locating engineer for the Great Northern Railway. In 1890, while surveying its route, he discovered the pass that now bears his name.

U.S. 30 and I-84 covered parts of the Oregon Trail in Oregon's Blue Mountains. At a place called Deadman's Pass, a stone marker commemorated the efforts of a pioneer, Ezra Meeker, to save the trail's route from obscurity. Meeker had first trekked it in a covered wagon in 1852 and lived long enough—he died at ninety-eight—to fly over it in a U.S. Army biplane in 1924.

I'd been reading the "scroll" of *On the Road*, a much raunchier and more exuberant book than the partly censored version I'd read years before. Kerouac was writing about his travels in 1947–49, almost exactly a century after Francis Parkman published *The Oregon Trail*. Everything had changed in a mere one hundred years. Kerouac's America is recognizable to us today: paved highways, towns, cities, gas stations, wild sex, drugs, booze, and jazz (rock 'n' roll had yet to come). Parkman's America, with its plainsmen and trappers and Indians hunting buffalo across trackless prairies, seemed as distant as ancient Greece. It was certainly as extinct.

And yet that had been Meeker's America as well, and he'd gone from the prairie schooner to the airplane in his lifetime. As we sped at seventy miles an hour over the ruts of wagons lucky to have made seventy a week, the chasm between Meeker's time and mine collapsed down to a ditch. I felt as if I could jump right over it.

Bruneau Dunes looks like a chunk of Saudi Arabia transplanted to the high desert of Idaho. There, we sat with Lowell Messely outside his trailer and waited for the skies to throw the master switch and turn on the stars.

A short, affable man of seventy-eight, Lowell was a retired psychologist and had arrived at Bruneau Dunes for a forthcoming star party of fellow amateur astronomers.

"I retired in 1995, and was looking for something to do when my wife mentioned a star party. I went and got snake-bit. I bought my first telescope, and I've owned half a dozen since."

His present one, a Dobsonian reflector with a fifteen-inch mirror, was black and shiny and nearly seven feet long.

"I love to show people what's out there," he said as nighthawks strafed the desert for insects. "Most people are excited about it, but astronomy scares some people. Religious people mostly. What's up there contradicts their theology, like the idea that the universe was created in seven days six thousand years ago. With this scope, I can see a galaxy forty million light-years away, and that frightens them. They just walk away."

At about ten, the Milky Way appeared, the stars so crowded I could not make out some well-known constellations. Lowell cranked his scope straight up, toward the constellation Hercules, and fetched a stepladder— the viewfinder was nearly six feet above. I stood on the first rung. In the eyepiece's circle was M13, a stunning globular cluster twenty-six thousand light-years away. It looked like a huge chandelier with thousands of glowing bulbs.

Round about midnight, he trained the scope on the constellation Andromeda, hopped up the ladder, and inserted a high-power eyepiece. A few degrees above Andromeda's third star, a faint white blur appeared: the galaxy he'd spoken of earlier, NGC 202. We gazed at archaic light, light that had begun its journey across the cosmos ages before hunter-gatherers armed with deer femurs walked the earth.

"If you didn't know what it was, you wouldn't know what you're looking at," Lowell said. "It's just a smudge. Forty million light-years! If someone in that galaxy is observing ours, they'll be seeing it as it was forty million years ago."

Leslie and I had spent the day hiking the dunes in ninety-five-degree heat, and we were flagging. We thanked Lowell for all he'd shown us and said good night.

Just before I turned in, I looked out the window and saw him, still at his scope in the cool desert night, peering out across oceans of time and space. An old man, alone, immersed in the majesty and beauty of creation. Willa Cather said it best: "That is happiness, to be dissolved into something complete and great."

———

We'd become roads scholars and for the next five days attended seminars on desert highways. Idaho 51 morphed into Nevada 225, the blacktop stringing through the Shoshone reservation and the Owyhee Desert into the Independence Mountains, then merging with I-80 at Elko. I-80 carried us to U.S. 93 south across the Great Basin, an ancient ocean that's now a sea of sand, sage, and brittlebush.

We stopped for the night in Ely, Nevada, and from there followed U.S. 6/50: three hundred miles of next-to-nothing dubbed "the Loneliest Road in America" by *Life* magazine in 1986. The American Automobile Association warned motorists not to drive it unless they were confident of their survival skills. Feeling confident, I set the truck on cruise control, and with the highway shooting bullet-true ahead, I had the weird feeling that we were standing still and the road was moving, conveying us to wherever it led.

———

Roads scholarship would have to include New Mexico 53, which approximates the route of an east-west trail traveled for centuries by Indians, Spanish conquistadores, and Anglo pioneers. It passes a great sandstone promontory called Inscription Rock for the glyphs, names, initials, dates, and fragmentary stories chiseled into its smooth face.

The oldest dated inscription says the following: PASSED BY HERE, THE GOVERNOR DON JUAN DE OÑATE FROM THE DISCOVERY OF THE SEA OF THE SOUTH ON THE 16TH DAY OF APRIL, 1605.

In 1598, on the orders of King Philip of Spain, Oñate led five hundred Spanish settlers north from Mexico and across the Rio Grande into what's now the United States. He established a colony, which he christened Santa Fé de Nuevo México. The king appointed him its governor. His successor, Governor Don Pedro de Peralta, founded a settlement at the foot of the Sangre de Cristo Mountains, proclaimed it the provincial capital, and saddled it with the cumbersome name La Villa Real de la

Santa Fé de San Francisco de Asis (the Royal Town of the Holy Faith of Saint Francis of Assisi). That's wisely been pared down to Santa Fe.

Our journey would officially end in Breckenridge, Texas, but it seemed fitting to make Santa Fe its ceremonial end. There was a practical reason for this decision: Leslie's leave of absence would soon expire, she had to get back to her office, and Santa Fe was the nearest town with a major airport.

The other reason lay in the twenty-five words Don Juan de Oñate carved into Inscription Rock. They preface a counternarrative to the Anglo-Saxon story that the American saga unfolded from east to west. For Spanish-speaking peoples, European settlement advanced from south to north. The province of Nuevo Mexico was established nine years before Jamestown and twenty-two years before William Bradford planted his pilgrim foot on Plymouth Rock. And Santa Fe's founding in 1610 makes it the oldest capital in the modern United States. We couldn't think of a better place to mark the end of the longest road.

We stayed four days, in a campground on an old ranch outside the city. I was curious if any descendants of the Oñate expedition lived in the city, and found my way to Joe Lujan. Square-shouldered, black-haired, fifty-eight years old, Lujan works in the state historical museum, housed in the former Palace of the Governors. His ancestors were among the colonists who'd followed Oñate in 1598, and he was proud of it.

"We predate the *Mayflower*," he said. "We have first families that have been here more than four hundred years. We speak a unique dialect in northern New Mexico, an archaic Spanish that resembles the Spanish spoken in the sixteenth century."

Was he ever irritated by the Anglo dominance of our national story, the idea that American civilization began with the Massachusetts Bay Colony and marched westward?

He was, but nowhere near as much as he used to be. "I started school in the late fifties, and we were all led to believe that we had to stop speaking Spanish and learn about all the stuff that happened back East and forget about where we came from—it was no longer important. They tried to de-Hispanicize us. All that changed with the civil rights acts in the midsixties, bilingual education and all that."

Santa Fe was such a mosaic of Anglo and Spaniard and Indian, of new immigrants from Mexico and venerable families like his. What was the mortar that kept all those racial and cultural tiles in place?

"There's a lot of tolerance out here," Lujan said. "For the most part, all the cultures pretty much get along. I don't know if it's our space. We're not all crowded in. It's the roaming space out here, and I think that goes for the West in general."

I asked if that could go for the country in general. He wasn't sure; he thought so.

"It's probably our laws and our Christian values, our tolerance. This country was built by everybody, not just one group or nationality. They've all contributed something. You know, I see the Native Americans here, the older men, a lot of veterans, and proud of it. It's their country, too. It's probably more their country."

———

I find this note in my journal for September 3: "We're winding it up! Leslie leaves Sunday a.m. The trip to Breckenridge and then home to CT will be lonesome without her."

And it was. Half an hour after kissing her good-bye at the airport, I found myself turning to say something to her and felt her absence as a tangible thing when I looked at the empty passenger seat. After traveling so far together, after living literally side by side for three and a half months, it was as if some part of myself were missing.

I missed her all the way down U.S. 84 through the great, open solitudes of the New Mexican rangelands to Fort Sumner, where Billy the Kid was buried, and then east across the even greater solitudes of the Llano Estacado, the Staked Plain, then south again, the small towns—Lariat, Muleshoe, Littlefield—clinging to the asphalt ribbon as if threatened by the Llano's annihilating emptiness. I missed her still more in Lubbock, where I called it quits for the day. She phoned late in the night to say that she'd made it safely home. Her disembodied voice made me wish the truck could grow wings and fly me back to her side and to my own bed in my own house.

Eighty miles out of Lubbock, I picked up U.S. 180 east, a high wind blasting across the stretched-out land, dust devils pirouetting in the distance. More towns—Snyder, Roby, Anson—and over the Clear Fork of the Brazos, more creek than river in the worst drought Texas and Oklahoma had experienced since the thirties. Triple-digit temperatures, no rain for months, range fires consuming grass that crunched underfoot like brown paper bags. "Like the dust bowl days all over again," an Oklahoman had told me in Santa Fe. Funston, Albany, and finally Brecken-ridge.

I checked into a motel, where my gut reacted to fourteen weeks of road food, questionable water, handling sick dogs, and sheer exhaustion. I promptly threw up breakfast.

I splashed cold water on my face, rinsed my mouth with Listerine, and hauled Ethel her last three miles to the east end of town, where Erica Sherwood and her husband, Jef, ran a silk-screen and embroidery shop that sold uniforms to sports teams in their neck of Texas. Erica came out, and towering over me the onetime point guard for Baylor University gave me a welcoming hug.

Ethel, the beautiful lady, had acquired a few bruises, not surprisingly. A lot of detours and side trips had made the journey much longer than expected. Ethel had been taken over every kind of road for a total of 16,241 miles—two-thirds of the way around the world. After unhitching for the last time, I spent about two hours off-loading her and spiffing her up, inside and out. Then I closed the door, and she was no longer mine, no longer Ethel but merely a trailer made of metal, rubber, and wood, a lifeless thing without the power to delight or exasperate.

Later on, Erica and Jef treated me to Texas-style hospitality. They bought me dinner at a TexMex restaurant and invited me to go dove shooting on Erica's stepfather's ranch the next day. I accepted. Anxious as I was to get home, I couldn't face three more days on the road without a break.

That night, we had a glass of wine apiece in the family den—a 1948 Airstream that Erica had renovated to its original luster. The brutal heat had abated, and we sat outside, under the trailer's awning. My hosts wanted to hear my traveler's tale. I said it would take me till dawn. So I hit a few highlights, and somewhere in that fractured narrative I mentioned that I'd set out to discover people's thoughts on what kept our immense, scrambled nation in one piece. I told them about Dean Cannon's schol-arly analysis, and Carol Springer's idea that it was a belief, not necessarily based on evidence, that we had more in common than we had differ-ences, and a quip I'd heard from a college kid in Tuscaloosa: the glue was professional sports.

"What do you think?" asked Erica.

My answer was inspired by the night of stargazing with Lowell Mes-sely in Idaho and a comment made by Analiese Apel, the Montana wrangler: "The country definitely is in disarray. At the same time, to grow as a country, we need to have conflict, and conflict is healthy, conflict is good."

"Conflict is what holds a star together," I said. Cosmologists call it *dynamic disequilibrium*, a tension between gravity, which pulls a star toward collapse, and thermonuclear fusion, which releases tremendous energy that sends the star's matter expanding outward. If gravity dominates, the star is crushed down into a black hole; if fusion wins out, it explodes into dust.

Almost from its birth, America had been in a state of "dynamic disequilibrium" between the Jeffersonian force, which aims toward an expansion of individual liberty ("the government that governs least governs best") and the Hamiltonian force, which pulls the citizen toward centralized, federal power. As a star exists between physical extremes, so does America between its political extremes. But this isn't the mushy "middle of the road" so favored by moderates. (As a Texas legislator once put it, all you find in the middle of the road are yellow lines and dead armadillos.) No, it's the perpetual conflict of extremes that generates the binding force. Today it's the Tea Party, We-Don't-Need-No-Stinking-Government righties and the Let's-Regulate-Everything, Nanny-State lefties. Tomorrow, there will be other labels. By whatever name, neither should be allowed to overcome the other. Too much Jefferson leads to anarchy, too much Hamilton to tyranny.

Jef's and Erica's quizzical frowns told me that they found the analogy between astrophysics and politics a little far-fetched.

"Well, Erica, what are your thoughts?"

"About what you said or what keeps us together?"

"What keeps us together."

"Hope," she said. "Isn't that what it's always been?"

POSTSCRIPT

IN MEMORY OF
AURORA SAGE
JULY 10, 1998–DECEMBER 21, 2011
STILL HUNTING